THE APPRECIATION OF
MODERN FRENCH POETRY

THE APPRECIATION OF MODERN FRENCH POETRY (1850–1950)

BY

PETER BROOME

Senior Lecturer in French, Queen's University, Belfast

AND

GRAHAM CHESTERS

Lecturer in French at the University of Hull

CAMBRIDGE UNIVERSITY PRESS

CAMBRIDGE

LONDON · NEW YORK · MELBOURNE

Published by the Syndics of the Cambridge University Press
The Pitt Building, Trumpington Street, Cambridge CB2 1RP
Bentley House, 200 Euston Road, London NW1 2DB
32 East 57th Street, New York, NY 10022, USA
296 Beaconsfield Parade, Middle Park, Melbourne 3206, Australia

First published 1976

Printed in Great Britain
at the University Printing House, Cambridge
(Euan Phillips, University Printer)

Library of Congress Cataloguing in Publication Data

Broome, Peter, 1937–
  The appreciation of modern French poetry, 1850–1950.
  A companion volume to An Anthology of modern French poetry,
1850–1950, edited by P. Broome and G. Chesters.
  Bibliography: p.
  Includes index.
  1. French poetry – 19th century – History and criticism. 2.
French poetry – 20th century – History and criticism. I. Chesters,
Graham, joint author. II. An Anthology of modern French poetry,
1850–1950. III. Title.
PQ437.B7   841'.8'09   75–40768
ISBN 0 521 20792 4 hard covers
ISBN 0 521 20930 7 paperback.

CONTENTS

v

Contents

PREFACE

The present work, *The Appreciation of Modern French Poetry*, is a companion volume to *An Anthology of Modern French Poetry*. It is hoped that, together, these two volumes will provide a comprehensive and stimulating approach to a hundred of the richest years of French poetry, from 1850 to 1950.

In this volume our broad aim has been to invite the reader into a closer, more active reading, not only of French verse, but of poetry in general. The Introduction is a detailed illustration of some of the workings of poetic form and style: here, we have not attempted to list the rules of French versification or define all the technical aspects of prosody as they have developed throughout its history – this has been done at greater length by more competent critics – but simply to draw attention to the suggestive effects that certain formal features can create or enhance in particular contexts. It is important to recognize an *enjambement*, tell *rimes croisées* from *rimes embrassées*, and scan a pentasyllabic line. But this knowledge is virtually useless without the ability to appreciate the various poetic designs to which they can contribute when appropriately chosen and sensitively applied. There is no absolute key in this respect. One cannot say that octosyllables, by their very nature, have such and such a quality, that *enjambement* or regular rhythm will invariably produce this or that effect, or that the repetition of an 'l' sound always evokes a particular mood. All that one can venture is that, according to the poet's intentions or intuitions, these can be made to blend into, and lend their weight to, an infinity of different patterns and unities. For this reason, we have chosen to emphasize suggestion rather than syllabification, symmetry rather than caesuras, and to illustrate in context rather than classify. Clearly, we cannot pretend to show all that the intricacies of poetic form can bring to life; and the headings under which we have studied different aspects of style and technique are arbitrary in that these aspects must inevitably intermingle: the effectiveness of an image in a beautiful stanza will depend, not on its self-contained properties, but on its position within a specific verse-form, the way in which rhythm stresses its most significant word or picks out its most harmonious sounds, its ability to cast light on other words, draw them together or set them in opposition and so on. But our purpose will have been served if, from this small selection of developed examples, the reader comes to appreciate all the more that the techniques of poetry are not stiff rules or soulless restrictions, but delicate manipulations, conscious or unconscious, coaxing language to divulge all its potential – for meaning and suggestion, sound and rhythm.

vii

Preface

The Commentaries which follow the Introduction turn from the question of what to look for in poetry in general and suggest a method of approaching particular poems. The works analysed are by the poets who figure in the companion volume, *An Anthology of Modern French Poetry*, thus preparing the ground, by a close reading of individual texts, for the wider selection which appears elsewhere. We have chosen to study *two* pieces by each poet in order to give some idea of how one poem can illuminate another and of the network of relations extending further into the author's work. Though detailed, these commentaries are not intended as fully fashioned or model *explications de texte*. We would prefer to call them guided commentaries or preliminary *explications*. Rather than present the student with a fully rounded and somewhat prohibitive end-product, we have tried to invite him into the problems and more tentative intuitions of the stages of approach. We have sought a method which combines comment and question, which elaborates on certain details and draws attention to others, in such a way that the reader, guided into the poem image by image and stage by stage, will ultimately compose his own appreciation. The exercise calls for and depends upon his participation.

It is important to stress, finally, that we are not *right* in our comments on these poems or in the notes to be found in the anthology volume (the poems of which we also refer to here at frequent intervals). Readers will, quite justifiably, disagree with aspects of our interpretations; but this does not matter and is even desirable. For our intention is basically a modest one. We have simply enjoyed the poems and tried to cultivate some awareness of the sources of that enjoyment. We have hoped to touch off enquiry and response and, in some small measure, make French poetry an adventure in reading and a delight in words.

P. B.
G. C.

ACKNOWLEDGEMENTS

The authors and publisher would like to thank Editions Gallimard for permission to quote material which is their copyright, as follows: *Non, l'amour n'est pas mort* and *Comme une main à l'instant de la mort* by Robert Desnos from *Domaine public*; *L'Amoureuse* and *Sans âge* by Paul Eluard from *Choix de poèmes* (1951); *Icebergs* and *Clown* by Henri Michaux from *L'Espace du dedans* (1966); *Montévidéo* and *Haute mer* by Jules Supervielle from *Choix de poèmes* (1947); *La Ceinture* and *Le Cimetière marin* by Paul Valéry from *Œuvres*, 'Bibliothèque de la Pléiade' (1957).

For Di and Anne

INTRODUCTION

THE LANGUAGE OF POETRY

As a first step towards determining the kind of language that poetry speaks, it is useful to call on the traditional distinction between poetry and prose. It has been argued that there is a difference of subject-matter, and that there are themes or ideas particularly appropriate to poetry and to which prose, by its more pedestrian nature, cannot do justice. Indeed, over the centuries, certain subjects have come to be associated with poetic expression: the love of nature, worship of the divine, the inevitability of death, laments on the passage of time, addresses to the loved one; whereas literary prose has often concerned itself with the exposition of intellectual ideas, the description of social milieux, the narration of events or the detailed portraiture of real or fictional characters. The less literary prose-forms, such as everyday journalism, pamphlets or scientific treatises, are even further removed from poetry and accentuate its more refined and exceptional nature. But this is not a reason for assuming that such traditional subjects of verse are in themselves a crucial constituent of the definition of poetry. Perhaps it is because they evoke a highly individual response and a deep emotional commitment that poets have felt inspired to contain and ennoble them in a memorable form; and perhaps the subject is only a stimulus for something more complex. Valéry, a pre-eminent poetic theorist, has said, 'Le *sujet* d'un poème lui est aussi étranger et aussi important que l'est à un homme, son *nom*'. A man's name is an important label or identification-mark, by which he is recognized and which gives him an official existence and perhaps even an ancestry, but which of itself says little about the complexity of features which go to make his personality. The subject of a poem, in Valéry's view, has the same limited status.

This brings us, then, to the question of whether it is primarily intensity of personal emotion which gives poetry its depth of character. The Romantic poets in particular, Hugo, Lamartine, Vigny, Musset, made their poems the vehicle for an exploration of their own states of feeling, with the 'moi' and its tribulations becoming the main focus of attention. Often their work is an apparently direct and sincere communication with a sympathetic reader, a strong outpouring of emotions meant to be shared; at other times it acts more as a private outlet for their joy and grief, enthusiasm and depression, with the poetic Muse the only true friend and consolation. Lamartine, in his Preface to the *Méditations*, summed up a contemporary mood:

Ce n'était pas un art, c'était un soulagement de mon propre cœur, qui se berçait de ses propres sanglots. Je ne pensais à personne en écrivant ces vers, si ce n'est à un ombre et à Dieu, les vers étaient un gémissement et un cri de l'âme.

It is certain that the attraction of Romantic poetry for many a reader lie in an immediate response to this dramatized expression of common huma emotions: love, hate, fear, contentment, pain, bitterness, awe, nostalgia But one wonders how often readers have confused quality of feeling an quality of poetic writing. Is there, in fact, a special register of poetic emotions any more than there is a special range of subjects, peculiarly appropriat to poetry? And are sincerity and intensity of feeling any guarantee of great ness in a work of art? It is again Valéry who has said that 'L'expression d sentiment vrai est toujours banale', meaning by this that sincerity of inspir ation has to pass through the filter of technique before it is purified into art and that anyone who thinks to by-pass this process and translate a heart-fel message directly onto the page will inevitably fall into the commonplace. It is worth remembering that even Verlaine, so often appreciated for his naïvety and simplicity, has created a subtly calculated illusion of sincerity and spontaneity. The emotions in his poetry are not identical to those of his life. They are literary emotions, created on the page, which have their own special intensity. Indeed, it would seem that an emotive subject and a burning desire to express exceptional feelings are not *in themselves* enough to create poetry.

Some may say that it is a grandeur in the source of inspiration which gives poetry its tone. Hugo, for instance, has an epic conception of poetry, seen in his ambition to write *La Légende des siècles* and in his use of titles such as *Dieu* and *La Fin de Satan*; many of his pieces have a Biblical or prophetic atmosphere and seek to plumb the depths of divine purposes. Baudelaire's *Les Fleurs du mal* presents an infinitely nuanced staging of the battle between the forces of good and evil, the satanical and the divine impulses in human nature. Rimbaud has considered the poet's function as that of a prophet or visionary, abandoning his mind and senses to super-natural intuitions beyond the reach of everyday perception. Even the self-mocking Apollinaire conceives of himself at times as a kind of universal mind and an agent of progress; and Eluard shares the Surrealist ideal of transfiguring the face of reality by the power of the imagination, seeing all men united in a fresh and luminous vision of the world. All of these aims are grandiose and enlist the resources of a high idealism. But are they any more grandiose than Pascal's fragmentary prose-texts enquiring into the existence of God and man's place in the universe, or Proust's attempt in his many-volumed novel to explore the labyrinth of memory and make the conquest of time past? Certainly, subjects of such scope are not exclusive to poetry, nor does poetry concern itself exclusively with the grandiose and high-flown. The seventeenth-century poet Saint-Amant found enough inspiration in the qualities of a melon to celebrate it in a long poem of great verve and linguistic colour which cannot be underestimated as a work of art because of the apparent triviality of the subject. In our own day, Francis Ponge has adopted 'le parti pris des choses', choosing to write of the most commonplace objects, a snail, a loaf of broad, a pebble, a glass of water, and still remains one of the most imaginatively refreshing poets of recent times. In a somewhat different vein, a poem like Baudelaire's *Une Charogne* takes as its starting-point the most disgusting image of carnal reality, that of a rotting corpse which,

> Les jambes en l'air, comme une femme lubrique,
> Brûlante et suant les poisons,
> Ouvrait d'une facon nonchalante et cynique
> Son ventre plein d'exhalaisons.

But, as Baudelaire himself has said, 'C'est un des privilèges prodigieux de l'Art que l'horrible, artistement exprimé, devienne beauté, et que la douleur, rhythmée et cadencée, remplisse l'esprit d'une *joie calme*'; and in this poem in particular he transcends the baseness of the original subject-matter through a play of association and image, suggestions of music and rhythm. Rimbaud provides an illustration of another kind. Many of his earlier satirical poems take a delight in emphasizing mediocrity and vulgarity, in the case of *A la musique*, that of the self-important local bourgeoisie:

> Epatant sur son banc les rondeurs de ses reins,
> Un bourgeois à boutons clairs, bedaine flamande,
> Savoure son onnaing d'où le tabac par brins
> Déborde – vous savez, c'est de la contrebande.

This is 'unpoetic' material and the tone throughout is decidedly unelevated. But it is undoubtedly poetry, dependent on its telling alliterations and positioning of effects within a concentrated formal context.

Perhaps, then, it is to the idea of style and form that one must turn to find the essence of poetry. It is almost a commonplace to say that the main stylistic difference between prose and poetry is that one is an art of statement while the other is an art of suggestion. More subtly, Valéry speaks of the difference between walking and dancing: one proceeds to its destination with no particular concern for grace and the magic of movement in themselves, the other works its charm in a concentrated play of rhythm, movement, gesture and indirect expression which forms a captivating harmony in its own right and has no need for a further utilitarian purpose and justification. Suggestion, which cultivates the implicit rather than the explicit, may depend on many things. It may conjure up an atmosphere which works on the reader's sensitivity far more emphatically than any precise message. This is certainly the case with Baudelaire who, in a plan for a literary work, gave this intention: 'Noyer le tout dans une atmosphère anormale et songeuse'. Such an atmosphere is often enhanced by a less

precise vocabulary, one more open to a variety of interpretations and associations. Some words may be ambiguous in themselves, as in the case of the
word 'ombres' in Hugo's lines:

> Quelqu'un qu'entourent les ombres
> Montera mes marches sombres,

where one does not know whether the mysterious 'Quelqu'un' is surrounded
by shades of the dead or simply by the dark shadows of an underground
vault. Or a suggestive ambiguity may stem from the lack of punctuation,
as in the poetry of Mallarmé and Apollinaire, where one is not always sure
of the exact relationship between the words, which seem to hover between
alternative meanings. Other words may have such richness of implication in
the context that they can hardly be translated: in the opening line of
Baudelaire's *La Chevelure*, 'O toison, moutonnant jusque sur l'encolure',
'moutonnant', descriptive of the woman's hair, unites the various ideas of
fleeciness of texture, waviness of outline and sensuous rhythmic movement.
In other instances a poet may choose a word, in preference to a familiar
synonym, for its comparative rareness, or group it with another word in
a way which surprises our normal reading habits. In the phrase 'O parfum
chargé de nonchaloir', again from *La Chevelure*, the word 'nonchaloir'
has an uncommon archaic aura and, linked with 'chargé', creates a poetic
blend of airy lightness and heavy torpor. A single word may occasionally be
repeated in different settings, as in Hugo's *Je suis fait d'ombre et de marbre...*
where '...les pieds noirs de l'arbre' is followed two stanzas later by '...les
pieds ailés des fêtes' and '...les pieds nus de l'amour': in this case, the
repetition makes one doubly responsive to the figurative possibilities of the
word 'pieds'. This lights another facet of the distinction between prose and
poetry. One is a more intellectual, the other a more imaginative medium.
Baudelaire has emphasized the central rôle of imagination, saying 'Il ne
faut pas confondre la sensibilité de l'imagination avec celle du cœur'. Prose,
in its attempt to maintain the outline of its message, relies primarily on the
literal and directly communicative use of language. Poetry, more concerned
with texture, tone and what have been called 'indirections' rather than
directions, exploits to a far greater extent its allusive and figurative potential.
Allusion sometimes takes the form of mythological, Biblical or traditional
reference, as in Hugo's *Booz endormi* in which one reads:

> Et ce songe était tel, que Booz vit un chêne
> Qui, sorti de son ventre, allait jusqu'au ciel bleu;
> Une race y montait comme une longue chaîne;
> Un roi chantait en bas, en haut mourait un Dieu.

Here, elliptically told, is the Biblical story of the stem of Jesse and the
descendance of Jesus from David, which most readers would be able to
recall and expand. At other times allusive language is an oblique mode of

expression, a veiled statement suggesting more than meets the eye. For instance, in the final tercet of Verlaine's *Mon Rêve familier*,

> Son regard est pareil au regard des statues,
> Et, pour sa voix, lointaine, et calme, et grave, elle a
> L'inflexion des voix chères qui se sont tues,

the haunting woman's voice is described by reference to persons not given a definite identity and we are left with the hint of a hidden drama which is developed no further. But above all poetry gains its distinction from the richness of its figurative expression and imagery. On the simplest level, a poet like Baudelaire may speak of 'l'automne des idées', 'l'abîme de ta couche' or 'le vent furibond de la concupiscence', phrases in which the words 'automne', 'abîme' and 'vent', are taken out of their literal usage and given widened connotations. His more complex imagery, simile or metaphor, is all the more evocative. Woman's hair becomes 'mer d'ébène' or 'forêt aromatique'; his mistress's walk takes on the qualities of 'un serpent qui danse/Au bout d'un bâton' or 'un beau vaisseau qui prend le large'; rain appears as the bars of a prison, hope as a bat flitting in the musty darkness, and Anguish as a despot planting its black flag into the poet's skull – all images which project the mind beyond common realities and prosaic conception into a multiple suggestive realm. Poetic vision is generally more alive to analogy than is prose: Baudelaire's imagination was preoccupied with *correspondances*, subtly interrelated impressions, while Mallarmé was haunted by what he called 'le démon de l'analogie', not things in themselves, but the mysterious principle that forges new links and parallels between different objects and perceptions. It is remarkable that, in the years immediately following 1870, all the greatest French poets (Mallarmé, Verlaine, Rimbaud) looked upon poetry as an instrument to convey intuitions of an order beyond the everyday face of reality, seeking a new form of expression which, avoiding statement and mere description, would evoke a complexity of impressions so vaguely apprehended as to defy the language of reason and rhetoric. 'Peindre non la chose, mais l'effet qu'elle produit' was Mallarmé's poetic aim: that is to depict, not objects, but that indefinable aura which emanates from them but does not have a precise name or contour. Similarly, Verlaine, having exhorted the aspiring poet in these terms, 'Prends l'éloquence et tords-lui son cou', proposes his ideal of

> ...la chose envolée
> Qu'on sent qui fuit d'une âme en allée
> Vers d'autres cieux à d'autres amours:

something fleeting and ethereal with an intangible spiritual source and destination. Rimbaud also pursued a new concept of expression, saying, 'Cette langue sera de l'âme pour l'âme': not art for art's sake, but soul for soul's sake, a language abandoning superficial description and clearly formulated intellectual ideas in order to suggest, by an imaginative and apparently irrational style, the mystery and excitement of spiritual discovery It is at this moment that French poetry is at its most refined and subtle a an art of suggestion, and shows itself contemptuous of the more functiona and explicit uses of language.

But one should not confuse poetic suggestion with stylistic vagueness Nor should one look on the poet essentially as a spiritual dreamer. Valéry warns that

La véritable condition d'un véritable poète est ce qu'il y a de plus distinct de l'état de rêve (. . .) Celui même qui veut écrire son rêve se doit d'être infiniment éveillé (. . .) Et plus la proie que l'on convoite est-elle inquiète et fugitive, plus faut-il de présence et de volonté pour la rendre éternellement présente, dans son attitude éternellement fuyante,

words which remind us that the poet, however obscure and evasive his inspiration, applies himself as a lucid and wilful artist. It is equally true that poetry, however imprecise and unlimited in its connotations, is a strictly condensed and carefully patterned art-form. Whereas the aesthetic structures of prose tend to be built on broader pillars (different stages of an argument, different episodes of narrative development or recurrent leit-motifs), those of poetry take shape closer to the individual word. In this compact mould, whether it is sonnet or long ballad, the poet focuses his sensitivity on the tiniest details. He sets word against word, consciously or unconsciously weighing in his mind such questions as their euphonic qualities, their contribution to the overall musical texture, their place in the rhythmical motions, and the way in which they form expressive patterns, highlighting each other and facets of the theme. Even modern poets writing free verse have not been able to abandon formal considerations, and despite its apparent ability to roam at will, their work still depends on recurrent rhythmical movements, the deliberate positioning of elements, and the concentrated interplay of sound with sound and image with image. It is important to recognize that the technical conventions, metre, rhyme and verse-form, which constitute the limited framework of poetry are not sterile restrictions. They enhance the colouring, balance and interdependence of the words and images, giving the whole a necessary cohesion and making it more memorable. Baudelaire defended the rules of versification and the formal demands of rhetorical expression as a spur to originality and not a halter placed upon it. Valéry has extolled the creative value of rhyme, saying that it is far more likely that rhyme will engender a literary idea than that a preconceived idea will produce a rhyme. More forcibly, Valéry writes that 'Les belles œuvres sont filles de leur forme, *qui naît avant elles*'. In a comparison of the two texts by Baudelaire entitled *L'Invitation au voyage*, the first a poem and the other poetic prose, one sees the crucial rôle played by strict form in the definition of poetry. The prose passage is longer and ess dense, it names objects and places more explicitly, and although it is full of rich language and poetic image, these do not cling to each other with the same compelling magnetism. The effect of the poem, on the other hand, depends on its closely repetitive metrical structure, the charm of its rhythm, the insistent rhymes and sound-echoes, the stylized refrain.

This introductory discussion has moved from what could be broadly called the inspiration of poetry to the kind of language and form through which this inspiration gains expression. Critics have been fascinated by the age-old question of the relationship between inspiration and technique, content and form, subject-matter and style. It has been said that 'l'art ne fait que des vers, le cœur seul est poète', a point of view with which many a Romantic poet would have sympathized. One can appreciate that, without a depth of emotion or lyrical intensity to motivate it, a poem may well appear dry and soulless, a mere technical exercise. Poetry depends on a certain kind of 'enthusiasm' with the power to kindle feelings and imagination. The shortcoming of much verse of the Parnassian period of French poetry, which was in reaction against the eloquent confessionals of the heart and grand didacticism of the Romantics, is its apparent lack of personal involvement, its concentration on limited ornamental themes and its cult of 'art for art's sake', formal perfection above all else. On the other hand, one cannot imagine poetry, however passionately inspired, without the carefully concerted effects produced by the organizing artistic mind. Valéry has described the modern poet in these terms: 'Ce n'est plus le délirant échevelé, celui qui écrit tout un poème dans une nuit de fièvre, c'est un froid savant, presque un algébriste, au service d'un rêveur affiné'. Historically, there have been fluctuations of taste and developments of poetic theory, at one time stressing the importance of subject-matter and quality of inspiration, at other times seeing the essence of poetry in more purely aesthetic attributes. The only conclusion one can suggest in this continuing debate is that great poetry will always be a unique blend of the two. It is a poetry in which there is complete reciprocity between content and form: the subject so intimately modelled with the expression that to extract this subject would leave one with only the hollow summary of a theme, and the form so self-cohesive and necessary that to change a word, syllable or sound would destroy the perfection of its balance. Valéry defines the poem as 'cette hésitation prolongée entre le son et le sens', a state of suspended animation in which one's response is so delicately balanced between musicality and meaning that to lean towards one and to try to speak of it in isolation leaves both the poem and one's appreciation impoverished.

METRE AND RHYTHM

The basic structural principle of French verse is the poetic line with a fixed number of syllables. Unlike his English counterpart, who has traditionally

had to keep in mind a certain number of *stresses* in composing his poeti
line, the French poet has observed a *syllabic* equality between the lines o
his poem; and whereas, for Wordsworth or Shelley, the number of syllable
is subordinate to the patterns of stress, for Hugo or Baudelaire the syllable
constitute the invariable framework within which to distribute his play o
accentuation.

One of the initial problems for the reader of French verse is the countin
of the syllables which constitute a particular metre. The most central aspect
of this problem is the value of the mute 'e'. Summed up in the most rudimentary form, the rules are that within the body of the verse the mute 'e
of a word *is* counted as a syllable if followed by a consonant (including ar
unpronounced 's' or 'nt') or aspirate 'h'; that it is *not* counted when followed
by, and elided into, a vowel or mute 'h'; and that a mute 'e' is *not* counted
when it occurs at the end of a line. As illustration, it is helpful to consider
the following decasyllabic stanza from Verlaine's *L'Heure du berger*:

$$\overset{1}{\text{Les}} \overset{2}{\text{chats-huants}} \overset{3}{\text{s}}\overset{4}{\text{'éveil}}\overset{5}{\textit{l}}\overset{6}{\textit{ent}}, \overset{7}{\text{et}} \overset{8}{\text{sans}} \overset{9}{\text{bruit}} \overset{10}{}$$

Les chats-huants s'éveillent, et sans bruit

Rament l'air noir avec leurs ailes lourd(es),

Et le zénith s'emplit de lueurs sourd(es).

Blanche, Vénus émerg(e), et c'est la Nuit.

It will be noticed that the terminal rhymes 'lourdes' and 'sourdes' lose the
syllabic value of their mute 'e', as does the internal 'émerge', even though
separated by punctuation from the vowel into which it elides. The verb-
ending of 's'éveillent', on the other hand, though similarly followed by
punctuation and the conjunction 'et', counts as a full syllable, as do the 'e'
mutes of 'Rament' and 'Blanche'. One might then look at examples, less
common, of lines including an aspirate or mute 'h', such as

Superb(e), elle humait voluptueusement   (Baudelaire)

or

Feignent d'être le rire de la lun(e) hilar(e)   (Apollinaire).

In the Baudelaire line, the mute 'e' of 'Superbe' falls, while that of 'elle',
preceding the aspirate 'h' of 'humait', has a full syllabic value. In
Apollinaire's line, after a series of 'e' mutes followed by consonants, 'lune'
is elided into 'hilare', with its mute 'h'.

An associated difficulty in determining the number of syllables in a line
is that of knowing whether two or more successive vowels within a word

count as one or more syllables. For instance, in the following couplet by Hugo,

> Ma laideur, vagu(e) effroi des as*tres* soucieux,
> Perc(e) à travers ma nuit et va salir les cieux,

the '-cieux' of 'soucieux' counts as two syllables, but the noun 'cieux' as only one; and similarly in Verlaine's line,

> Mourez parmi la voix que la Prièr(e) emport(e),

the '-ière' ending constitutes two syllables, whereas the same ending counts only as one in Baudelaire's

> Le chat sur le carreau cherchant u*ne* litièr(e).

One even finds the same word used with varying syllabic value, as in

> Mê*le* dans leur sépulchr(e) au miasm(e) insalubr(e)   (Hugo)

and

> Envo*le*-toi bien loin de ces mias*mes* morbid(es)   (Baudelaire).

The rules governing this aspect of syllabification depend on a variety of factors (the Latin origins of words, whether the syllable is a suffix or an integral part of the stem of the word, etc.), and a good deal of latitude has crept in to confuse the situation since the middle of the nineteenth century, in verse which has adopted conversational rather than literary rhythms. It is not within our scope here to deal in depth with a problem on which manuals of prosody have spent chapters. But some consideration of this basic principle of composition of French metre has been necessary before one can come to appreciate the values of rhythm. Perhaps the best advice, for cases of particular doubt, is that the reader, having determined the overall metrical pattern chosen by the poet, should then ascertain how many syllables an individual word has in the given context.

It is slightly easier to give some brief advice on determining the placing of accentuation within a line, since, almost without exception, French words are stressed on their final syllable. This rule presumes that final 'e' mutes can never be stressed, so that in Verlaine's line 'C'est l'extase langoureuse', for example, the accent falls on '-ta-' and '-reu-'. As in the rhythms of speech, those syllables receiving most emphasis belong to words which carry extra significance. This means that, in general, prepositions, conjunctions, auxiliary verbs, possessive adjectives play a backstage part in the stress distribution of a line; whereas adverbs, adjectives, major verbs and especially nouns more commonly receive the glare of the footlights. One further point about stress is that the longer the pause, the more obvious the stress on the preceding syllable (again ignoring 'e' mutes). Syllables which close phrases, sentences, breath-groups, metrical structures, are all liable to carry emphasis.

Such details of versification may suggest a poetry which is rigid and mechanical. But one must remember that they represent simply the necessary framework within which French poets have exercised a subtle and pliable art. Central to this art are the suggestive and compelling variation of rhythm. Broadly speaking, rhythm can be defined as the way in which the poet varies the distribution of his stresses within a particular poetic line or movement, creating an interplay of unaccentuated and accentuated syllables in order to reinforce his expression of emotion or theme. Rhythm, then, is intimately wedded to the writer's feelings, giving them added intensity and resonance; and whereas metre is a measurement imposed from without, rhythm comes from within, the variable pulse which infuses life into the subject-matter. Indeed it has been said that the Alexandrine line is not composed of twelve syllables, but of 'douze espaces sonores' (and one could add 'douze espaces accentuels') 'dont chacun réclame sa vie'. The poet Paul Claudel has compared the poetic line to a chain of hills: a fascinating contour-map with differences of distance and height between the phonetic peaks. He also calls rhythm 'une espèce de danse poétique' which can draw one in contagiously and intoxicate. Together, metre and rhythm set up, not an antagonism, but a kind of collaborative tension: the one representing regularity, order and predictability, the other representing surprise and variation. Put in another way, metre is the 'grammatical' rules imposed on the poem; rhythm is the 'stylistic' liberties available within these rules. With this distinction in mind, it is perhaps best now to abandon theoretical discussion and see rhythm at work within specific poems.

In the final line of Hugo's despondent poem *Veni, vidi, vixi*, which reads

> Afin que je m'en aille/et que je disparaisse!,

there is a perfectly balanced use of the twelve-syllable line (the Alexandrine), with the stress falling on the sixth and twelfth syllables. The effect of this is to direct emphasis on the verbs indicating departure, with no secondary stresses to give relief to the dispirited mood, while the divided symmetry of the line adds to the conclusiveness of the poet's feelings. But rhythmical balance can take many other forms. For instance, one finds the following line at the end of Hugo's *Le Satyre*:

> Place à Tout! Je suis Pan; Jupiter! à genoux.

In this case, the accentuation falls on the third, sixth, ninth and twelfth syllables, enhancing (by its curt, regular beat) the insistent, authoritative tone of this finale which announces a dramatic change of gods and the dawning of a new era. In Baudelaire's description of oncoming evening in *Paysage*, the awareness of an analogy between

> L'étoile dans l'azur, la lampe à la fenêtre

is reinforced by the parallel rhythm in the two *hémistiches* (the two halves of the line) which, in stressing the second and the sixth, the eighth and the twelfth syllables, helps to link 'l'étoile' with 'la lampe' and 'l'azur' with 'la fenêtre'. A similar rhythmical pattern can be seen in Eluard's line,

> Les fleurs sont desséchées, les graines sont perdues,

where the words 'fleurs' and 'graines', 'desséchées' and 'perdues' are given a reinforced relationship with each other by the repetitive syntax, positioning and stress. So far we have looked only at Alexandrines. It would be helpful, before leaving this question of symmetrical accentuation, to take the example of a different poetic line. One of Verlaine's poems from *Sagesse* begins,

> Les chères mains qui furent miennes.

Here, the octosyllabic line is accentuated with perfect regularity on the second, fourth, sixth and eighth syllables: together with the careful placing of the alliterations of che*res*' and 'fu*rent*', '*m*ains' and '*m*iennes', this even and undisturbed cadence helps to contribute to the serene, devotional opening of the poem.

Traditionally, French verse (especially the longer poetic lines such as the Alexandrine) has had a rhythmical pause or 'caesura' within the line. In the seventeenth century, when the Alexandrine dominated poetry, it was virtually obligatory to have this pause after the sixth syllable, so that there were at least two major stresses: on the sixth and twelfth syllables. The Romantic poets of the early nineteenth century gave much more pliability to this convention; brought into use Alexandrines broken into three, as opposed to two, main rhythmical groups; and, in general, introduced a new and unpredictable variety into the handling of rhythm. Hugo's poem *Le Satyre*, already quoted, offers an interesting illustration:

> On se rencontre, ô choc hideux! les deux armées
> Se heurtent, de la même épouvante enflammées,
> Car la rage guerrière est un gouffre d'effroi.

The first line (divided $4 + 4 + 4$) gives a rather chopped, disjointed effect, appropriate to the idea of opposing forces coming together. The second (divided $2 + 7 + 3$) is rhythmically wayward, straying from a recognizable regular pattern, and helps to suggest violence and the confusion of the mêlée. The third returns to a more standard scheme with a central caesura ($3 + 3/3 + 3$), as it moves from direct description of the heat of the battle to a more general comment on the nature of war. This brief extract shows clearly how rhythmical stress is governed by the needs of the inspiration and cannot be ascribed a fixed place in the metrical framework.

It is not uncommon for the poet to begin his line dramatically with an initial stress. Apollinaire starts *Vendémiaire* with the words,

> Hommes de l'avenir souvenez-vous de moi:

this is an oratorical introduction, designed to arrest the reader's attention, and needs a strong initial impact. The first line of Rimbaud's *Les Effarés* seeks to paint a starkly outlined picture in contrasting colours, an effect aided by the vigour of the opening monosyllable:

> Noirs dans la neige et dans la brume.

In Cros's poem *Vision* one finds the lines

> Et caché, je te regarde,
> Blanche, dans l'eau babillarde.

Here, the force given to the word 'Blanche' by its position and stress suggests the revelation of white flesh and the lingering attention of the onlooker. One of the pieces in Supervielle's *La Fable du Monde* begins

> Nuit en moi, nuit au dehors,

where the dominant position of the word 'Nuit', as well as its repetition in this short heptasyllabic line, emphasizes the fateful, omnipresent quality of night or darkness. It is not only the first syllable of a line which can be exploited in this way. Because of the importance which the central caesura has held in the tradition of French verse, the seventh syllable of an Alexandrine has often been seen as the beginning of the second *hémistiche*, a new section of the poetic development, and this, too, can be stressed to give unexpected rhythmical variation. For instance, in Baudelaire's tercet

> Que ce soit dans la nuit / et dans la solitude,
> Que ce soit dans la rue / et dans la multitude,
> Son fantôme dans l'air / danse comme un flambeau,

after two lines which match each other in symmetry and in which the stress on the sixth and the twelfth syllables seems reliably established, the final line throws sudden emphasis on the seventh syllable, in a verb which creates a strong impression of vitality and dramatizes the ghostly apparition. Rimbaud uses a similar device but to different effect in *Bal des pendus*:

> Belzébuth enragé / racle ses violons.

Here the poet wishes to suggest a devilish noise, and the rhythmical position of 'racle' (to say nothing of its onomatopoeic qualities) makes a major contribution to the clumsiness and cacophony. The last two examples have shown the seventh syllable usurping the major stress, but without eliminating completely the effect of the sixth syllable and the caesural pause. In the following lines from Cros's sonnet *Délabrement*, on the other hand,

> Que la pluie et le vent par la fenêtre ouverte
> Couvrent de moisissure âcre et de mousse verte
> Tous ces débris...,

the words 'Couvrent de moisissure âcre' flow on to the seventh syllable

and do not respect a theoretical central caesura: this gives more force to
the adjective 'âcre' and more expressiveness to the poet's distaste. At other
times, the regularity of the verse is broken by a poet's use of two consecutive
stresses, other than those straddling the caesura of an Alexandrine. In this
extract from a Verlaine poem,

> L'échelonnement des haies
> Moutonne à l'infini, mer
> Claire dans le brouillard clair...,

an association between the sea and the idea of infinity is forged, not only
by the rather artificial juxtaposition of the two words, but by the double
accentuation (on '...infini, mer') at the end of the line. The accents in this
line from Apollinaire's *Les Sapins* fall in a similar position, setting a final
seal on the picture of boats slipping away down the Rhine as seen from a
distant hill-side:

> Les bateaux qui sur le Rhin voguent.

It will have been noticed, in one or two of the examples quoted (for
instance, Cros's '*Blanche*, dans l'eau babillarde' and Baudelaire's '...*danse
comme un flambeau*'), that the stressed syllable is given added force by the
fact that it is followed by a mute 'e'. It is an important feature of French verse
that the mute 'e', rather than being pronounced as a separate syllable in
its own right, tends to have the effect of lengthening the previous one. In
Verlaine's lines,

> Il *pleure* dans mon cœur
> Comme il pleut sur la ville

the impression of melancholy is intensified by what would be a prolonged or
'dying' reading of the word 'pleure' (in contrast with the brevity of 'pleut',
which does not possess the same emotional resonance). At other times,
however, the mute 'e' can be read in a way which gives a bouncy cadence to
the verse. Supervielle exploits this possibility when he writes,

> Puis soulève son étendard
> Qu'une éternel*le* flam*me* lèche.

In the second line, where he wishes to convey both the flapping of a banner
and the flickering or lapping of flames, there is a rhythmic alternation of
heavily stressed syllables and lightly rebounding mute 'e's. There is a similar
effect in his line

> Aux fol*les* pha*ses* de l'écume,

but here his intention is to evoke the up-and-down or to-and-fro motions
of the foam-capped sea.

No introduction to the use of rhythm in French verse would be adequate without considering also the use of the *vers impair* (five, seven, nine syllables and so on). Verlaine has described the imparisyllabic line as

> Plus vague et plus soluble dans l'air,
> Sans rien en lui qui pèse ou qui pose.

One can illustrate partially what he means by quoting the following heptasyllabic stanza from the *Fêtes galantes*:

> Fondons nos âmes, nos cœurs
> Et nos sens extasiés,
> Parmi les vagues langueurs
> Des pins et des arbousiers.

Here it is impossible to fix a central caesura or divide the lines into equal rhythmical segments: in the first line the accent falls on the second, fourth and seventh syllables; in the next on the third and seventh; in the following one on the fourth and seventh; and in the final one on the second and seventh. This means that, in this case, there is a very shifting pattern of accentuation and that, in any *vers impair*, there will be a rhythmical inequality within the individual line. It cannot be stressed with that firm and positive regularity that one finds in Hugo's Alexandrine,

> Répondez, vallon pur, répondez, solitude;

or even in Verlaine's own

> Voici des fruits, des fleurs, des feuilles et des branches.

As a result it dissolves the predictable patterns of rhetorical stress and is conducive to that blurring of outlines to which Verlaine is so attracted. A further interesting illustration of a mobile use of rhythm in a seven-syllable line is found in the first of his *Ariettes oubliées*, which begins:

> C'est l'extase langoureuse,
> C'est la fatigue amoureuse,
> C'est tous les frissons des bois
> Parmi l'étreinte des brises....

The major accent here slips subtly from the third, to the fourth, to the fifth syllables in the opening three lines: this introduces variety and almost imperceptible change into what is a deceptively repetitive formula, thus avoiding monotony and giving the reader the impression of being carried gradually deeper into some unnamed mystery.

We began by defining rhythm as a variable pulse. Whether in parisyllabic or imparisyllabic verse, in traditional Alexandrines or experimental free verse, its function is to give vitality to the metrical skeleton and set up a stimulating relationship between the fixed and the free, the anticipated and the unexpected. Our final example is from Supervielle:

Un cheval blanc découvrait l'homme
Qui s'avançait à petit bruit,
Avec la Terre autour de lui
Tournant pour son cœur astrologue.

After three octosyllabic lines all accented on the fourth and eighth syllables and giving a simple narrative structure, there is a surprise-effect: the reader loses his footing in an unexpected rhythm which helps to evoke the giddiness of a planet in motion and a fathomless universe.

USES OF VERSE-FORM

One cannot attribute a particular effect to a particular metrical line. There is no key which says, for instance, that an Alexandrine always carries with it a spirit of nobility or that an octosyllabic line must inevitably be brisk and racy. But obviously a good poet chooses his verse-form to do maximum justice to his theme, seeking an affinity between form and content.

If one considers firstly the Alexandrine, one can see why many French poets have shown a predilection for it. Its expansive quality allows scope for the fairly full development of an idea or expression of emotion within the single line, while its twelve syllables lend themselves mathematically to the greatest variety of even rhythmical divisions. Only the Alexandrine allows Hugo so many accumulated stresses, recurring at such regular emphatic intervals, in his line:

Tuons! Frappons! Damnons! J'ai peur! J'ai froid! J'ai faim!

It is an appropriate vehicle for such dramatic surges of energy. Similarly, it supports well the elevated tone and relentless *souffle* of rhetoric, as in

Nous crions vers vous, Père! O Dieu bon, punissez!
Car vous êtes l'espoir de ceux qu'on a chassés,
Car vous êtes patrie à celui qu'on exile,
Car vous êtes le port, la demeure et l'asile! (Hugo).

Its equally balanced parts provide a perfect mould for the forging of parallels and antithesis: in Baudelaire's line,

Doux comme les hautbois, verts comme les prairies *} division*

one is made aware of a kind of identity between the two impressions, despite the fact that they deal with different areas of sense-perception; while in Hugo's *Booz endormi*, the basic contrast between the qualities of youth and age is underlined by the structure of

Car le jeune homme est beau, mais le vieillard est grand.

At other times, the Alexandrine may simply be used to give double stress to a theme or emotion, as in

Mon sillon? Le voilà. Ma gerbe? La voici (Hugo);

to extend an image, as in

Tes baisers sont un philtre et ta bouche une amphore   (Baudelaire);

or to make a forceful distinction between two different states, in this case a present and a future:

Le Monde a soif d'amour: tu viendras l'apaiser   (Rimbaud).

Verlaine's attitude to the Alexandrine line during the course of his poetic career is a very revealing one. Verlaine is often thought of as one of the great poetic innovators of the nineteenth century, experimenting (especially in *Romances sans paroles*) with slender and tenuous verse-forms and irregular rhythms in the attempt to convey wavering states of mind and indefinite landscapes. In the collection *Sagesse*, however, written as a consequence of his imprisonment and conversion to the Catholic faith, he returns to the Alexandrine as his main poetic line. This coincides with a new-found firmness of belief, a more elevated or didactic tone associated with more explicit religious themes, and a desire to re-establish himself within a traditional order. The lines

> Il pleure dans mon cœur
> Comme il pleut sur la ville.
> Quelle est cette langueur
> Qui pénètre mon cœur?
> (*Romances sans paroles*)

have a simple melancholy and a direct melodic appeal; but they do not have the grander sweep, formality and tone of authority which the Alexandrines allow in:

> Donnez-leur, ô mon Dieu, la résignation,
> Toute forte douceur, l'ordre et l'intelligence,
> Afin qu'au jour suprême ils gagnent l'indulgence
> De l'Agneau formidable en la neuve Sion   (*Sagesse*).

The octosyllabic line, on the other hand, tends to be used to different effect. Like the six-syllable line, it does not provide scope for the weightier cumulative effect, for the lengthy development of idea, emotion or simile which one finds in the Alexandrine. Consequently, it is more appropriate to the lighter lyric and the comparatively direct narrative style. Apollinaire's poem *L'Adieu* gives a good illustration of its use:

> J'ai cueilli ce brin de bruyère
> L'automne est morte souviens-t'en
> Nous ne nous verrons plus sur terre
> Odeur du temps brin de bruyère
> Et souviens-toi que je t'attends.

Here, the lyrical emotions are expressed in a simple, unpretentious way, in

n economical style which slips swiftly from notation to notation and
between descriptive fragment and personal nostalgia: the octosyllabic line
certainly contributes to the brevity and poignancy of this almost over-hasty
little poem (one of the themes of which is the rapid passage of time). Supervielle chooses the same line in *Une étoile tire de l'arc*, which begins:

> Toutes les brebis de la lune
> Tourbillonnent vers ma prairie
> Et tous les poissons de la lune
> Plongent loin dans ma rêverie.

In the case of this imaginative fable, the octosyllable projects one briskly
through the stage-by-stage narrative progression in which each grammatical
part of the sentence is clearly allocated to its individual line: one is not left
to ponder too deeply on this childlike fantasy. The octosyllabic line, as one
can see if one compares these examples with the earlier Alexandrines, is a
freer, more casual verse-form, and its rhythm (especially as used by modern
poets) is unpredictable – no doubt because it would soon degenerate into
sheer doggerel if it were stressed consistently in a 4 + 4 pattern.

Lines of less than six syllables are infrequent and because of their rarity
tend to be used for a more deliberate or exceptional purpose. Two examples
of the four-syllable line are particularly interesting. In Verlaine's *Walcourt*
we find this stanza:

> Guinguettes claires,
> Bières, clameurs,
> Servantes chères
> A tous fumeurs!

Here it has been the poet's intention to create an impressionistic descriptive
effect, like those of Renoir or Monet, with tiny fast-moving touches of the
brush to capture the effervescent spirit of a beer-garden. In Apollinaire's
Hôtels, on the other hand,

> La chambre est veuve
> Chacun pour soi
> Présence neuve
> On paye au mois,

the four-syllable line is used, not to paint a fluid, mobile picture, but in a
stiff, staccato way, in order to suggest the solitude and impersonality of
modern hotel life. The rhythm is monotonously accentuated on every
second and fourth syllable; each line is self-contained, helping to evoke
compartmentalized life; and the final line is very reminiscent of the curt
notice one might find on a hotel door.

Although it is a suspect procedure to try to define, in absolute terms, the
difference between a twelve syllable line and a ten, or between a ten and an
eight, there are cases where one can safely say that a poet has chosen a

combination of lines of different length and used them cleverly to give extr
relief to his theme. Baudelaire's *Le Chat* is such an example:

> Viens, mon beau chat, sur mon cœur amoureux;
> Retiens les griffes de ta patte,
> Et laisse-moi plonger dans tes beaux yeux,
> Mêlés de métal et d'agate.

In the first longer line, the poet uses romantic vocabulary, carried on a
heavily cadenced anapaestic rhythm ('...mon beau chat, sur mon cœu
amoureux'). The eight-syllable line brings a contrast: after the suggestior
of a languid loving nature, it strikes a note of tension and cruelty, and botl
line and rhythm are more contracted. The next two lines reiterate thi
effect: the idea of pleasurable self-abandonment and the inviting beauty
of the eyes, conveyed by the longer line, is counteracted by the image o
unyielding metallic hardness forcefully condensed in the shorter one.

Sometimes one finds a mixture of parisyllabic and imparisyllabic lines
Verlaine's *Colombine* from the *Fêtes galantes* is a gymnastic little poem, ir
which he playfully juggles with his verse-form:

> Léandre le sot,
> Pierrot qui d'un saut
> De puce
> Franchit le buisson,
> Cassandre sous son
> Capuce...

The pentasyllabic line in itself is rhythmically asymmetrical, but the verse
is made even more capricious by the surprise introduction of a two-syllable
line which appears like a jack-in-the-box (one should remember that Verlaine
is here describing the antics of pantomime figures). The words 'De puce'
and 'Capuce' are typographically positioned to give a suggestive visual
effect: in the first case, imitating Pierrot's movement, they jump out of line,
while 'Capuce', tucked away on its own, helps to conjure up a picture of
Cassandre huddled inside his hood.

This brings us to the use which poets have made of the imparisyllabic
line throughout whole poems. Again Verlaine provides some of the most
interesting illustrations since, together with Rimbaud in the early 1870s,
he made a deliberate attempt to elasticate some of the most respected
conventions of French verse. One curious example is his *Sonnet boiteux*,
so called because its thirteen-syllable line perversely avoids the balance of
the classical Alexandrine and hobbles awkwardly beyond the usual confines:

> Ah! vraiment c'est triste, ah! vraiment ça finit trop mal.
> Il n'est pas permis d'être à ce point infortuné,
> Ah! vraiment c'est trop la mort du naïf animal
> Qui voit tout son sang couler sous son regard fané.

he theme here, appropriately, is that of suffering and misfortune which ave gone beyond a reasonable limit, and a dulled consciousness which can aguely see its own life seeping away beyond its control. But this verse-form, which seems to have no reliable backbone and no clear contour, is one of ne rarest in French poetry and can hardly be quoted as a model. Perhaps he most common *vers impair* is the five-syllable line. *Soleils couchants*, y the same poet, illustrates a characteristic use of it:

> Une aube affaiblie
> Verse par les champs
> La mélancolie
> Des soleils couchants.

By its brevity and its rhythmical incompleteness, it lends itself to this kind of uninterrupted 'run-on' effect, by which the description of a pallid dawn enveloping the fields, a feeling of melancholy, and the associative image of sunset do not stand apart but flow over one into the other.

This example touches on another aspect of the use of verse-form, namely, *enjambement*. *Enjambement* occurs when the sense of a phrase is not fully expressed within an individual line, but needs to 'step over' into the next line before it is complete. *Rejet* is the term applied to that part of the *enjambement* which is 'thrown over' to the following line. Poets have been able to exploit *enjambement* as a poetic device because, in failing to respect the more traditional procedure of bringing the sense-unit to an end at the terminal rhyme, it directs attention to itself as an irregularity. For instance, Baudelaire creates a surprise-effect in the transition from the quatrains to the tercets in his sonnet *Recueillement*, where the *enjambement* is not made between the lines within a stanza but between one stanza and the next (traditionally kept apart at this point in the sonnet):

> Pendant que des mortels la multitude vile,
> Sous le fouet du plaisir, ce bourreau sans merci,
> Va cueillir des remords dans la fête servile,
> Ma Douleur, donne-moi la main; viens par ici,
>
> Loin d'eux. Vois se pencher les défuntes Années,
> Sur les balcons du ciel, en robes surannées;
> Surgir du fond des eaux le Regret souriant.

The *rejet* here is all the more effective, as the sense seems to be complete with 'viens par ici', only to be carried on, even if briefly, in the next stanza. It thus bites into the tercet and breaks the anticipated unity of structure. By setting the words 'Loin d'eux' at a distance, Baudelaire makes all the more emphatic his desire to be apart from 'la multitude vile' and alone with his pain. In Verlaine's descriptive poem *L'Heure du berger*, the idea of the earth sinking to sleep as the night-time mist rises is given an added rhythmical weight by means of *enjambement*:

> Dans un brouillard qui danse, la prairie
> S'endort fumeuse, et la grenouille crie...

Many dramatic uses of *enjambement* occur in Rimbaud's poetry. The la**?**
two lines of *Le Dormeur du val*, for instance, read:

> Il dort dans le soleil, la main sur sa poitrine
> Tranquille. Il a deux trous rouges au côté droit.

In this case, the adjective 'Tranquille' is isolated as the *rejet* and charge**?**
with potential irony, which explodes when one realizes that this soldier **?**
not just asleep on a warm summer's day, but dead.

One should not leave the consideration of uses of verse-form without **?**
few examples of the contribution that the choice of a particular stanza**?**
form can make to the success of a poem. There are times when the use o**?**
the rhyming couplet can give a lyrical simplicity and musical saturation to **?**
theme, as in Verlaine's

> O triste, triste était mon âme
> A cause, à cause d'une femme.
>
> Je ne me suis pas consolé
> Bien que mon cœur s'en soit allé... ;

or an uninhibited narrative progression (and, in this case, a certain clarity
of outline and forthrightness to the allegorical figure and his actions):

> Bon chevalier masqué qui chevauche en silence,
> Le Malheur a percé mon vieux cœur de sa lance.
>
> Le sang de mon vieux cœur n'a fait qu'un jet vermeil,
> Puis s'est évaporé sur les fleurs, au soleil.
>
> L'ombre éteignit mes yeux, un cri vint à ma bouche,
> Et mon vieux cœur est mort dans un frisson farouche   (*Sagesse*).

Baudelaire adopts an interesting verse-form in *L'Invitation au voyage*: the
long twelve-line stanza, switching between lines of five and seven syllables,
gives an expansiveness to the imaginative vision and a sinuous mobility.
The refrain, on the other hand, brings it back periodically to a central focus.
In addition, the refrain

> Là, tout n'est qu'ordre et beauté,
> Luxe, calme et volupté

carries with it a lulling incantatory quality, and its recurrence suggests
the reassuring existence of a changeless ideal. Verlaine's use of a refrain
in the second of his poems entitled *Streets* provides a noticeable contrast.
Here the effect is not lulling and dreamy, but brisk and energetic. With
each appearance, the refrain brings a note of forced gaiety in the present,
to contrast with the more nostalgic reminiscences from the past, and sets
up a dubious interplay of feelings:

Dansons la gigue!

J'aimais surtout ses jolis yeux,
Plus clairs que l'étoile des cieux.
J'aimais ses yeux malicieux.

Dansons la gigue!

Elle avait des façons vraiment
De désoler un pauvre amant,
Que c'en était vraiment charmant!

Dansons la gigue!

Although not quite the same as a refrain, a repeated (or approximately repeated) line within a stanza can be employed to great advantage. Baudelaire is a master of this art. The repeated line in the second stanza of *Le Balcon*,

Les soirs illuminés par l'ardeur du charbon,
Et les soirs au balcon, voilés de vapeurs roses.
Que ton sein m'était doux! que ton cœur m'était bon!
Nous avons dit souvent d'impérissables choses
Les soirs illuminés par l'ardeur du charbon

enhances the luxurious atmosphere, gives a well-rounded fullness to the poem and increases the sense of harmony and contentment. In *L'Irréparable*, on the other hand, the repeated line does not bring about a sense of fulfilment but rather, thanks to subtle modifications, an unsettling and disquieting mood:

Pouvons-nous étouffer le vieux, le long Remords,
Qui vit, s'agite et se tortille,
Et se nourrit de nous comme le ver des morts,
Comme du chêne la chenille?
Pouvons-nous étouffer l'implacable Remords?

The substitution of the abstract and emphatic 'implacable' for the more commonplace adjectives 'vieux…long' intensifies one's impression of the insatiable nature of Remorse, and turns the initial question into a rhetorical one. The last two examples have been of five-line stanzas, whereas the quatrain is the standard verse in French. This extra line can and usually does give a different quality to a stanza, as, for instance, in Baudelaire's *La Chevelure*, where there is not only a greater concentration of rhyme, but also a greater headiness of atmosphere, density of imagery and a feeling of superabundance:

O toison, moutonnant jusque sur l'encolure!
O boucles! O parfum chargé de nonchaloir!
Extase! Pour peupler ce soir l'alcôve obscure
Des souvenirs dormant dans cette chevelure,
Je la veux agiter dans l'air comme un mouchoir!

There are many different stanza-forms in French verse, some fixed, som
variable, some traditional, some experimental. It would take a volume t
show them all used in expert hands. But this limited introduction will hav
encouraged insights into this particular aspect of the collusion of conter
and form.

SONORITY *fulness + deepness of soun*

Poetry, more than any other literary genre, has exploited the musica
possibilities of language. Verlaine has called for 'De la musique avan
toute chose' and attempted to create a poetry which would be 'la chanso
grise', by which the reader is lulled into a vague and penetrating musica
mood which appeals to the ear more than the intellect. And though Ver
laine's poetry is an exceptional example of the art of poetic song, poetry i
general has always depended on the technique of musical juxtaposition
Verlaine's apparently effortless melodies, his spontaneity and fluidity, ar
the product of a carefully patterned artifice; and, paradoxically, the impre
cision which seems to dissolve the framework of his poems stems from
fine sense of musical order.

The principal source of sonority in French verse has traditionally beer
the terminal rhyme. It is the recurrent rhyme-pattern which gives not only
structural regularity to the poem, but also musical harmony and the satisfaction of hearing sounds echoing each other at anticipated intervals. In
general terms, rhyme ensures the musical cohesion of the verse. More
colourfully the poet Claudel calls it a lighthouse at the end of a headland,
communicating across the space of the page with the lights on other points.
But since it is a necessary convention 'indispensable à notre art français'
as Verlaine has said, one can rarely discern in its phonetic qualities a specific
effect designed by the poet – hence the examples which follow, illustrative
as they are, do not prove that rhyme is always meaningful, and students
should beware of trying to read too much into the different rhyme-schemes
of French verse.

Rimes plates is the term applied to rhymes which come at the end of two
consecutive lines. By their proximity, they have a more close-knit musical
resonance than rhymes at a further distance from each other. Cros uses
them in his poem *La Vision du grand canal royal des deux mers*, where,
in the opening couplets, he wishes to sound the rousing note of a fanfare:

> Envole-toi chanson, va dire au Roi de France
> Mon rêve lumineux, ma suprême espérance!
>
> Je chante, ô ma Patrie, en des vers doux et lents
> La ceinture d'azur attachée à tes flancs,
>
> Le liquide chemin de Bordeaux à Narbonne
> Qu'abreuvent tour à tour et l'Aude et la Garonne.

n Baudelaire's sonnet *L'Aube spirituelle*, on the other hand, the intention
as been to create a final fanfare, and the *rimes plates* of the last two lines
after the *rimes embrassées* used throughout the octet) help to provide the
equired musical flourish and give a sense of completion satisfying to the
ar:

> Le soleil a noirci la flamme des bougies;
> Ainsi, toujours vainqueur, ton fantôme est pareil,
> Ame resplendissante, à l'immortel soleil!

A similar example is to be found in Rimbaud's *Chanson de la plus haute
our*:

> Oisive jeunesse
> A tout asservie,
> Par délicatesse
> J'ai perdu ma vie.
> Ah! Que le temps vienne
> Où les cœurs s'éprennent.

Here the *rimes plates* mark the change from retrospective analysis of his
own life to a rather desperate wish for the future, and round off the stanza
with added intensity.

Rimes croisées are rhymes which alternate *abab*; while *rimes embrassées*
are a pair of rhymes embraced or surrounded on either side by another pair
of rhymes to form the pattern *abba*. It is almost impossible to say what
effect is created by one form or the other. It is perhaps more satisfying to
refer to an instance where a poet has made a switch from one form to another
in a very telling way. In *Soleils couchants* Verlaine maintains alternating
rhymes for twelve of his sixteen lines, then suddenly, after the appearance of
the most unsettling images in the poem, switches to *rimes embrassées*,
making one aware of a change of register and plunging one unexpectedly
into a disturbing conclusion.

Since the earliest days of French poetry, a distinction has been made
between so-called masculine and feminine rhymes; and from the sixteenth
century onwards it has been the tradition to alternate these two types of
rhyme, that is, to ensure that one masculine pair of rhymes is not followed
by another masculine pair, or a feminine by another feminine. Quite simply,
a masculine rhyme (regardless of the actual gender of the word) is one which
does not end in a mute 'e', whereas a feminine rhyme is one that does.
Critics have suggested that masculine rhymes, which end more abruptly on a
consonant or stressed vowel sound (e.g. 'espagnol...rossignol' or 'bassin...
dessein'), tend to be clipped, curt and devoid of echo; and that feminine
rhymes, thanks to their following mute 'e' which is not counted as a syllable
(e.g. 'grêles...ailes' or 's'effacent...rêvassent'), have a final reverberation
after their accented syllable which slightly prolongs, softens and 'aerates'
their effect. One can read numerous poems in which there is no discernible

difference in effect between the masculine and feminine rhymes, but this is nevertheless a distinction which can be cleverly exploited. Here is a stanza of masculine rhymes (many poets have now dispensed with the strict rule of alternation) by Supervielle:

> Pour avoir mis le pied
> Sur le cœur de la nuit
> Je suis un homme pris
> Dans les rets étoilés (*Vivre*).

In this case the idea of an automatic succession of cause and effect and the poet's frank recognition of the inevitable are enhanced by the unrelieved sharpness of the terminal rhymes. One should then compare this with a stanza of feminine rhymes from Verlaine:

> Tourbillonnent dans l'extase
> D'une lune rose et grise,
> Et la mandoline jase
> Parmi les frissons de brise (*Mandoline*),

where the 'e' mutes at the end of the lines combine with those within the verse to produce an unhurried rhythm, and the drowsy sibilants of the rhyming words seem to linger. In other instances, it is not the intrinsic properties of the masculine or feminine rhyme which catch the attention, but the way in which the poet has used their alternation to underline two different aspects of his theme. In the first stanza of Cros's *Cueillette*:

> C'était un vrai petit voyou,
> Elle venait on ne sait d'où,
> Moi, je l'aimais comme une bête.
> Oh! la jeunesse, quelle fête!

the masculine rhymes are reserved for the more offhand, colloquial and pejorative description, whereas the feminine ones accompany a more enthusiastic and, in the final line, more hyperbolic expression of his personal emotions. The first two couplets from Verlaine's *Spleen* are equally illustrative:

> Les roses étaient toutes rouges,
> Et les lierres étaient tout noirs.
>
> Chère, pour peu que tu te bouges,
> Renaissent tous mes désespoirs.

Here the rhymes seem to be distributed thematically: 'rouges' and 'bouges', with their more delicate, prolonged effect, are linked with the theme of love (red roses and the address to the dear one); while the rhyming of 'noirs' and 'désespoirs' accentuates the more negative undertones. In this way, the duality of the subject-matter is supported by the dual nature of the rhyming.

One other feature of rhyme in French verse needs to be considered. This
is the distinction between *rimes faibles*, *rimes suffisantes* and *rimes riches*.
The *rime faible* is nothing more than an assonance (an identity of vowel
sound) occurring in the rhyming position, such as those in the poem *Vivre*
by Supervielle just quoted: 'pieds...étoilés' and 'nuit...pris'. A *rime
suffisante* consists of two identical sounds, normally a vowel and an accompanying consonant (that is, in terms of sound and not spelling), such as
'bête...fête', 'rouges...bouges' or 'asservie...vie'. A *rime riche* is a
rhyme which provides more common elements than the two which are
necessary to make up a *rime suffisante*, as, for example, in 'France...
espérance', 'grise...brise' or 'espagnol...rossignol'. Sometimes poets have
purposely weakened the effect of their rhymes, often in order to reduce their
obtrusiveness and the rigidity of the verse and to turn the emphasis to more
subtle internal qualities (of rhythm, sound or image). Verlaine does this in
many poems, either by using internal rhymes which diminish the importance
of the terminal ones, or by the use of *rimes faibles*, or by an exceptional
indulgence in *enjambement* which causes the voice to glide over the terminal
rhymes. This can be seen partly as a reaction against Hugo, who wrote:

> Mes strophes sont comme les balles
> Aux coups meurtriers et fréquents.
> Mes deux rimes sont deux cymbales
> Qui sonnent sur les fronts des camps.

In more recent years, Supervielle has written a good deal of poetry which
is stitched only by very tenuous rhymes, assonances and approximate
sounds: in this way he draws more attention to the oddities of his imaginative
vision and his surprise-images which enjoy an added measure of freedom
from the constraints of verse-form. At other times, poets have cultivated
very rich rhymes, and in general the effect of these is easier to gauge. It
may be a humorous effect, deliberately ridiculing the excesses of verse
technique, as in this parody of his own style by Verlaine (which not only
uses *rime riche* but also goes to extremes with internal rhyme):

> Des romances sans paroles ont,
> D'un accord discord ensemble et frais,
> Agacé ce cœur fadasse exprès,
> O le son, le frisson qu'elles ont!
> (*A la manière de Paul Verlaine*).

It may be to convey satire, as when Rimbaud links the verb 'rachète' with
'Monsieur Hachette!'; or to express revolt and disgust and to shock con-
servative readers, as when the same poet writes of '...des hoquets bachiques'
and 'des sursauts stomachiques'. Or it may be simply to gain a greater
musical richness and consistency, as in Baudelaire's *Parfum exotique*, the
tercets of which are the most lavish:

> Guidé par ton odeur vers de charmants climats,
> Je vois un port rempli de voiles et de mâts
> Encor tout fatigués par la vague marine,
>
> Pendant que le parfum des verts tamariniers,
> Qui circule dans l'air et m'enfle la narine,
> Se mêle dans mon âme au chant des mariniers.

One of the most important attributes of rhyme is the way in which it high-lights the author's meaning by linking key-words. Baudelaire is a mine of such examples. The final tercet of the sonnet *Avec ses vêtements ondoyants et nacrés...* reads:

> Où tout n'est qu'or, acier, lumière et diamants,
> Resplendit à jamais, comme un astre inutile,
> La froide majesté de la femme stérile.

Here the rhyme, in pairing two associated words, gives an incontrovertible force to the idea of sterility (and one also notices the internal rhyme of 'maje*sté*...*sté*rile', which helps to interweave the two ideas of regal distance and a barren relationship). In the following stanza from *Le Serpent qui danse*:

> Comme un navire qui s'éveille
> Au vent du matin,
> Mon âme rêveuse appareille
> Pour un ciel lointain,

the feminine rhymes link the two terms of the comparison, making one more aware of the interchange between the ideas of 'navire' and 'appareille', 'rêveuse' and 's'éveille'. The quatrains of the sonnet *Sed non satiata* are a particularly rich illustration of rhyming:

> Bizarre déité, brune comme les nuits,
> Au parfum mélangé de musc et de havane,
> Œuvre de quelque obi, le Faust de la savane,
> Sorcière au flanc d'ébène, enfant des noirs minuits,
>
> Je préfère au constance, à l'opium, aux nuits,
> L'élixir de ta bouche où l'amour se pavane;
> Quand vers toi mes désirs partent en caravane,
> Tes yeux sont la citerne où boivent mes ennuis.

The rhymes 'havane...savane...pavane...caravane', all rich rhymes, are exotic and contribute to the effect of foreignness and mystery emanating from this woman, while the masculine rhymes are all associated with ideas of darkness, dark moods or the dark attractions of intoxication, which suggest another side of her nature. Sometimes, it is internal rhyme which is introduced to fuse ideas or images, as in this stanza from *Chant d'automne*, where loving qualities, sisterly affection and sweetness are picked out phonetically in the body of the verse:

> Et pourtant aimez-moi, tendre *cœur*! soyez mère,
> Même pour un ingrat, même pour un méchant;
> Amante *ou sœur*, soyez la *douceur* éphémère
> D'un glorieux automne ou d'un soleil couchant.

At other times, internal rhyme serves to give a varied or disturbed rhythmical reading by acting as competition to the terminal rhyme-scheme or at least breaking its authority to some extent. But more often it simply helps to give a much richer musical texture to a poem, as in a line like 'Sur les b*or*ds *du*vetés de vos mèches t*or*dues' from *La Chevelure.*

Rhyme, however, is not the only source of sonority in poetry. One must also consider such less formal devices as alliteration, assonance, onomato-poeia and expressive combinations of sounds. Alliteration is usually taken to mean the repetition of a consonant sound, while assonance refers to the repetition of a vowel. More often than not, especially in the rich context of poetry, they are found working in conjunction. One of the most famous illustrations comes from Hugo's *Booz endormi*:

> Un frais parfum sortait des touffes d'asphodèle;
> Les souffles de la nuit flottaient sur Galgala,

two lines of perfectly positioned alliterative effect which, in their context, are highly expressive of a hushed night-time atmosphere, a lightly perfumed air and only the slightest breeze. There are many conspicuous examples in Rimbaud's *Le Bateau ivre*, not all of which work to one and the same end. For instance, like the description quoted from Hugo, the line

> Pussent forcer le mufle aux Océans poussifs

is onomatopoeic, suggesting by its sound a violent, hissing, frothing ocean. The sounds of the following line, on the other hand,

> Fermentent les rousseurs amères de l'amour

cannot be said to be directly related to the meaning or to conjure up any particular descriptive impression (although the energy of the recurrent 'r' might be evocative of a seething or fermentation); but the repetitive sounds in 'amères...amours' are especially instrumental in bringing out the contrast between love and bitterness, and in general the heavy use of the sound 'r', falling at rhythmic intervals, draws attention to this line, which contains one of the most curious and startling sense-perceptions of the whole poem. In this further example,

> Et des taches de vins bleus et des vomissures
> Me lava, dispersant gouvernail et grappin,

the alliteration clenches together the two nouns 'gouvernail' and 'grappin', the two associated symbols of the whole restrictive world to be rejected, and adds vigour and tautness to this description of a crucial turning-point in the poet's experience. Another emphatic combination of sounds occurs in

> Je courus! Et les Péninsules démarrées
> N'ont pas subi tohu-bohus plus triomphants,

where the poet wishes to evoke the turbulent bobbing of a floating object on the waves and the feeling of exhilaration. Rimbaud, a particularly dynamic and energetic poet, usually handles language in a flamboyant way. One should turn finally to a more discreet poet like Verlaine, whose use of sounds is more musical and structural than dramatically expressive. One line which we have already quoted,

> Les chères mains qui furent miennes

shows how alliteration may be positioned to create symmetry and a graceful balance. The following stanza of a poem from *Sagesse* illustrates some of Verlaine's most delicate musicalities (even though he was later to refer to it scathingly as 'cette musicaillerie, sans talent aucun'):

> Ecoutez la chanson bien douce
> Qui ne pleure que pour vous plaire.
> Elle est discrète, elle est légère:
> Un frisson d'eau sur de la mousse.

The first line contains assonance, its echo being felt all the more in the brief octosyllabic line; the second has a rich alliteration, nicely balanced with the sounds recurring in virtually the same order, which picks out the two emotional words 'pleure' and 'plaire' representing the pain of love and the pleasures of love; the third uses syntactical repetition, with each part perfectly modelled on the other and the same vowel-sound played and replayed; the final line moves closer to onomatopoeia, the word 'frisson' being onomatopoeic in itself but made all the more so here by the return of the sounds 'r' and 's' and the accompanying image of slightly ruffled water.

One could accumulate *ad infinitum* illustrations of sound-patterns in poetry. It is important to recognize that few will lend themselves to a definite interpretation linking them to the poet's emotion and thought (though critics have tried to make tables of correspondences between the different sounds and a certain range of associations which go with them). But there can be no doubt that poetry weaves analogies between sound and sense (a line like 'Infinis bercements du loisir embaumé' undeniably works its charm on both levels simultaneously), that the poem declines to be a mere messenger and becomes a 'sonorous object' in its own right, and that, without a responsiveness to the musical resources of language and to the sense of order which patterns them, one remains excluded from an area of appreciation central to poetry.

WORDS AND THEIR TONES

Turning from the sounds of words and their place in the musical patterning of the verse, one might now consider words and their flavours and the different atmospheres they help to establish. For poetry, despite a common misapprehension that it uses a narrow range of vocabulary, has exploited the widest possible variety of tones, from the highest to the lowest, the rarest to the most familiar. Certainly, at different periods of its history, French verse has drawn on a limited store of words and phrases deemed to be particularly poetic: words pertaining to nature such as 'l'azur' or 'la voûte étoilée' for the sky, 'Vénus' or 'la reine des ombres' describing the moon, 'aquilon', 'zéphyr' or 'bise' for various types of wind, 'onde' or 'flots' for the sea, 'aurore' instead of 'aube', and 'astres' rather than 'étoiles' for the stars; words relating to the emotions such as 'feu' and 'flamme' meaning love, 'courroux' as a more noble variant for 'colère', and 'tourments', 'supplices' or 'maux' to describe emotional pain; and a host of other decorous synonyms or periphrases such as 'éclore', 'gésir', 'trépas' or 'la course de nos jours'. But poets are by definition adventurers in language, and poetry has never been caught for long in the doldrums of cliché and stereotype.

Indeed, good poetry has always been in conscious or unconscious reaction against the commonplaces of a previous era; and a full appreciation of any poet's originality will depend on a knowledge of what has preceded him in terms of traditional poetic vocabulary, favoured expression and consecrated image. For instance, one cannot properly estimate Hugo's revolutionary impact on poetic expression in the first half of the nineteenth century, unless one sees the relevance of this extract from his own *art poétique*, *Réponse à un acte d'accusation*:

> La langue était l'état avant quatrevingt-neuf;
> Les mots, bien ou mal nés, vivaient parqués en castes;
> Les uns, nobles, hantent les Phèdres, les Jocastes,
> Les Méropes, ayant le décorum pour loi,
> Et montant à Versaille aux carrosses du roi;
> Les autres, tas de gueux, drôles patibulaires,
> Habitant les patois; quelques-uns aux galères
> Dans l'argot; dévoués à tous les genres bas;
> Déchirés en haillons dans les halles; sans bas,
> Sans perruque; créés pour la prose et la farce;
> Populace du style au fond de l'ombre éparse.

There is a biting contrast here between the different 'castes' of words: on the one hand, the aristocracy, in stockings and wigs, travelling in regal carriages and fraternizing with literary nobility ('Phèdre', 'Jocaste' and 'Mérope' were all heroines in classical tragedies); on the other hand, the proletariat, in rags and tatters, clapped in irons and relegated to a literary

dungeon where it makes only low-class acquaintances of dubious value
The unsubstantial verb 'hantent' and the somewhat effete 'décorum' ring
ironically in the company of such gross words as 'tas de gueux, drôles
patibulaires', words hardly to be found in a play by Racine. Hugo then
expands the image of pulling down the Bastille, releasing the unkempt and
undignified rabble of condemned words and giving them their rightful place
in the new poetic society; and describes his own contribution to the newly
liberated literature in these terms:

> . . .j'ai brisé tous les carcans de fer
> Qui liaient le mot peuple, et tiré de l'enfer
> Tous les vieux mots damnés, légions sépulcrales;
> J'ai de la périphrase écrasé les spirales.

Similarly, some of the implications of Rimbaud's *Ma Bohème* will be
missed, if one is unaware that such words as 'idéal', 'Muse', 'ombres fantastiques' and 'lyre' form part of the well-worn vocabulary of Romantic poetry
and that Rimbaud's use of them here is a light-hearted parody. Rimbaud is
indeed notorious for his self-conscious rebellion against the style of well-
reputed poets. In *Les Mains de Jeanne-Marie* he takes the subject-matter
and verse-form of an earlier poem by Gautier entitled *Etude de mains*, but
gives these his own characteristic vocabulary and flavour. Two stanzas of
Gautier's poem describing a sculptured hand read:

> Sous le baiser neigeux saisie
> Comme un lis par l'aube argenté,
> Comme une blanche poésie
> S'épanouissait sa beauté.
>
> Dans l'éclat de sa pâleur mate
> Elle étalait sur le velours
> Son élégance délicate
> Et ses doigts fins aux anneaux lourds.

These finely written lines, symptomatic of the *l'art pour l'art* mood, are
elegant and decorative, fixing against a rich background (silver light,
luxurious velvet, extravagant rings) the pictorial qualities of the hand (its
whiteness and graceful flower-like shape). Some of the words ('poésie',
'beauté', 'élégance') represent the Parnassian ideal of artistic perfection;
others ('neigeux', 'lis', 'aube'), though more concrete, are traditional
symbols of a purity unsullied by the mundane. Rimbaud's description of
hands is a startling contrast and could hardly be less conventional:

> Ont-elles pris les crêmes brunes
> Sur les mares des voluptés?
> Ont-elles trempé dans des lunes
> Aux étangs de sérénités?
> (. . .)

Mains chasseresses des diptères
Dont bombinent les bleuisons
Aurorales, vers les nectaires?
Mains décanteuses de poisons?

Instead of the untouchable quality and refined pallor, there is the suggestion of brown scum which these hands have scooped up, not from any ordinary pond, but from the surface of a murkier pool of sensual pleasures. Instead of the clear visual quality and explicit similes, Rimbaud's metaphors here are enigmatic: one can only hazard a guess whether these hands have plucked at reflected moons in stagnant waters and symbolize a kind of madness. Instead of the unambiguous lily whiteness lit by dawn or superficially displayed on a velvet background, one has hands of a dubious colour, a combination of creamy brown and livid moonlight, which have soaked themselves in unknown depths. The second stanza shows Rimbaud in even more inventive vein: the scientific terms ('diptères', 'nectaires') and neologisms ('bombinent', 'bleuisons') contrast vividly with Gautier's traditional poetic vocabulary; juxtaposed with the idea of dawn is the image of the glossy blue bodies of buzzing insects; and the hands, which lose the sculptured and statuesque quality found in Gautier's poem, become dynamic, involved perhaps in some mysterious, unsavoury pursuit and animated by a nefarious spirit. Looking further ahead in the poem *Les Mains de Jeanne-Marie*, one realizes that Rimbaud's female figure is no model posing for the artist's eye, but a woman committed to the revolutionary struggle of the 1871 Commune, putting her hand to the gun and to the barricade. This reinforces one's awareness of two different poetic moments and two different poetic vocabularies.

In the same way, if one sees the historical relevance of the sharply contrasted linguistic tones in Apollinaire's poem *La Chanson du mal-aimé*, one appreciates all the more the poet's special position at a crossroads between established literary influences and a blatant modernistic trend, between one century and the next. The following stanzas, part of the final movement of the poem, give a good illustration of a tension between ancient and modern or, as Apollinaire himself puts it in *La jolie rousse*, 'cette longue querelle de la tradition et de l'invention/De l'Ordre et de l'Aventure':

Près d'un château sans châtelaine
La barque aux barcarols chantants
Sur un lac blanc et sous l'haleine
Des vents qui tremblent au printemps
Voguait cygne mourant sirène
(...)
Soirs de Paris ivres du gin
Flambant de l'électricité
Les tramways feux verts sur l'échine

Musiquent au long des portées
De rails leur folie de machines.

The first stanza, with its castle and absent mistress, strikes a medieval note. The word 'sirène' harks back to classical mythology. The image of the dying swan, evocative of the death of beauty and purity, is a traditional one. More particularly, the description creates an atmosphere reminiscent of mid- and late nineteenth-century poetry: Verlaine, for instance, writes a poem beginning 'Mystiques barcarolles...'; the words 'Le vent dans la plaine/Suspend son haleine' appear as the epigraph to the first of his *Ariettes oubliées*; and throughout his work he shows a taste for pallid settings, quivering movements on the face of nature, drifting moods and dying tones. Apollinaire might also be echoing the English poet Tennyson who, in his *Morte d'Arthur*, describes the ceremonial barge taking the dying king to Avilion as being like a great white swan, carolling as she goes to her death. With Apollinaire's second stanza, however, comes a complete change of vocabulary: the undefined 'château' and natural setting make way for a geographical proper-name and a modern urban scene alive with mechanical innovations; the stately 'barque' and graceful boating songs are replaced by ungainly trams and their frenetic music, the smoothness of the lake by the hardness of metal rails, and the monochrome whiteness of water and swan by the garish clash of red and green. There are dissonant foreign words, words boldly forged, words with an aggressive, uncompromising energy.

These examples, from Hugo, Rimbaud and Apollinaire, illustrate the same point: that a knowledge of fluctuating tastes in poetic vocabulary can enrich one's response to individual poems and to a poet's handling of style and language in general. The three poets quoted have all been aware of the need to revitalize poetry by calling on a range of expression distinct from that of a preceding era. The existence of poetry depends on such a process of rejection and renewal, and one finds Eluard, as late as 1952, virtually echoing Hugo's thought:

Rien de plus affreux que le langage poétisé, que des mots trop jolis gracieusement liés à d'autres perles. La poésie véritable s'accommode de nudités crues, de planches qui ne sont pas de salut, de larmes qui ne sont pas irisées. Elle sait qu'il y a des déserts de sable et des déserts de boue, des parquets cirés, des chevelures décoiffées, des mains rugueuses, des victimes puantes, des héros misérables, des idiots superbes, toutes les sortes de chiens, des balais, des fleurs dans l'herbe, des fleurs sur les tombes. Car la poésie est dans la vie.

But a full-scale study of words in an historical perspective stretches beyond the reach of this brief section; and putting aside the question of specific moments in the development of poetic language, we propose simply to examine some of the different shades of vocabulary encountered in poetry and the particular colouring they can help to give.

In Baudelaire's *Harmonie du soir*, there is a formal religious terminology ('encensoir...reposoir...ostensoir') which is very tightly patterned: re-inforcing each other in a rhyming relationship, these words give a strong air of ceremonial solemnity, although the theme of the poem is not explicitly religious. The atmosphere of Verlaine's poem beginning 'Les chères mains qui furent miennes' depends equally on its sequence of religious vocabulary, which surrounds the image of the hands with an intense suggestive aura and invites one to see them as those, not just of a loved one, but of a mysterious spiritual intercessor:

> Remords si cher, peine très bonne,
> Rêves bénis, mains consacrées
> O ces mains, ces mains vénérées,
> Faites le geste qui pardonne!

Hugo's poetry, too, shows a strongly defined religious inspiration. Sometimes this finds expression in widely recognizable Christian vocabulary and imagery, such as 'archange', 'colombe', 'firmament', 'Amour' or the lines

> Elle eut un fils, prions tous,
> Dieu le prit sur ses genoux
> (*La Chanson du spectre*);

at other times in images fashioned on the Biblical model, as in *Booz endormi*:

> Il n'avait pas de fange dans l'eau de son moulin;
> Il n'avait pas d'enfer dans le feu de sa forge.

But, whereas Baudelaire and the Verlaine of *Sagesse* can be set in a more specific Catholic tradition, Hugo, 'le poète le mieux doué pour exprimer le mystère de la vie' as Baudelaire has called him, pursues his meditations on a vaster and more universal plane; and one of the most distinctive features of his poetic vocabulary is his taste for portentous words with grandiose reverberations. Lines like

> Son embouchure, gouffre où plongeait mon regard,
> Cercle de l'Inconnu ténébreux et hagard,
> Pleine de cette horreur que le mystère exhale,
> M'apparaissait ainsi qu'une offre colossale
> D'entrer dans l'ombre où Dieu même est évanoui
> (*La Trompette du Jugement*)

are remarkable for the accumulation of words suggesting the immeasurable ('gouffre', 'plongeait', 'colossale'), the obscure ('Inconnu', 'ténébreux', 'mystère', 'ombre') and the awesome ('hagard', 'horreur'). 'Dieu' as a concept is introduced, but seems of little stature compared with the engulfing cosmic forces which leave the mind floundering.

Poetry with religious or spiritual overtones sometimes retreats into a more esoteric mode of expression, and its use of vocabulary might be called hermetic. Mallarmé's work gives numerous examples of this. He forges many obscure phrases from comparatively commonplace vocabulary: 'l'unanime pli' or 'blanc vol fermé' meaning a fan, 'le suicide beau' describing sunset, or 'la considérable touffe' referring to woman's hair. But, as in the following sestet from his sonnet *Ses purs ongles*..., he also favours the use of the rare and archaic:

> Mais proche la croisée au nord vacante, un or
> Agonise selon peut-être le décor
> Des licornes ruant du feu contre une nixe,
>
> Elle, défunte nue en le miroir, encor
> Que, dans l'oubli fermé par le cadre, se fixe
> De scintillations sitôt le septuor.

Here one slips into the most enigmatic of atmospheres: the cryptic details of the unicorns and the nymph seem to be the emblems of some legendary confrontation; there is the suggestion of an astronomical mystery (the 'septet of scintillations' referring to the constellation known as the Plough, found in the northern sky); and several of the words have more than one level of meaning ('croisée' is a casement-window or a meeting-point; 'vacante' is partly a synonym for 'ouverte' but adds the unusual idea of the window being empty; 'septuor' is usually a musical term, but is used here to describe the visual conglomeration of seven stars). The syntax is so tortuous, moreover, that one is left uncertain of the grammatical relationship between the words. One's final impression in a poem of this kind is that of moving in a universe of private signs where language points in many directions but does not lead anywhere conclusive.

Metaphysical themes or an attempt to suggest a mystery beyond the everyday face of things are often accompanied by a measure of abstract and semi-philosophical vocabulary. This is apparent in the following characteristic example from Hugo:

> Autour de lui le temps et l'espace et le nombre
> Et la forme et le bruit expiraient, en créant
> L'unité formidable et noire du néant.
> Le spectre Rien levait sa tête hors du gouffre
>   (*Et Nox facta est*).

But such vocabulary will not always carry the same poetic tone. Whereas Hugo's abstract language, for instance, is rarely divorced from the sombre, ominous and incomprehensible and aims at provoking an emotional tremor, that of Paul Valéry produces a more serene and measured intellectual balance. This verse from *Le Cimetière marin* is an elegant illustration:

> Quel pur travail de fins éclairs consume
> Maint diamant d'imperceptible écume,
> Et quelle paix semble se concevoir!

Quand sur l'abîme un soleil se repose,
Ouvrages purs d'une éternelle cause,
Le Temps scintille et le Songe est savoir.

Throughout this stanza, there is an increasing concentration of abstract
vocabulary ('pur', 'paix', 'éternelle cause', 'Temps', 'Songe', 'savoir').
The last line is the culmination of the meditative sequence, condensing in
absolute terms the essence of the purity, peace and eternity apprehended in
the surface of the sea struck by brilliant sun. Its aphoristic philosophical
form gives an immutability to what is elsewhere perceived as incessant
activity, and a firmer intellectual conclusion to what has been partly described in luminous visual terms. It is worth noting, though, that poets,
for fear of depriving their work of colour and substance, seldom extend the
use of abstract language beyond a reasonable limit. Here, in Valéry's poem,
the abstraction is set in relief by the rich visual quality seen especially in a
phrase like 'Le Temps scintille'. The point applies no less to Hugo: his
vague, resonant words would lose much of their effect if not periodically
crystallized in the stark concrete image. In the above example, the personified vision of Nothingness rearing its head from the abyss stands out all
the more dramatically against such 'bodiless' words as 'temps', 'espace',
'nombre', 'forme', 'unité' and 'néant'; and Hugo is renowned for lines like
'Le chaos est l'époux lascif de l'infini' which weld intangible concepts into
a highly sensual metaphor.

This takes us from religious, hermetic or abstract language to vocabulary
of a more sensual order. While Hugo's work often provokes a metaphysical
'frisson', it is Baudelaire who is generally considered as the supreme artist
of the physical and sensual 'frisson'; and where sexual imagery in Hugo
often animates a cosmic vision, that of a universe threatened by pent-up
forces ready to be unleashed, Baudelaire's sexual suggestions do not have
the same brute energy and are far more intimate and subtle. In this stanza
from *Le Chat*, the description of which prepares the way for a complete
analogy between cat and woman, the profusion of words denoting tactile
impressions creates a particularly sensuous atmosphere:

chat

Lorsque mes doigts caressent à loisir
Ta tête et ton dos élastique,
Et que ma main s'enivre du plaisir
De palper ton corps électrique.

Part of its subtlety is the way in which the feeling of physical involvement is
intensified, passing from 'caressent' to 'palper', from superficial and leisurely
stroking to a more intent and intoxicated physical exploration; from 'doigts'
to 'main' and from isolated parts of the body to the suggestion of a more
enveloping caress; from the lithe pliability of 'élastique' to the more highly
charged and vibrant response implicit in 'électrique'. Here, compressed in
a tautly developed framework, is a wide register of evocative physical

vocabulary. Rimbaud is also a poet with an acute awareness of the senses, having deliberately deranged his sense-perceptions in order to produce dramatic innovatory images. The example of *Voyelles* is among the best known:

> A, noir corset velu des mouches éclatantes
> Qui bombinent autour des puanteurs cruelles.

Here the reader runs the gauntlet of aggressive sensual images: visual (the contrast of 'noir' and 'éclatantes'), tactile (the soft, hairy texture of 'velu'), auditory (the forceful buzzing of 'bombinent'), olfactory (the invading stench of 'puanteurs cruelles'). Quite clearly, one has moved into an area of language and poetic tone different from Mallarmé's purified mysteries and Valéry's intellectual refinement.

In Rimbaud, it is only one step from a suggestive sensual vocabulary to a much cruder use of language, where the intention is not so much to appeal to the intellect, but to force the reader into a spontaneous reaction of shock, disgust or bewilderment. In the following extract from the poem *Accroupissements,*

> Autour, dort un fouillis de meubles abrutis
> Dans des haillons de crasse et sur de sales ventres;
> Des escabeaux, crapauds étranges, sont blottis
> Aux coins noirs: des buffets ont des gueules de chantres
> Qu'entrouvre un sommeil plein d'horribles appétits,

one is so bludgeoned by the accumulation of sordid words that the individual detail of this descriptive setting is submerged in an overall impression of murkiness and crapulence and can hardly be visualized. In his early satirical poems Rimbaud often delights in employing words not in polite usage ('...sa large croupe/Belle hideusement d'un ulcère à l'anus'), and especially in giving them an incongruous, mock-religious context ('Doux comme le Seigneur du cèdre et des hysopes, / Je pisse vers les cieux bruns...'). His work is also well sprinkled with colloquialisms which have a rough and ready tone, as in the 'Oh! là là! que d'amours splendides j'ai rêvées!' of *Ma Bohème* or the poem *Michel et Christine*, which begins, 'Zut alors, si le soleil quitte ces bords!' But one should not, of course, see these features as a condemnation of Rimbaud's poetry. They are merely symptoms of a linguistic energy and audacity of conception which are the hallmarks of his best work. Colloquial language and plebeian vocabulary, moreover, have become perfectly respectable ingredients of twentieth-century poetry. Apollinaire's poem *Les Femmes* is primarily an interweaving of different conversational voices, on a backcloth of Rhineland scenery, intended to convey the picturesque local colour of ordinary peasant folk caught in the middle of their everyday chatter. It is an early indication of this poet's interest in the realism of the spoken word, an interest developed to the full in his so-called *poèmes–conversations* such as *Lundi Rue Christine* (from *Calligrammes*), in which variegated snatches of 'live' conversation, some highly colloquial, burst in on the wavelength of the poem and then disappear just as unpredictably. Nor does Supervielle see any objection to the introduction of less favoured common-or-garden words into poetry. In his poem *Hommage à la vie*, he speaks of the pleasure he feels

> ...d'avoir tous ces mots
> Qui bougent dans la tête,
> De choisir les moins beaux
> Pour leur faire un peu fête,
> D'avoir senti la vie
> Hâtive et mal aimée,
> De l'avoir enfermée
> Dans cette poésie.

In another vein, quite distinct from the vulgar, exhibitionistic, blunt and colloquial, is Verlaine's taste for a vocabulary of half-tints and delicately shaded effects. The first two stanzas of *Cythère* bring out this contrast well:

> Un pavillon à claires-voies
> Abrite doucement nos joies
> Qu'éventent des rosiers amis;
>
> L'odeur des roses, faible, grâce
> Au vent léger d'été qui passe,
> Se mêle aux parfums qu'elle a mis.

All the sensations seem muted and faint: the lovers' haven is in a half-light, only the slightest breeze stirs the air and the scent of roses is almost imperceptible. The language of the poem *A la promenade* creates a very similar impression:

> Et le vent doux ride l'humble bassin,
> Et la lueur du soleil, qu'atténue
> L'ombre des bas tilleuls de l'avenue,
> Nous parvient bleue et mourante à dessein.

The sunlight is softened into a bluish, twilight hue through a screen of leaves, the wind is so gentle that it barely puckers the water's surface, and the objects themselves seem diminutive and self-effacing ('l'*humble* bassin', '*bas* tilleuls'). One notices particularly how the poet dims his effect with words like 'doucement', 'faible', 'léger', 'atténue' and 'mourante'. These are most characteristic of Verlaine, as are phrases like 'une lune rose et grise' (the indeterminate nuance rather than bold colour), 'un ciel d'automne attiédi' (a half-and-half impression of a sky somewhere between two seasons, two tones of light and two temperatures), 'épeuré quasiment' or 'quasi / Tristes sous leurs déguisements fantasques' (the inconclusive description of a state of mind which makes one wonder if what one detects is only a semblance), 'Comme des nuées / Flottent gris les chênes' (material objects which seem diluted and lacking in consistency), or 'la mandoline jase / Parmi les frissons de brise' (a music broken into tiny notes and dispersed on a tremulous breeze).

A final region of vocabulary which deserves special attention is that which could be broadly called rare and experimental. This can assume several guises. We have already seen Rimbaud's use of scientific vocabulary and neologism and Mallarmé's choice of the rare word for the occult context. In addition, poets sometimes have recourse to foreign words and to words entirely of their own invention. Whatever its specific poetic justification may be, such vocabulary draws attention to itself for its eccentricity. There is, for instance, the exoticism of the rare word in Rimbaud's sentence from *Après le déluge*, 'Les "mazagrans" fumèrent dans les estaminets', possibly chosen as much for its luxuriant sound and novelty as for any other reason. In *La Chanson du mal-aimé*, Apollinaire introduces the Greek-flavoured words 'argyraspides' and 'dendrophores' in close succession, no doubt with a secret delight in his own erudition, but also to draw more threads into the poem's firmly woven balance between modern experience and classical tradition. Occasionally, a poet goes even further and uses words and phrases taken unaltered from another language. Verlaine is particularly fond of English titles, such as *Nevermore, Birds in the Night, Green, Streets, Beams*, which deprive one of that clear insight into the subject-matter which titles normally provide: for the French reader, these will have a vague, disorientating quality, in keeping with Verlaine's affection for the poetic region 'Où l'Indécis au Précis se joint'. In *L'Eternité*, Rimbaud has the following stanza:

> Là pas d'espérance,
> Nul orietur.
> Science avec patience,
> Le supplice est sûr.

The Latin verb 'orietur', used as a noun and emphatically isolated in the short poetic line, lends an even more baffling note (and perhaps an obscure religious flavour) to a stanza composed of cryptic formulae. Apollinaire, with his love of surprise, climaxes his poem *La Synagogue* with what will be to most people an incomprehensible line of Hebrew: 'Hanoten ne Kamoth bagoim tholahoth baleoumim'. The effect here, as well as providing a touch of authentic local colour, is to put a mock-grandiose and ironic conclusion to his comic portrait of two quarrelling Jewish burghers ostensibly reconciled as they sing together in a religious service. All these examples show a desire on the part of the poet to stray from the well-trodden tracks of expression and provoke in the reader a slight linguistic shock. In the nineteenth century, no-one was more self-consciously experimental with vocabulary than Rimbaud: neologisms such as 'hargnosités', 'percaliser', trideurs', 'bleuités', 'nacreux', 'dérades', 'ithyphalliques' and 'pioupiesques' bound in his work. In the twentieth century none has ventured more effectively than Michaux into a realm of a freely invented vocabulary which oes even further than neologism. His sound-poem *Le grand Combat* rovides a fitting conclusion, since it throws a challenging question-mark ver the relationship between language and poetry:

> Il l'emparouille et l'endosque contre terre;
> Il le rague et le roupète jusqu'à son drâle;
> Il le pratèle et le libucque et lui barufle les ouillais;
> Il le tocarde et le marmine,
> Le manage rape à ri et ripe à ra.
> Enfin il l'écorcobalisse.

We have only dealt with a small sample from the range of poetic ocabulary. But this will serve as an introduction to the diversity of shades with which the poet can compose: sometimes he will use them singly (as in Verlaine's *Les chères mains*...), sometimes in a mixture (as in Apollinaire's *La Chanson du mal-aimé*); sometimes he will stay close to the conventional, ometimes he will cultivate the garish. It is central to literary criticism to ask why a writer has selected one word rather than another: has he wanted a word with wider religious associations, with a greater measure of obscurity, with a more grandiose sphere of reference, with a stronger air of familiarity, with a more provocative sensual quality? Choice, in this respect, is the ouchstone of the poet's art.

IMAGINATIVE VISION AND POETIC IMAGE

Since Hugo French poetry has been concerned more with seeing than with thinking, and in general it has aimed at provoking an imaginative rather than an intellectual response. The poet's imagination is his vital attribute, 'la reine des facultés' as Baudelaire said, a kind of sixth sense which commands and binds together all the others, or in Eluard's words 'la mère du progrès', the fertile force which brings change and novelty to reality. Through its use the poet can fulfil a rôle which Apollinaire saw as necessary: 'Les grands poètes et les grands artistes ont pour fonction sociale de renouveler sans cesse l'apparence que revêt la nature aux yeux des hommes. Sans les poètes, sans les artistes les hommes s'ennuieraient vite de la monotonie naturelle'. The prosaic recording of reality offers only boredom; the poetic task is to kindle through a supremely creative use of language a new vision of things. What is seen or felt to lie in or beyond reality will depend on the individual poet: for Hugo, it is at times a world of cosmic threat; for Baudelaire, an awe-inspiring 'ténébreuse et profonde unité'; for Rimbaud, a challenging universal 'là-bas' to be gate-crashed through hallucination and violent imaginative experience; for Mallarmé, either a pure

world of Ideas or a paralysing Nothingness; for Eluard, a brilliant Utopia,
realm which only habit prevents us from seeing. 'Je dis qu'il faut être *voyant*,
se faire *voyant*', proclaimed Rimbaud. Poetry is there to open one's eyes
even to the invisible.

   It was Baudelaire who characterized Hugo as 'l'homme le mieux doué...
pour exprimer par la poésie ce que j'appellerai le *mystère de la vie*', as th
translator not only of the more direct, picturesque aspects of Nature but
also of the inner, invisible 'forces de la vie universelle' which are obscurely
and fleetingly revealed to man. Under the crust of objects pulsates a univers,
which Hugo apprehends yet cannot penetrate. But his imaginative vision i
so powerful that his poetry often shudders with this feeling of hidden
mystery: foam on the sea becomes sinister sheep, the moon has sinister eyes,
clouds build an arch to celebrate night's victory over day, the sky take
on the form of a rotting corpse. Hugo's intuitions of the beyond are more
terrifying than those of Baudelaire who dreamed of a marvellous unity
behind the fragmentary, visible façade. Driven on by the need to order a
chaotic world by using his imagination, Baudelaire seeks analogies o
correspondances everywhere: 'Tout l'univers visible n'est qu'un magasir
d'images et de signes auxquels l'imagination donnera une place et une
valeur relative'. The touch-paper of vision is often ignited by his senses
the colour, scent and swirl of female hair conjure up a luminous, exotic
land; the sound of wood-choppers evokes images of fear; a perfume reminds him of green meadows. A fellow poet, Théophile Gautier, said of
him:

Il possède aussi le don de correspondance...c'est-à-dire qu'il sait découvrir par une
intuition secrète les rapports invisibles à d'autres et rapprocher ainsi, par des analogies
inattendues que seul le *voyant* peut saisir, les objets les plus éloignés et les plus opposés
en apparence.

Baudelaire sees with his senses and co-ordinates with his imagination.
   The visionary function of the poet is a constant theme after Baudelaire:
the poet is either 'l'homme chargé de voir divinement' in Mallarmé's definition or simply 'le voyant' in Rimbaud's. The imaginative vision is considered
not as a mere source of ornamental imagery, but as a means of knowing the
self and the universe. In his otherworldly poetry, Mallarmé shuns 'le réel
parce que vil', refuses to describe objects and concentrates on the struggle
to distil the essence of the universe into the symbols of his verse. Rimbaud
will only enthuse about reality after it has been distorted 'par un long,
immense et raisonné *dérèglement* de *tous les sens*'; looking back at his
poetic career, he remarks 'Je m'habituai à l'hallucination simple: je voyais
très franchement une mosquée à la place d'une usine'. It is by this wilful
bending of perception (as in *Voyelles*) that the poet exploits his imaginative
potential, explores the darkest recesses of his mind and ultimately penetrates
l'inconnu and the mysterious 'âme universelle'. Rimbaud's vision does not

olatilize objects until they virtually disappear, like that of Mallarmé, ﾟut rather bursts through to the unsuspected core of things to feel in them more dynamic sensuous life-force.

Not all poets share the ambition to pierce a mysterious metaphysical ｐattern through poetic vision. Valéry's imagination is the servant of his ｏwn intellect and his poetry is a careful, subtle exercise which tests the ｐower of his mind: 'une manœuvre de moi-même par moi-même'. Rather ﾑhan probing the beyond for some universal truth, Apollinaire's vision is ｍore at home transforming, in humorous or saddened but nearly always ｓurprising insights, the most 'unpoetic' elements of twentieth-century life: ﾑhe curious tailor's shop which becomes animated in *L'Emigrant de Landor Road*, the chit-chat interweaving with the expressions of the natural land-ｓcape in *Les Femmes*, the street-life of Paris which takes its place alongside ｌegend in *La Chanson du mal-aimé*, or the trench warfare transmuted into ｓpectacle in *Fête*. Supervielle who, like Hugo, gazes inquiringly into the ｃosmos does so in a less sombre and more fanciful mood, expressing in his ｖerse what he calls 'mon émerveillement devant le monde' and creating an *Alice in Wonderland*-like world rather than one of Gothic resonances.

Imaginative vision is also the keystone of Surrealist doctrine in the 1920s and 1930s, though whether accompanied by a belief in some mystical reality or simply concerned with reconciling man with all his covert poten-tial is not always certain. Through vision, the Surrealist poet taps the obscure source of energy within him, the subconscious, the dream-realm in which the collision of incongruous elements produces a cascade of sparks. The world, to use André Breton's word, is a *cryptogramme* to be explored in a much more dazzlingly irrational way than Baudelaire ever conceived. The result is a poetry which is unashamedly contradictory, which thrives on shock and claims to have direct relevance to our relations with reality since it leads the mind 'à se faire du monde et de lui-même une représentation moins opaque' (Breton).

It might be said that most poetry achieves to some degree the effect described by Breton. It makes us see things differently. Themes of love, death and time are renovated through the creative optics of the poet; the sights of nature (the sea, a falling leaf, a swan, dawn, pine-trees, icebergs, reflections in a river) reveal hidden riches of actual beauty or symbolic meaning; objects such as a fan, a cigar, a bridge radiate in the prism of the poetic imagination. Good poetry, invoking a special language, provokes a special vision: childlike, mystical, macabre, humorous, fanciful, illogical, myopic or whatever – but never prosaic.

The natural vehicle for this vision is the poetic image, by which is meant a figure of speech which draws together two ideas, two elements or two areas of association by comparison (not simply an image in the sense of a mental picture) and holds them there suggestively poised between difference

and identity. Imagery has always been an essential of poetry, adding a
ornamental glitter to the banal, explaining the intangible in terms of th
tangible, persuading by the unexpected appropriateness of its parallels o
seducing by its magical extensions and transformations of reality. T
convey the freshly-perceived, a poet will rarely invent new words or describ
at intricate length but will use old words in novel combinations and evok
by the shorthand of analogy. The double perspective inherent in analog
disturbs the reader's monocular vision. It is as if the poet were puttin
different but related photographs in the two frames of a stereoscope. Th
result may be an impression of depth and complex coincidence or simply o
rich confusion; but it will inevitably excite the retina.

Simile and metaphor are central to poetic expression. Both imply a per
ception of sameness, the first voicing similarity in explicit terms: 'Tor
souvenir en moi luit comme un ostensoir' (Baudelaire); the second eithe
claiming identity: 'Le chaos est l'époux lascif de l'infini' (Hugo), or, more
commonly, talking of an unstated object as if it were another: 'Ailes couvran
le monde de lumière, / Bateaux chargés du ciel et de la mer' where Eluard
is writing of his beloved's eyes. Personification, allegory, conceit and symbol
are specialized types of these two basic figures.

The simile is often felt to be less subtle than metaphor because it announces
its rôle quite overtly. It speaks of likeness but goes no further, and the word
'comme' stands as a thin but noticeable dividing-wall between the two
intended partners. Yet Baudelaire for whom poetry was a refined 'magie
suggestive' uses it generously; in fact, of all the words in *Les Fleurs du mal*,
comme is the thirteenth most frequently used (coming after a list of articles
and common prepositions). In his stated aim to 'glorifier le culte de l'image
he sees no reason to cover up the analytical nature of the simile and in
Avec ses vêtements ondoyants et nacrés... he even exploits this facet to give an
air of scientific detachment to his study of the woman. Moreover, an image
like that quoted above, 'Ton souvenir en moi luit comme un ostensoir', is
by no means a simple juxtaposition: while seeming to capture an intangible
mental impression in clearly visual terms, it is in fact a deep and complex
statement on the poet's memory as a hallowed chapel in which private
devotions take place, and on individual memories as objects of communion, invitations to spiritual refreshment and promises of salvation. One
has only to replace the word 'ostensoir' by 'phare' or 'coucher du soleil' to
realize the distinctive and multiple reverberations that each sets in motion
as opposed to the other. With the growing emphasis on suggestion rather
than statement, the simile has lost some ground in French poetry, although
the Surrealists have used it to contrast the comparative ingenuousness of
its form with the explosive analogy it can contain (in Eluard's *L'Amoureuse*,
for instance). The power of the metaphor, on the other hand, has been
more and more revered. To claim that 'A is B' in preference to 'A is like B'

s imaginatively bolder and less deferential to the rational notion of difference and identity. It seals things forcibly instead of placing them side by side
or our more leisured perusal. The form of the metaphor is also attractively
flexible: it can make its impact very concisely by a direct yoking of what are
called the tenor (the main idea) and the vehicle (the image-making consti-
uent), as in Hugo's *A celle qui est voilée*:

> Je sens en moi, douce frayeur,
> Frissonner toutes mes pensées,
> Feuilles de l'arbre intérieur;

or it can, by in a way substituting itself for and concealing the tenor, spark
off a dynamic process of interpretation in the reader's mind, as in Mallarmé's
Autre éventail where the fan might be a symbol of poetry (which is not
mentioned) or in Rimbaud's *Le Bateau ivre* where the adventures of the
boat suggest the poet's mystical journey (but one cannot be sure of this).
Metaphor can depend, too, on the implications of a single word transferred
from a usual context into an unusual one: the first noun in Verlaine's 'Les
sanglots longs / Des violons', the adjective in Apollinaire's 'La chambre est
veuve' or the verb of 'j'égrenais dans ma course / Des rimes' from Rimbaud's
Ma Bohème.

We all use images when we speak: *a traffic jam, a bottle-neck on the roads,
a pay-freeze* are all expressions which depend on metaphor. But their
imaginative appeal soon fades. Poetry seeks to avoid the 'dead' metaphors
of ordinary speech. Gautier, as we have seen, praises Baudelaire for his
'analogies inattendues' and his bringing together of 'les objets les plus
éloignés et les plus opposés en apparence'. Pierre Reverdy, the twentieth-
century poet, noted in 1918 that 'Plus les rapports des deux réalités rappro-
chées seront lointains et justes, plus l'image sera forte – plus elle aura de
puissance émotive et de réalité poétique'. And André Breton in 1953 talks
of images as 'certains traits de feu reliant deux éléments de la réalité de
catégories si éloignées l'une de l'autre que la raison se refuserait à les mettre
en rapport et qu'il faut s'être défait momentanément de tout esprit critique
pour leur permettre de se confronter'. It is clear from these statements that
an important, vivifying ingredient in the poetic image is the perception of an
unsuspected similarity in very dissimilar notions. The wider the distance
between tenor and vehicle, the more striking the image. In Baudelaire's
Le Cygne, for example, the bringing together of the swan and the negress
as symbols of exile achieves its effect partly because, on the one hand, there
is the white bird, struggling in the parched dust of a Parisian summer,
looking for water, and, on the other, the black woman, lost in the mud and
fog of a Parisian winter, dreaming of her native Africa. By demolishing the
barriers of logical perception, Rimbaud releases startling juxtapositions:

> J'ai vu le soleil bas, taché d'horreurs mystiques,
> Illuminant de longs figements violets,

> Pareils à des acteurs de drames très antiques
> Les flots roulant au loin leurs frissons de volets!

The reflections of the setting sun on the sea evoke images of violence and congealed blood, then of dignified actors and finally of domestic shutters quivering in the wind. The mind is pulled one way and then the other by the magnetic strength of Rimbaud's imagination, as it seeks to illustrate an underlying unity which defies single definition. Valéry's comparison of human brains with bursting pomegranates surprises by its somewhat grotesque interlinking of the cerebral and the vegetal; while Apollinaire's transformation of hard, lethal shells into soft, inviting woman's breasts first shocks the reader by its antitheses and amuses by the superhuman proportions of its vision, before ultimately leading into a suggestive awareness of the bond between war and erotic fantasies, dire realities and wishfulfilment. Although the content of the images in the poetry of Eluard and Desnos is rarely as arbitrary as Surrealist theory would have it, their similes and metaphors do take a long time, in Breton's words, 'à traduire en langage pratique'. But once one accepts that for Eluard love shatters our restricted vision, that the aura surrounding his mistress permeates all things, then images such as

> Tu es l'eau détournée de ses abîmes
> Tu es la terre qui prend racine
> Et sur laquelle tout s'établit

carry an emotional conviction which transcends logic. Once one accepts that for the poet of *La Voix de Robert Desnos* midnight is the magical hour, then the opening images in

> Si semblable à la fleur et au courant d'air
> au cours d'eau aux ombres passagères
> au sourire entrevu ce fameux soir à minuit
> si semblable à tout au bonheur et à la tristesse
> c'est le minuit passé dressant son torse nu au-dessus des
>   beffrois et des peupliers

possess the persuasive charm of incantation and can easily dispense with any strictly rational justification. These are both examples of an exalted 'unrealism', in which literal impossibilities and juxtapositions without apparent explanation become quite natural, and create a newly liberated world with its own laws.

If one were to schematize roughly the development of the poetic image since the middle of the nineteenth century, one could point to two salient features. Firstly, poets have stressed that imagery is powerful when it goes beyond the limited conceptual clutches of man's intellect: Gautier speaks of unexpectedness, Reverdy of 'puissance émotive', Breton of reason's inadequacy confronted with imaginative 'traits de feu'. Secondly,

n a continual search for renovation, poets have widened the gap between
enor and vehicle: aptness of an image, in the sense of its easily perceptible
oarallelisms, is a defunct notion. Eluard's 'La terre est bleue comme une
orange' provokes reaction by its sheer inaptness (it is perhaps only later
hat one responds to the simultaneous identity of the roundness of earth,
he curve of blue sky, the self-contained lushness of fruit, etc.); if one substi-
utes *ronde* for 'bleue', one has a banal, eminently forgettable simile. The
whole idea of a close identifiable bond between tenor and vehicle is upset
nere by the choice of a word which, clearly, breaks the accustomed trans-
'usion between the two.

   Eluard's image leads us to our final consideration. As the first line of a
ooem, dislodging the reader from his normal linguistic habits, it serves a
definite function. The rôles that images can play in the structure of a poem
are as numerous as the contexts in which they occur. One might distinguish,
however, at least three broad uses. Firstly, there is the clearly delineated,
conspicuous image which either bursts against a duller background or
condenses in a single insight various vague notions within a poem. In
A la faveur de la nuit, for example, Desnos suddenly introduces an image of
the wind as a cloak in a figurative sentence which contrasts with the rest of
the poem and coincides with the moment of drama as the window opens.
His concise image of the scales, pinpointed at the centre of *J'ai tant rêvé de
toi*, encapsulates, enriches and gives a mythical depth to the emotional
wavering of the man in love with an inaccessible woman. In the same way,
it is partly because the image is, by definition, a fusion of two ideas that it
lends itself naturally as a method of concluding a poem. The final stanza of
Hugo's *Booz endormi* joins the human and the divine, the microcosm and
the macrocosm, in the analogy of the crescent-moon and the harvester's
sickle. And Cros's last line 'Femme, femme, cercueil de chair!' intertwines
the ideas of death and sexuality which run through *Hiéroglyphe*, sealing
the poem with a compact metaphor. A second rôle is that of imagery not so
much as the visionary intensification of a theme, but as a creative element
in its own right, strangely freed from the dictatorship of idea and subject-
matter. The tumbling, multiple metaphors and similes in *Le Bateau ivre*
are not a dramatic elaboration or crystallization of an experience which
can be defined in separate terms; they are the actual *form* of that experience.
The same could be said of the imagery in Baudelaire's *La Chevelure* or
Eluard's *La courbe de tes yeux*..., where the metaphors, though initially
provoked by a privileged object of contemplation, seem to take flight of
their own accord, freed from any allegiance to an external poetic idea, and
governed by some self-generating internal law of analogy. A third function
lies in the use of the extended image to underpin the whole structural framework of a poem. Perhaps the best example of this is to be found in Baudelaire's *Harmonie du soir* in which the procession of devotional images

('encensoir...reposoir...ostensoir') parallels the movement of oncomin night, the growing spiritual anguish and the triumphant resurrection of th conclusion. Mallarmé in *Toute l'âme résumée*...fashions a whole poen on a single, clever analogy, that between writing literature and smoking cigar. And Apollinaire's initial perception of similarity between tim passing, love lost, and water flowing under a bridge, carries the reade through *Le Pont Mirabeau* in such a way that image and structure of th poem are inseparable.

Simile and metaphor are deceptively familiar devices, yet the skill witl which they are used is still a significant measure of a poet's greatness Aristotle, that traditional oracle for pronouncements on literary theory saw many qualities as being necessary to the poet; 'But', he said, 'the greates thing by far is to be master of metaphor'. Modern poetry has tended to prove him right.

THE STRUCTURE OF A POEM

One might define the structure of a poem as the patterns of development or artistic lines of force (gradually emerging from the organization of the verse-form, the play of imagery, the movements of sound and rhythm, the juxtaposition and sequence of effects) which shape and finally set in relief the thematic material. All poems follow some kind of logic, often artistic rather than intellectual, and no appreciation would be complete without some attempt to trace how subtly, dramatically, elegantly, suggestively and so on a poem unfurls to reach its conclusion.

Clearly, if one considers the poem as a supremely condensed verbal theatre, beginnings and endings have a particular importance in the structural development. The beginning gives the poem impetus and direction, often launching it in a striking or persuasive way. Hugo's 'Je suis fait d'ombre et de marbre' has a mysterious resonance, aided by the dense alliteration and the unequal rhythmical balance, which sets the tone for the sombre and unsettling atmosphere of the rest of the poem. Nerval's 'Je suis le ténébreux, – le veuf, – l'inconsolé' establishes a similar atmosphere of personal or psychological mystery, accented here by the halting syntax and made all the more intriguing by the compact multiple definition. In other contexts a single word can have a strong initial impact, as in Baudelaire's 'Pluviôse, irrité contre la ville entière' or Laforgue's 'Blocus sentimental!': in the first case the slight foreignness of the word, isolated as it is, gives a more awesome edge to the personification (to say nothing of its lugubrious sound or the restless assonance of '...irrité contre la ville' which follows); while in the latter 'Blocus' bursts explosively on the reader and, incongruously joined with an adjective like 'sentimental', foreshadows the blend of romanticism and modernism, sentiment and cynicism, which pervades the poem

s a whole. There is a shock-effect of a different kind in the first line of
Rimbaud's *Voyelles*, 'A noir, E blanc, I rouge, U vert, O bleu: voyelles'
r in Eluard's 'Elle est debout sur mes paupières'. Both challenge normal
perception: one by taking an elementary sequence known to every child,
twisting it inexplicably out of order and turning each familiar letter into a
cryptic cipher; the other by means of paradox and an upsetting of logic
which are a prelude to a surreal description of the effects of love. Many of
Mallarmé's poems have their own kind of initial obscurity, which gives the
opening lines the fascinating quality of a quest: 'Indomptablement a dû...',
though full of alliterative power and suggesting something of that 'vaulting
ambition which o'erleaps itself' which is the theme of the sonnet, remains
for a long time a syntactical enigma; while in 'Le vierge, le vivace et le bel
aujourd'hui' one is left unsure of the grammatical function of the words
whether 'vierge' and 'vivace' are adjectives qualifying 'aujourd'hui' or
nouns in their own right) and the desire for firm meaning is held in suspense.
In a less extreme way and in a mood richly sentimental rather than abstract,
Verlaine draws attention to the beginning of 'Il pleure dans mon cœur...'
by the unusual grammatical transposition which blends tears and rain as
if they were one and the same thing, simultaneously exterior and interior.
Quite frequently it is an exclamatory or invocatory form which infuses the
poem with a surge of energy: Mallarmé's 'O rêveuse...' has a pleading
intensity, coupled with a magical vagueness, which gives this feminine spirit
an undeniable yet nebulous dominance over all the ensuing patterns; and
Baudelaire's 'O toison, moutonnant jusque sur l'encolure!', followed by
similar rhythmic waves which envelop the reader ('O boucles! O parfum...'),
has a devotional or celebratory grandeur not usually addressed to such
sensual objects. Perhaps most often it is simply a musical or rhythmical
consistency which exerts the first spell on the reader, drawing him unobtrusively into the thematic richness, as with the melodic appeal of Verlaine's 'Il pleure dans mon cœur', the eerie sibilance and internal rhyme
(pressing home the idea of foreknowledge) in Apollinaire's 'La tzigane savait
d'avance', or the inviting anapaestic rhythm which carries the reader forward
in Desnos's 'Non, l'amour n'est pas mort en ce cœur et ces yeux...'.

The end of a poem, on the other hand, has as its aim to give a sense of the
consummate. It is here that all the interrelated aspects of theme, the suggestions of the imagery, the emotional intensity, the latent demands of logic
and the various tonal shadings are brought to some kind of fulfilment and
resolved. It is the point beyond which any further word would be superfluous. Rimbaud is an idiosyncratic master of the dramatic ending: the
stark precision of 'Il a deux trous rouges au côté droit' in *Le Dormeur du val*
is the complete answer to the graceful vitality and slightly precious poetic-
ization of nature in the earlier descriptions; the bathetic humour which
twists the end of *Ma Bohème* is the ideal graphic summary of his ambiguous

attitude to poetry, nature and himself; and the surprised matter-of-factness of 'Au réveil, il était midi', which stands as a sentence apart as the conclusion of *Aube*, emphatically conveys the transition from dream to reality and the fall back into real as opposed to mythical time. The last line of Apollinaire's famous long poem *Zone*, written for the most part in expansive rhyming couplets which overspill the traditional framework of the Alexandrine, is the sharp and elliptical 'Soleil cou coupé', the tautest image of the poem, having no matching rhyme in the immediate vicinity and rhyming only with itself. Michaux occasionally shows a taste for the single word finale 'La Nuit', 'et risible', 'Une', to show that a particular movement has expended its energy and subsided. Baudelaire's 'La froide majesté de la femme stérile', stiffened by the two internal rhymes, provides an unyielding, incontrovertible ending against which there is no appeal; while the last word of the line 'Causent sinistrement de leurs amours défunts', apart from the utter finality of its meaning, has a deadened nasal sound with no repercussions. A similar quality of finality is apparent in Hugo's 'Et quelqu'un les descendra', which takes the attention down into the depths where the vision began and leaves the poem on an ominous prophetic note; in Mallarmé's 'Musicienne du silence', hushed and prolonged, which provides an appropriately reverent and tranquil, as well as a paradoxical conclusion, or in 'Que vêt parmi l'exil inutile le Cygne', where the inversion dramatizes the absolute quality and mystery of this ideal representation of the swan; in Cros's 'Femme! femme! cercueil de chair!', where the brutal image prohibits any further development on the theme of woman; in Apollinaire's 'Parmi le bruit des flots et les derniers serments', with its lingering pathos and floating emotional void; in Supervielle's 'Et les fait choir au sombre fond', where the lengthened vowel of 'choir', slipping into the double-stressed nasal sound, seems to pull the poem down to the very ocean bed.

But beginnings and endings are not complete in themselves and do not have an autonomous life. They are, so to speak, the firm edges of the fabric of structure and not the whole of its intricate weave. 'La froide majesté de la femme stérile' is only so effective as the culminating line of the sestet because it is the antithesis of the initial 'Avec ses vêtements ondoyants et nacrés' and because Baudelaire's sonnet, in trying to describe the spell exercised by this idealized figure of woman, has passed inexorably from the attractions of sensual rhythm, movement and shimmering tones of light to a vaster vision of inhuman undulations, then to the idea of abstraction, enigma and inviolability, and finally to this image of mineral hardness, frigidity and sterility. Mallarmé's quietly climactic line 'Musicienne du silence', though graceful and musical in itself and attractive because of its self-contradictory nature, derives its full richness as the ultimate point of balance between the real and the ineffable from the fact that the female saint on the stained glass window and her symbolic musical instruments have faded, to be replaced in the second part of the poem by a supernatural intuition of a silent music played on the strings of light. Cros's 'Femme! femme! cercueil de chair!', striking as it is, is only fully meaningful as the final permutation of the trio 'L'amour, la mer, la mort', as a third and unexpectedly negative definition of woman, and in contrast to the opening line 'J'ai trois fenêtres à ma chambre', which gave no hint of enclosure or imprisonment. Similarly, Supervielle's 'Et les fait choir au sombre fond' comes as the despairing conclusion in a simple three-stanza poem which has moved in three neat stages from an upper ('Parmi les oiseaux et les lunes ... à la surface') to a middle ('Et les sillages sous-marins') to a lower stratum (' ... sombre fond'), and from intimations of light and a language to be read ('lunes...Et qu'on devine à la surface') to impenetrability ('l'aveugle témoignage') to complete darkness.

The structural patterns into which a poem can fall are unlimited. It may have a cyclical form, returning to its starting-point, as in Rimbaud's *Chanson de la plus haute tour* where the repetition of the first stanza at the end ('Oisive jeunesse / A tout asservie...') supports the idea of an imprisonment, a personal stagnation, an inability to advance in time or break a vicious circle. *Le Bateau ivre*, after plunging into a realm of imaginative perceptions which no single metaphor or unified vision can hold, eventually returns to the more deliberate navigational imagery (of cargo-boats and prison-ships) with which it began; and Valéry's *Le Cimetière marin*, at the conclusion of its deep and sinuous meditation, links up again with the very first image ('Ce toit tranquille, où marchent des colombes...Ce toit tranquille où picoraient des focs'), thus illustrating a comparison which the poet once made between the art of the diamond-cutter and the nature of poetry: the diamond-cutter shapes the facets so that the ray of light penetrating the gem can only come out again through the same facet, thus giving it its intense reflective glint, just as poetry, in Valéry's conception, might be defined as the 'retour du rayon spirituel aux mots d'entrée'. On the other hand, a poem may have an antithetical structure, with one part perfectly counterbalancing the other. Supervielle's *Sous le large* is just such a poem, two of its four stanzas leading from the nether depths to the light above and acting as a kind of request, the other two sinking down from surface to sea-bed and acting as the equally matched negative response. In a similar way, there may be a parallelism in the patterning of the stanzas or a mirroring effect. Baudelaire's *Le Chat* is a fine example of this: the quatrains of the sonnet describe the cat, passing from its fascinating but inhuman eyes to the languid but dangerous sensuality of its body; the tercets then switch quite brusquely, as if a new image had been superimposed, to the figure of woman, moving again in sequence from the coldly penetrating eyes to the inviting but untrustworthy effluvia emanating from her dusky body. Here the natural two-part division of the sonnet form sets up a re flective interplay, a perfectly balanced *correspondance*, between the feline an female natures, with the greater concentration of the sestet giving a slightl sharper dramatic edge to the image of the woman and a climactic tensio to the poem as a whole. Most poems reveal a stage-by-stage deepening intensification or personalization of theme, closely related to the move ments and modifications of form (or sometimes it is more appropriate t speak of a progressive narrowing or widening of focus). Several of Verlaine' poems provide an interesting illustration. The first of his *Ariettes oubliée* begins in the most impersonal mood with a series of indefinite statement ('C'est l'extase...C'est la fatigue...C'est tous les frissons...') which d little to define the object in question; the next stanza, with its more precis verbs, moves slightly closer to definition ('Cela gazouille et susurre, / Cel ressemble...'), becoming more varied in grammatical form and more personalized (with the exclamation 'O le frêle et frais murmure!' and the reference to an addressee 'Tu dirais...'); the third stanza finally identifie the neuter 'ce' as 'Cette âme...', and proceeds to become more restless plaintive and openly lyrical in nature (the 'moi' and its tormented relations show themselves in 'C'est la nôtre, n'est-ce pas?/La mienne, dis...') as well as more agitated and broken in form. A similar development from impersonal description to emotional involvement, from the suggestion o an objective pattern of harmony to the exclamation of his own personal disharmony, dictates the structure of the well-known *Le ciel est, par-dessus le toit*..., where two stanzas of calm description with a repetitive syntax ('...dans le ciel qu'on voit...sur l'arbre qu'on voit') give way to one of personal commentary with a more insistent form ('Mon Dieu, mon Dieu...'), and ultimately to one full of remorse and self-criticism, which turns back on the self and loses all composure and serenity of style. It is useful finally to return to the example of the sonnet, the divided structure of which has traditionally lent itself to a significant change of register, an adjustment or intensification of theme. In Baudelaire's *Correspondances*, where the octet concerns itself with the more grandiose and abstract theme of the mysterious pattern of purposes running through Nature, making it a symbolic language to be read, and then with the way in which the sense perceptions receiving these messages can fuse together in an awareness of a superior unity, the sestet concentrates on just one of these senses, showing in more lyrical terms how it becomes a stimulus for the artist's imagination, the key to a journey of unlimited association. Cros's *Conquérant* devotes the stouter structure of the octet to the self-imagined potency of the male overlord, while the more slender and irregular tercets describe the flittering world of female courtesans, the final stanza dramatizing a single figure, unique in her ethereal quality and lack of fear. One of Mallarmé's specialities is the isolation of a couplet at the end of a sonnet: in *Toute l'âme résumée*...

cleverly suggests the ash flicked off from the end of a cigar and brings the poem to an appropriate conclusion; in *Au seul souci de voyager*... it isolates the helmsman of the boat as an heroic symbol, simultaneously humanizing and generalizing the essential themes.

One further point needs to be made: that the structure of a rich poem can be read along many paths, and is ultimately the sum of these paths. It is rarely adequate to apply the terms 'cyclical form' or 'parallel patterning' as a description of the whole, as these are usually only part of the tracery. Again one can choose no better illustration than Baudelaire. *La Chevelure* begins with a description of woman's hair in animal terms ('toison'), its curls and its perfume, and ends with similar references ('mèches tordues... senteurs confondues...crinière lourde'), so that there is the semblance of a return to the original inspiration, which in turn explains the mood of the final stanza with its desperate urge to prolong or reproduce the experience. Within this framework one can detect an imaginative development from darkness ('l'alcôve obscure...tes profondeurs, forêt aromatique') to light ('éblouissant rêve...dans l'or et dans la moire...ciel pur') and back to comparative darkness ('noir océan...ténèbres tendues'), the 'luminous' stanza being situated at the very centre of the poem as the climax of transport and purified vision. Supporting this development are the successive transformations of the metaphor of the hair, 'overprinting' each other in a cumulative way: the fleeciness and luxuriance of the scented 'toison' is extended in the image 'forêt aromatique', the vegetal qualities of which then expand into 'mer d'ébène', which finally in its own right emerges as 'noir océan', before reverting to 'cheveux', 'mèches' and 'crinière' in the penultimate stages. At the same time there is another very significant structural pattern: the first, third, fifth and seventh stanzas all have future tenses or a forceful expression of future intention ('Pour peupler...Je la veux agiter', 'J'irai là-bas...soyez la houle', 'Je plongerai...saura vous retrouver', 'Sèmera le rubis...Afin qu'à mon désir'), while the second, fourth and sixth are entirely in the self-sufficient present. The result is a perfectly measured ebb and flow of will-power and abandonment of the will, desire and contentment; and a subtle alternating movement joins that of the progressive curve or parabola of thematic development. In the same way, in *L'Invitation au voyage*, one can explore several patterns, one progressing and deepening in the three main stanzas, another oscillating as one is lulled backwards and forwards between the long verse and the refrain: these combine, delicately and uncertainly, to guarantee the spell of the poem as a whole.

FREE-FORM POETRY

Together with a new concept of imagination and the poetic image, and the widening cultivation of poetry as a 'sorcellerie évocatoire' rather than an act of communication, the emergence of free verse is probably the mos important development of modern poetry.

Writing to a correspondent in 1886, at a moment in French poetry whic is responding to Baudelaire's question,

> Quel est celui de nous qui n'a pas, dans ses jours d'ambition, rêvé le miracle d'un prose poétique, musicale sans rythme ni rime, assez souple et assez heurtée pou s'adapter aux mouvements lyriques de l'âme, aux ondulations de la rêverie, aux soubre sauts de la conscience?,

which has savoured the liberty of Verlaine's delicate dilutions of verse form, and is nearly ripe for the impact of Rimbaud's dazzlingly rapi prose-poems in the *Illuminations*, Laforgue says: 'J'oublie de rimer, j'oubli le nombre des syllabes, j'oublie la distribution des strophes, mes ligne commencent à la marge comme de la prose'. Laforgue's *Derniers vers* ar an intriguing illustration of what he calls elsewhere 'le genre somnambule' poems proceeding in a free play of association, governed by some rhythmi and phonetic instinct rather than the meticulous control of the versifier

Apollinaire, in 1908, a period of self-conscious artistic experiment i which Cubism was dismantling the familiar contours of reality to recompose it in new angular shapes and Futurism was soon to be attuning itself to the frantic pulse and metamorphoses of the nascent twentieth century, write 'Pardonnez-moi mon ignorance / Pardonnez-moi de ne plus connaître l'ancien jeu des vers'. Then in 1918, in what has been seen as a poetic testa ment, he again pleads his inability to satisfy the demands of a traditiona ideal of aesthetic harmony, an ordered arrangement corresponding to a belief in an ordered universe, and shows his allegiance to new realities and their voracious appetite for new structures:

> Vous dont la bouche est faite à l'image de celle de Dieu
> Bouche qui est l'ordre même
> Soyez indulgents quand vous nous comparez
> A ceux qui furent la perfection de l'ordre
> Nous qui quêtons partout l'aventure
> (...)
> Il y a là des feux nouveaux des couleurs jamais vues
> Mille phantasmes impondérables
> Auxquels il faut donner de la réalité   (*La jolie rousse*).

Eluard, inspired by the Surrealist intention of the 1920s and 1930s to demolish all restrictions, prosodic, imaginative and mental, and to perform in poetry the miraculous reconciliation of contradictions (conscious and subconscious, reason and imagination, reality and surreality, life and death) and so restore the mind passionately to its whole nature, makes the following dramatic statement through the voice of an imagined author:

> Dès maintenant, le poète sait que tout doit lui servir. L'hallucination, la candeur, la fureur, la mémoire, ce Protée lunatique, les vieilles histoires, l'actualité, la table et

ncrier, les paysages inconnus, la nuit tournée, les souvenirs inopinés, les prophéties
: la passion, les conflagrations d'idées, de sentiments, d'objets, la nudité aveugle,
réalité crue, l'allégement des systèmes, le dérèglement de la logique jusqu'à l'absurde,
ısage de l'absurde jusqu'à l'indomptable raison, c'est cela – et non l'assemblage
ius ou moins savant, plus ou moins heureux des voyelles, des consonnes, des syllabes,
:s mots – qui concourt à l'harmonie d'un poème.

/hat is meant here is that harmony depends primarily on the structures of
ision, the conciliatory patterns which fuse all the disparate and conflicting
natter of life, and not on the unreal and somehow 'bodiless' structures of
ersification.

Michaux, very much a law unto himself in the picture of contemporary
oetry, has adopted the following curious quotation from a fourteenth-
entury Oriental writer as the epigraph to his essays, *Passages*:

.oyu, le religieux, dit: seule une personne de compréhension réduite désire arranger
:s choses en séries complètes.

.'est l'incomplétude qui est désirable. En tout, mauvaise est la régularité.

)ans les palais d'autrefois, on laissait toujours un bâtiment inachevé, obligatoirement.

Although referring in the first instance to the restricting inclinations of the
iuman mind, these words are equally relevant to Michaux's ideal of art,
vhich refuses the regularity of fixed metres and recurrent verse-patterns
ind shuns the finished and harmonious quality of the traditionally well-
ounded masterpiece. One should add, prompted here by the word 'religieux',
that Michaux's 'unfinished' structures and their formal lawlessness are
not a mere act of rebellion or perversity, but the most pliable means of
:linging close to, and authentically representing, those currents of infinitude
which create the stresses and the joys of much of his poetry. A chosen verse-
'orm could only erect barriers against what he considers to be the living
ict of poetry, unpredictable and demanding constant invention: the equivalent of poking a stick into a moving wheel.

The question now arises: what, if anything, distinguishes free-form
poetry from mere rhythmic or highly imaged prose; what, if anything,
guarantees that it remains poetry? For no-one more than Michaux challenges
the watertightness of the distinction. Mallarmé once said, 'Le vers est
partout dans la langue où il y a rhythme, partout, excepté dans les affiches
et à la quatrième page des journaux (...) Toutes les fois qu'il y a effort
au style, il y a versification'. But this seems too easy an identification to
satisfy the searching critic. Any stylistic conquest which prises language
out of the utilitarian grasp into the palm of Beauty and the effect of which,
to quote Mallarmé again, is to 'Donner un sens plus pur aux mots de la
tribu' may well be a poetic use of language, but is this the same as saying
that it makes a poem? Or have definitions become so problematical by the
mid-twentieth century that it is hardly relevant to speak of a 'poem', as a

fully fashioned artistic entity having firmly dictated contours, but only a 'poetry'? Verlaine, for his part, could not conceive of poetry without rhyme or at least a compelling musical consistency: 'Rimez faiblement, assonez si vous voulez, mais rimez ou assonez, pas de vers sans cela'. On another occasion he gave a slightly different response to the contemporary encroachments of *vers libre*, saying, 'Pour qu'il y ait vers, il faut qu'il y ait rythme. A présent on fait des vers à mille pattes!'. But it is clear that both rhyme and formal versification have disappeared from the work of many significant contemporary French poets. What has replaced them to give individual writings that poetic self-justification which sets them apart from prose? If it is simply aesthetic rhythm or devices such as rhetorical repetition, the is this in itself enough to differentiate poetry from swaying oratory or the cadences of religious litany? One can only suggest an answer to these questions by looking more closely at a selection of the most representative illustrations.

Laforgue's *L'Hiver qui vient*, perhaps an example of *vers libéré* rather than *vers libre*, dispenses with fixed line lengths, just as it dispenses with predictable syllabic patterns of rhyme. Instead, the lines find their own length, propelled by emotive ideas of varying intensity and duration, and the rhyme surges and relapses at irregular intervals. But it is a poem which still respects Verlaine's desire for musicality, with rhymes, assonances and repetitions tumbling in profusion. More important than this to its effect however, are a convincing lyrical tension which charges the atmosphere an enveloping rhythm which provokes a feeling of turbulence and confusion an acute imagery which turns reality into vision, and a complex play of leitmotifs which sends the mind backwards and forwards to gather together more and more of the stitching. In short, it is a rich and cohesive orchestration, even if an intuitive one.

Apollinaire's *Liens* is a far less expansive poem. Lines like 'Cordes faites de cris' and 'Araignées-Pontifes' are curt, severed and in themselves unpoetic. Nor, apart from an occasional loose contact, is there any matching interplay of rhymes or continuous rhythm to smooth them together. But height and depth, horizontal and vertical planes, time and space, impersonal and personal communications converge dynamically at the dense crossroads of the poem, as the image of cords meets with the lashwork of railway-lines, submarine cables, spiders' webs, the criss-cross of bridges, rainfall combing out the tangled skeins of the smoke, centuries hanged from the gallows as a new age is proclaimed, and so on. It is a fascinating piece of faceting, alive with radiations and reflections, of a kind rarely, if ever, found in prose.

Eluard, while abandoning rhyme, often maintains a regular syllabic structure. But in a poem such as *Tu te lèves l'eau se déplie . . .*, this, too, disappears. In their place one finds a series of balanced initial repetitions

'Tu te lèves...Tu te couches...Tu es l'eau...Tu es la terre...Tu fais les bulles...Tu chantes des hymnes...') which give a measured unity and devotional quality; a purified lyrical mood which never once halts to describe itself but seems airborne in the ethereal perfection of the object that it contemplates; a magical use of language which takes everything that it touches out of the realm of humdrum logic and makes it a source of metaphors; and a finely controlled structure, which begins as a simple musical ritual, relinquishes the initial assonances as it expands to a climax, and finally becomes slight and understated as the poem rests in an utterly neat yet paradoxical conclusion. There is no feeling here of a technical loss.

Michaux, in his poetry, has given a new importance to rhythm, showing that it can become a structural backbone as firm as that of versification, capable of producing climax and anticlimax. The dramatic tension of *Clown* could be plotted in a kind of poetic graph, commencing as a thin rising line (vibrating regularly and with increasing emphasis), developing into a shapeless bulge (agitated and almost explosive), and finally breaking up into a succession of calmer falling waves (more and more spaced out before vanishing from the page). But it would be an impoverishment to suggest that rhythm alone propels this poem and holds it together, just as it would to reduce *Dans la nuit* to a mere exercise in incantatory repetition. For *Clown* is a compact poetic arena in which repetitions, colourful and violent vocabulary, evocative rhythms, fluctuations of emotion, rare and suggestive imagery, and a profound central metaphor (that of the clown) engage in a collision of language which, by its sheer density and dynamism, soars beyond prose.

Some of the poems of Desnos come closer than any others in this anthology to the inspired prose of love-letters. Were their effect to depend simply on one or two stock devices, repeated *ad infinitum*, one would perhaps call them prose. But this is not the case. They are a rare conjunction of unpretentious sentimentality and impassionated rhetoric, plain language and surreal imagery, reassuring refrains or repeated patterns and surprising twists of thought and emotion. Above all, like the poems of Eluard, they have an enchanted atmosphere which dissolves reality, makes the cumbersome dainty and leaves the utilitarian shamefaced. Nor is this an enchantment which could spread its developments long-windedly over page after page: like wonders worked within the fairy-ring, its effect depends upon the limited context and condensed formula which are the poem.

It becomes clear, when one looks at twentieth-century poetry, that poetic vision has become more important than poetic sentiment, imagery more important than embellished description, and rhythm more important than rules of prosody. But this does not prove that the essentials of poetry have become any less essential: the respect for the sonority and texture of words, and the love of the powers of suggestion released by their contact; the impetus of the lyrical mood, the heightened feeling and perception, withou which words would be flaccid; the sensitivity of observation, emotio imagination and language working in creative co-ordination. Indeed it ha been said that there is no such thing as *free* verse. There is good poetry an bad poetry. And good poetry, whether in verse-form or not, is always sent ment and vision, rhythm and sound, pattern and meaning collaborating i exceptional harmony.

So we return to the threshold of the original secret, perhaps as impene trable as ever.

WHAT IS POETRY?

To restore some of the subtlety to what we have necessarily examine piecemeal, this is the place to silence the voice of the critic and make roon for the intuitions of the poets themselves, their words being perhaps th best answer to the question 'What is poetry?', and the best introduction t any poetic anthology:

Hugo:

Le domaine de la poésie est illimité. Sous le monde réel, il existe un monde idéal, qu se montre resplendissant à l'œil de ceux que des méditations graves ont accoutumé à voir dans les choses plus que les choses.

> Le poète en des jours impies
> Vient préparer des jours meilleurs.
> Il est l'homme des utopies;
> Les pieds ici, les yeux ailleurs.
> C'est lui qui sur toutes les têtes,
> En tout temps, pareil aux prophètes,
> Dans sa main, où tout peut tenir,
> Doit, qu'on l'insulte ou qu'on le loue,
> Comme une torche qu'il secoue,
> Faire flamboyer l'avenir.

Nerval:

Décadence et chute! tu copies la nature avec froideur (...) Enfant, l'art n'est point là: il consiste à créer (...) Souviens-toi des vieux Égyptiens, des artistes hardis et naïfs de l'Assyrie. N'ont-ils pas arraché des flancs du granit ces sphinx, ces cyno-céphales, ces divinités de basalte?

Je chantais en marchant, un hymne mystérieux dont je croyais me souvenir comme l'ayant entendu dans quelque autre existence, qui me remplissait d'une joie ineffable.

la dernière folie qui me restera probablement, ce sera de me croire poëte: c'est à la critique de m'en guérir.

Baudelaire:

La poésie, pour peu qu'on veuille descendre en soi-même, interroger son âme, rappeler ses souvenirs d'enthousiasme, n'a pas d'autre but qu'elle-même; elle ne peut pas en

voir d'autre, et aucun poème ne sera si grand, si noble, si véritablement digne du
om de poème, que celui qui aura été écrit uniquement pour le plaisir d'écrire un
oème.

a poésie est ce qu'il y a de plus réel, c'est ce qui n'est complètement vrai que dans
n autre monde.

y a dans le mot, dans le *verbe*, quelque chose de *sacré* qui nous défend d'en faire un
u de hasard. Manier savamment une langue, c'est pratiquer une espèce de sorcellerie
vocatoire.

out homme bien portant peut se passer de manger pendant deux jours, – de poésie,
amais.

Mallarmé:

a poésie est l'expression, par le langage humain ramené à son rhythme essentiel, du
ens mystérieux des aspects de l'existence: elle doue ainsi d'authenticité notre séjour
t constitue la seule tâche spirituelle.

Ce n'est point avec des idées qu'on fait des sonnets, Degas, c'est avec des mots.

a poésie consistant à *créer*, il faut prendre dans l'âme humaine des états, des lueurs
d'une pureté si absolue que, bien chantés et bien mis en lumière, cela constitue en
effet les joyaux de l'homme...

Nommer un objet, c'est supprimer les trois quarts de la jouissance du poème qui est
aite du bonheur de deviner peu à peu; le *suggérer*, voilà le rêve.

evoquer, dans une ombre exprès, l'objet tu, par des mots allusifs, jamais directs.

t toutes les paroles s'effacer devant les sensations...

Donner un sens plus pur aux mots de la tribu.

Cros:

> J'ai bâti dans ma fantaisie
> Un théâtre aux décors divers:
> –Magiques palais, grands bois verts –
> Pour y jouer ma poésie.
>
> Mais si je dérange parfois
> La sérénité des cieux froids,
> Si des sons d'acier ou de cuivre
> Ou d'or, vibrent dans mes chansons,
> Pardonne ces hautes façons,
> C'est que je me hâte de vivre.

Verlaine:

> De la musique encore et toujours!
> Que ton vers soit la chose envolée
> Qu'on sent qui fuit d'une âme en allée
> Vers d'autres cieux à d'autres amours.
>
> Que ton vers soit la bonne aventure
> Eparse au vent crispé du matin
> Qui va fleurant la menthe et le thym...
> Et tout le reste est littérature.

Rimbaud:

La première étude de l'homme qui veut être poète est sa propre connaissance, entière
il cherche son âme, il l'inspecte, il la tente, l'apprend. Dès qu'il la sait, il do
la cultiver...

Le Poète se fait *voyant* par un long, immense et raisonné *dérèglement* de *tous les sen*
Toutes les formes d'amour, de souffrance, de folie; il cherche lui-même, il épuise e
lui tous les poisons, pour n'en garder que les quintessences. Ineffable torture où il
besoin de toute la foi, de toute la force surhumaine, où il devient entre tous le gran
malade, le grand criminel, le grand maudit, – et le suprême Savant! – Car il arrive
l'*inconnu*! Puisqu'il a cultivé son âme, déjà riche, plus qu'aucun! Il arrive à l'inconn
et quand, affolé, il finirait par perdre l'intelligence de ses visions, il les a vues! Qu'
crève dans son bondissement par les choses inouïes et innombrables: viendront d'autre
horribles travailleurs; ils commenceront par les horizons où l'autre s'est affaissé!

Cette langue sera de l'âme pour l'âme, résumant tout, parfums, sons, couleurs...

J'écrivais des silences, des nuits, je notais l'inexprimable. Je fixais des vertiges.

Laforgue:

Une poésie n'est pas un sentiment que l'on communique tel que conçu avant la plume
Avouons le petit bonheur de la rime, et les déviations occasionnées par les trouvailles
la symphonie imprévue vient escorter le *motif*...

Je rêve de la poésie qui ne dise rien, mais soit des bouts de rêverie sans suite. Quand o
veut dire, exposer, démontrer quelque chose, il y a la prose.

Valéry:

Tout autre est la fonction de la poésie. Tandis que le fond unique est exigible de la
prose, c'est ici la forme unique qui ordonne et survit. C'est le son, c'est le rythme, c
sont les rapprochements physiques des mots, leurs effets d'induction ou leurs influence
mutuelles qui dominent, aux dépens de leur propriété de se consommer en un sen
défini et certain. Il faut donc que dans un poème le sens ne puisse l'emporter sur la
forme et la détruire sans retour; c'est au contraire le retour, la forme conservée, ou
plutôt exactement reproduite comme unique et nécessaire expression de l'état ou de la
pensée qu'elle vient d'engendrer au lecteur, qui est le ressort de la puissance poétique.
Un beau vers renaît indéfiniment de ses cendres, il redevient, – comme l'effet de son
effet, – cause harmonique de soi-même.

...c'est une erreur contraire à la nature de la poésie, et qui lui serait même mortelle,
que de prétendre qu'à tout poème correspond un sens véritable, unique, et conforme
ou identique à quelque pensée de l'auteur.

Un poème doit être une fête de l'Intellect. Il ne peut être autre chose.

Fête: c'est un jeu, mais solennel, mais réglé, mais significatif; image de ce qu'on n'est
pas d'ordinaire...

Mettre ou *faire mettre en prose un poème; faire d'un poème un matériel d'instruction ou
d'examens*, ne sont pas de moindres actes d'hérésie.

Apollinaire:

C'est que poésie et création ne sont qu'une même chose; on ne doit appeler poète

e celui qui invente, celui qui crée, dans la mesure où l'homme peut créer. Le poète
t celui qui découvre de nouvelles joies, fussent-elles pénibles à supporter. On peut
re poète dans tous les domaines: il suffit que l'on soit aventureux et que l'on aille à
découverte.

es poètes ne sont pas seulement les hommes du beau. Ils sont encore et surtout les
ommes du vrai, en tant qu'il permet de pénétrer dans l'inconnu, si bien que la surprise,
nattendu, est un des principaux ressorts de la poésie d'aujourd'hui.

u lis les prospectus les catalogues les affiches qui chantent tout haut
oilà la poésie ce matin...

upervielle:

'état de poésie me vient alors d'une sorte de confusion magique où les idées et les
nages se mettent à vivre, abandonnent leurs arêtes, soit pour faire des avances à
'autres images – dans ce domaine tout voisine, rien n'est vraiment éloigné – soit pour
ubir de profondes métamorphoses qui les rendent méconnaissables. Cependant pour
esprit, mélangé de rêves, les contraires n'existent plus: l'affirmation et la négation
eviennent une même chose et aussi le passé et l'avenir, le désespoir et l'espérance, la
olie et la raison, la mort et la vie. Le chant intérieur s'élève...

> Et d'avoir tous ces mots
> Qui bougent dans la tête,
> De choisir les moins beaux
> Pour leur faire un peu fête.

Eluard:

Le poète est celui qui inspire bien plus que celui qui est inspiré.

La poésie ne se fera chair et sang qu'à partir du moment où elle sera réciproque. Cette
éciprocité est entièrement fonction de l'égalité du bonheur entre les hommes.

Michaux:

Or, la poésie est un cadeau de la nature, une grâce, pas un travail. La seule ambition de
aire un poème suffit à le tuer.

> Pour noyer le mal,
> le mal et les angles des choses,
> et l'impératif des choses,
> et le dur et le calleux des choses,
> et le poids et l'encombrement des choses,
> et presque tout des choses,
> sauf le passage des choses,
> sauf le fluide des choses,
> et la couleur et le parfum des choses,
> et le touffu et la complicité parfois des choses...

Art des désirs, non des réalisations. Art des générosités, non des engagements. Art des
horizons et de l'expansion, non des enclos. Art dont le message partout ailleurs serait
utopie. *Art de l'élan.*

Desnos:

La poésie peut parler de tout en toute liberté. Essayez un peu pour voir, poètes renais-
sants, mes amis, pour voir que vous n'êtes pas libres.

Nous sommes les arborescences qui fleurissent sur les déserts des jardins cérébraux.

SUGGESTIONS FOR FURTHER READING

THE NATURE OF POETRY

Bosquet A., *Verbe et vertige*, Hachette, 1961.

Brémond H., *La Poésie pure*, Grasset, 1926.

Claudel P., *Réflexions sur la poésie*, (Collection Idées, 29), Gallimard, 1963.

Dufrenne M., *Le Poétique*, Presses universitaires de France, 1963.

Eluard P., *Les Sentiers et les routes de la poésie* in *Œuvres complètes* t. ii, (Bibliothèqu de la Pléiade), Gallimard, 1968, pp. 525–643.

Gibson R., *Modern French Poets on Poetry*, Cambridge University Press, 1961.

Gutmann R.-A., *Introduction à la lecture des poètes français*, Nizet, 1946.

Jean G., *La Poésie*, Edns. du Seuil, 1966.

Mallarmé S., *Propos sur la poésie*, Edns. du Rocher, 1953.

Mallarmé S., *Crise de vers* in *Œuvres complètes*, (Bibliothèque de la Pléiade), Gallimar 1945, pp. 360–8.

Mounin G., *Poésie et société*, Presses universitaires de France, 1962.

Onimus J., *La Connaissance poétique*, Desclée de Brouwer, 1966.

Renard J.-C., *Notes sur la poésie*, Edns. du Seuil, 1970.

Valéry P., Various texts under the heading 'Théorie poétique et esthétique' in *Œuvre* t. i, (Bibliothèque de la Pléiade), Gallimard, 1957, pp. 1153–418.

THE STRUCTURE AND TECHNIQUES OF FRENCH VERSE

Caminade P., *Image et métaphore*, Bordas, 1970.

Cohen J., *Structure du langage poétique*, Flammarion, 1966.

Delbouille P., *Poésie et sonorités*, Les Belles Lettres, 1961.

Deloffre F., *Le Vers français*, Société d'édition d'enseignement supérieur, 1973.

Elwert Th., *La Versification française*, Klincksieck, 1965.

Gauthier M., *Système euphonique et rythmique du vers français*, Klincksieck, 1974.

Ghyka M., *Essai sur le rythme*, Gallimard, 1952.

Grammont M., *Petit traité de versification française*, (Collection U), Colin, 1965.

Guiraud P., *La Versification*, (Que sais-je?, 1377), Presses universitaires de France, 1970.

Guiraud P., *Langage et versification d'après l'œuvre de Paul Valéry*, Klincksieck, 1953.

Kastner L. E., *A History of French Versification*, Clarendon Press, 1903.

Mazaleyrat J., *Pour une étude rythmique du vers français moderne: notes bibliographiques*, Minard, 1963.

Mazaleyrat J., *Eléments de métrique française*, (Collection U2), Colin, 1974.

Meschonnic H., (ed.) *Poétique du vers français* (issue no. 23 of *Langue française*, September, 1974).

Morier H., *Dictionnaire de poétique et de rhétorique*, Presses universitaires de France, 1961.

Parent M., (ed.) *Le Vers français au XXe siècle*, Klincksieck, 1967.

Spire A., *Plaisir poétique et plaisir musculaire*, Corti, 1949.

Thomas L.-P., *Le Vers moderne: ses moyens d'expression, son esthétique*, Académie royale de langue et de littérature françaises de Belgique, 1943.

CRITICAL APPROACHES AND METHODS OF ANALYSIS

Cahiers d'analyse textuelle, Nos. 1– , Les Belles Lettres, 1959– .

Chaillet J., *Etudes de grammaire et de style*, Bordas, 1969 (2 vols.).

Delas D. and Filliolet J., *Linguistique et poétique*, (Collection Langue et langage), Larousse, 1973.

Howarth W. D. and Walton C. L., *Explications: the technique of French literary appreciation*, Oxford University Press, 1971,

Jakobson R., *Questions de poétique*, Edns. du Seuil, 1973.

Meschonnic H., *Pour la poétique*, Gallimard, 1970–3 (3 vols.).

Niel A., *L'Analyse structurale des textes*, Mame, 1973.

Nurse P. H., *The Art of Criticism: essays in French literary analysis*, Edinburgh University Press, 1969.

Pouget P., *L'Explication française au baccalauréat*, Hachette, 1952.

Riffaterre M., *Essais de stylistique structurale*, Flammarion, 1971.

Schlumberger B. J., *L'Explication littéraire*, Harrap, 1951.

Wetherill P. M., *The Literary text: an examination of critical methods*, Blackwell, 1974.

COMMENTARIES

Victor Hugo

(1802–1885)

Pasteurs et troupeaux

Le vallon où je vais tous les jours est charmant,
Serein, abandonné, seul sous le firmament,
Plein de ronces en fleurs; c'est un sourire triste.
Il vous fait oublier que quelque chose existe,   4
Et sans le bruit des champs remplis de travailleurs,
On ne saurait plus là si quelqu'un vit ailleurs.
Là, l'ombre fait l'amour; l'idylle naturelle
Rit; le bouvreuil avec le verdier s'y querelle,   8
Et la fauvette y met de travers son bonnet;
C'est tantôt l'aubépine et tantôt le genêt;
De noirs granits bourrus, puis des mousses riantes;
Car Dieu fait un poëme avec des variantes;   12
Comme le vieil Homère, il rabâche parfois,
Mais c'est avec les fleurs, les monts, l'onde et les bois!
Une petite mare est là, ridant sa face,
Prenant des airs de flot pour la fourmi qui passe,   16
Ironie étalée au milieu du gazon,
Qu'ignore l'océan grondant à l'horizon.
J'y rencontre parfois sur la roche hideuse
Un doux être; quinze ans, yeux bleus, pieds nus, gardeuse   20
De chèvres, habitant, au fond d'un ravin noir,
Un vieux chaume croulant qui s'étoile le soir;
Ses sœurs sont au logis et filent leur quenouille;
Elle essuie aux roseaux ses pieds que l'étang mouille;   24
Chèvres, brebis, béliers, paissent; quand, sombre esprit,
J'apparais, le pauvre ange a peur, et me sourit;
Et moi, je la salue, elle étant l'innocence.
Ses agneaux, dans le pré plein de fleurs qui l'encense,   28
Bondissent, et chacun, au soleil s'empourprant,
Laisse aux buissons, à qui la bise le reprend,
Un peu de sa toison, comme un flocon d'écume.
Je passe, enfant, troupeau, s'effacent dans la brume;   32

Le crépuscule étend sur les longs sillons gris
Ses ailes de fantôme et de chauve-souris;
J'entends encore au loin dans la plaine ouvrière
Chanter derrière moi la douce chevrière, 36
Et, là-bas, devant moi, le vieux gardien pensif
De l'écume, du flot, de l'algue, du récif,
Et des vagues sans trêve et sans fin remuées,
Le pâtre promontoire au chapeau de nuées, 40
S'accoude et rêve au bruit de tous les infinis,
Et, dans l'ascension des nuages bénis,
Regarde se lever la lune triomphale,
Pendant que l'ombre tremble, et que l'âpre rafale 44
Disperse à tous les vents avec son souffle amer
La laine des moutons sinistres de la mer.

Pasteurs et troupeaux

Lines 1–18. Hugo has created a distinctive place for himself in French poetry as a painter of nature, able to seize vast patterns of meaning behind its apparently innocuous scenes and tiny details, responsive to its symbolic and religious texture, massively sympathetic to its ambiguities, dualities and changes of mood.

The opening descriptive section of this poem is a fine illustration. The setting has all the qualities of a serene haven set apart from the agitation of the world and conducive to solitary meditation of which the Romantic poets were so fond. Hugo begins with a particularly generous interplay of sounds to draw one into the charm of this valley (the prominent assonance of 'Serein...Plein', the alliterations and echo of 'charmant...chose...champs', etc.). The prevailing spirit of harmony is dramatized in the succinct image, 'l'ombre fait l'amour', which dispels any disquieting connotations the word 'ombre' might spread in other contexts – an impression of freedom from cares or sombre considerations which is immediately reinforced by the following image (built on the similar pattern of an abstract quality or force given a human expression), 'l'idylle naturelle / Rit': what effect does Hugo's use of the *rejet* have here?

But while speaking of harmony and serenity, the poet is developing suggestions of contrast and opposition. The early metaphor, 'c'est un sourire triste', summarizing as it does the opening lines of description, contains an element of the unexpected and invites one to take a second look at the juxtaposition of 'ronces' and 'fleurs' and their possible symbolic significance (cf. the flower in *J'ai cueilli cette fleur...* and the setting in which it grows). One notices the antithesis, even though only a benign one, between '...fait l'amour' and '...s'y querelle', the clash of temperament (and colour) between 'bouvreuil' and 'verdier', the contrast between the forbidding hardness of granite and the light, soft texture of moss. In Hugo's description, too, there are opposing tones: study the way in which he combines both here and further in the poem the grandiose and the simple, the serious and the whimsical. (What part does personification play; what effect is created by the translation of natural features of the landscape into human terms; how do you react to the comparison of God to Homer?) Lines 15–18, which conclude this introductory description, are a particularly forceful example of both contrast and correspondence: contrast between the expanse and multiplicity of the face of nature ('...les fleurs, les monts, l'onde et les bois!') and the particularity of the 'petite mare'; contrast and correspondence between the pool's tiny stature and the force and vastness of 'l'océan grondant à l'horizon', of which it is only a miniature replica. Why do you think Hugo chooses the word 'ironie' here?

Lines 19–31. The coming into prominence of the poet himself, after the long descriptive overture, marks a new development and a deeper level of theme. Note how Hugo creates dramatic emphasis at this juncture (especially by the *enjambement* and *rejet*, and the constrained hiatus of 'roche hideuse' followed by the easy liaison of 'doux être'). The contrast here between the harsh, graceless rock and a delicate being intensifies, since it introduces a suggestive human element, the earlier contrast between 'granits bourrus' and 'mousses riantes'. How effective do you find the description of the young girl (is there a change of rhythm)? Is it obvious that Hugo intends this portrait to have more a symbolic than a visual value?

This phase of the poem still depends, essentially, on the force of its oppositions, some more prominent than others: the dark of 'ravin noir' and the symbolic light of human life ('...qui s'étoile le soir'), the apparent solidity and permanence of rock and the precariousness and transience of man-made structures ('...vieux chaume croulant'); or, on a richer human level, the industrious domesticity of the girl's sisters and her own sympathetic union with the spirit of nature, and, most significant, the candour and naïvety of the girl and the depth of experience and sombreness of thought of the poet himself (the light and dark of 'ange' and 'sombre esprit': cf. this kind of confrontation in *A celle qui est voilée*). Note how, as a master of the dramatic situation, Hugo has organized his verse-form (lines 25–7) to underline the importance of this encounter and to convey the momentary surprise of the poet's appearance (an effect which differs markedly from the balanced use of the Alexandrine in such lines as 'C'est tantôt l'aubépine et tantôt le genêt').

The description of the lambs, traditionally suggestive of innocence and purity (cf. Verlaine's *L'échelonnement des haies*...), enhances the unreal aura. Each is bathed in a rich purplish light. Each in turn, as if in a ritual, leaves tufts of its fleece caught on the bushes, to be taken away on the winds as a kind of sacrificial offering into the vastness of nature. The suggestion of a religious atmosphere causes one to reconsider '...ses pieds que l'étang mouille' and 'le pré...qui l'encense', which imply a natural ceremony of communion. It is here, too, that the title *Pasteurs et troupeaux* and the religious connotations of the word 'agneau' come to life. Examine the richness of the final image, so neatly presented, which links the fleece with flecks of foam and blends landscape and premonitions of the sea. It is noticeable that both this stage of the poem and the preceding one end with similar references and the idea of a correspondence or reflective interplay.

Lines 32–46. The movement of the poet on his walk or pilgrimage ('Je passe...') brings on the final change of scene and atmosphere (how would you define this change; what does the echo between '...passe' and '...s'effacent' contribute; do you find the picture of oncoming twilight melodramatic or quite subtle?). One becomes aware that the poem is passing unobtrusively from sunlight to sunset, and from twilight eventually to nightfall (a common progression in Hugo's poetry, often used to illustrate in an atmospheric way the cycle of life from youth to age or the collapse of the superficial décor to reveal the tenebrous underside of life).

Attention is drawn, in this dimmer solitude, to the rôle of the poet, who is not only a passing spirit ('J'y rencontre...J'apparais...Je passe'), that is, almost an apparition himself and a slightly phantomatic presence (cf. '...sombre esprit'), but also a contemplative mind set apart from the workaday world (cf. '...au loin dans la plaine ouvrière' and '...sans le bruit des champs remplis de travailleurs') and a kind of link between two worlds ('J'entends encore au loin... derrière moi...Et là-bas, devant moi').

It is from line 37 onwards that the plural title *Pasteurs et troupeaux* assumes its full significance, in that the figure of the young girl goat-herd (who was 'ange' and 'innocence') is superseded by a vaster and more mysterious shepherd-figure (cf. in *Booz endormi* the parallel images of the reaper, one human and one divine). Again Hugo makes careful use of corresponding and contrasting patterns. The idea of '...gardeuse / De chèvres' is expanded in the echoing '...vieux gardien pensif / De l'écume' (the words 'gardeuse' and 'gardien' representing different shades of the same function): the parallel structure of the two phrases stands out emphatically, and an *enjambement* which appeared gratuitous in its original banal context now acquires a firmer justification. Whereas the earlier enumeration 'Chèvres, brebis, béliers, paissent' gave an impression of tranquillity, the present lines (by the variety of vowel-sounds, the *enjambement*, the run-on line and the restless repetition of 'sans trêve et sans fin') suggest a more awesome, turbulent and less containable flock which needs constant vigilance. In revealing that this shepherd is, in fact, the headland looking out to sea (cf. Rimbaud's 'Péninsules démarrées' in *Le Bateau ivre*), Hugo again uses personification to magnificent effect, humanizing the inanimate and introducing a picturesque touch which makes the figure unexpectedly rustic and familiar. The gaze of this shepherd, however, is not merely watching over its flock but probing the depths of the infinite. It is here that the poem begins to take on its deepest contemplative tone ('...pensif...rêve...regarde'). The words 'vieux *gardien* pensif' and '*pâtre* promontoire' (an image of great verbal audacity) form a clear analogy with the young girl and her function. Perhaps they have an even deeper and more complex metaphorical link with the poet himself ('vieux *gardien pensif*', 'pâtre *promontoire*').

The opposition of dark and light briefly sketched out in the image of the black ravine and the star-like gleam of the cottage also returns expanded and enriched. The rising moon and the illuminated clouds (why the epithet 'bénis'?) are set against the darkening night. There is thus an intimation of divine light and serene order counterbalancing the waywardness, disorder, murkiness and chaos which it is the shepherd's task to watch over. But the spectacle of heavenly light has its triumph only for a moment. For the last three lines show at their most intense the dark (cf. 'l'ombre fait l'amour' with 'l'ombre tremble'), the harsh (cf. 'la bise' with 'l'âpre rafale') and the ominous (cf. the first descriptive word of the poem, 'charmant', with the final one, 'sinistres'). The cosiness and seclusion of the little valley, with all its diminutive life-forms, gives way to the frightening open expanses of the sea. What was a vague reference to sadness in 'un sourire triste' is now given more sombre intensity, and the distant premonition of 'l'océan grondant à l'horizon' is fulfilled. Notice the crucial positioning of the words 'Le vallon' and 'la mer' in the structural patterning of the poem as a whole, and the progressively widening vision (the tiny insect passing by the pond, the girl at the edge of the pool, the headland jutting into the infinite sea, and the poet who spans all these different perspectives and has the ultimate vision).

Study in detail the final image: in what way does it bring to a culmination what has preceded (cf. the final image in *Booz endormi*); how effectively has

Hugo developed, especially in view of the earlier simile linking 'toison' and 'flocon d'écume', the linguistic association in French between fleece and foaming breakers ('moutons' in this sense meaning 'white horses')? These final lines bring together, in a structural relief which balances perfectly that of lines 30–1, aspects of the sky ('la bise...l'âpre rafale'), things of the earth ('toison...laine') and images of the sea ('flocon d'écume...moutons sinistres de la mer'). They send the mind plunging beyond one mere element into the realm of universal analogy, and conjure up a deep instinctive *frisson* at all that lies behind the décor of human life: the powerful, the fathomless, the obscure.

Je suis fait d'ombre et de marbre . . .

Je suis fait d'ombre et de marbre.
Comme les pieds noirs de l'arbre,
Je m'enfonce dans la nuit.
J'écoute; je suis sous terre;
D'en bas je dis au tonnerre: 6
Attends! ne fais pas de bruit.

Moi qu'on nomme le poète,
Je suis dans la nuit muette
L'escalier mystérieux;
Je suis l'escalier Ténèbres;
Dans mes spirales funèbres   12
L'ombre ouvre ses vagues yeux.

Les flambeaux deviendront cierges.
Respectez mes degrés vierges,
Passez, les joyeux du jour!
Mes marches ne sont pas faites
Pour les pieds ailés des fêtes,   18
Pour les pieds nus de l'amour.

Devant ma profondeur blême
Tout tremble, les spectres même
Ont des gouttes de sueur.
Je viens de la tombe morte;
J'aboutis à cette porte   24
Par où passe une lueur.

Le banquet rit et flamboie.
Les maîtres sont dans la joie
Sur leur trône ensanglanté;
Tout les sert, tout les encense;
Et la femme à leur puissance   30
Mesure sa nudité.

Laissez la clef et le pène.
Je suis l'escalier; la peine
Médite; l'heure viendra;
Quelqu'un qu'entourent les ombres
Montera mes marches sombres,
Et quelqu'un les descendra.

36

Je suis fait d'ombre et de marbre...

Stanza 1. It is significant that, in his Preface to the collection *Les Contemplations*, Hugo wrote, 'Ce livre doit être lu comme on lirait le livre d'un mort'. One could say the same of this poem, composed in the same period.

Consider the impact of the opening line, so emphatic in form (its brevity and monosyllabic curtness, its assertive, almost categorical, tone) yet so indeterminate in meaning (the mystifying metaphor resembling a riddle). How suggestive do you find the image '...d'ombre et de marbre', with its contrasting qualities, its regal and sepulchral associations? In what way might it be seen as a definition of the poet's nature? The following image ('Comme les pieds noirs de l'arbre...') enriches the metaphorical dimension: it introduces the idea of descent, the murky intermingling of roots (the groping tentacles on which the strength of the tree as a whole depends) and subterranean darkness, and suggests the poetic mind delving into the depths. With its balance of the impalpable and the concrete, it reinforces the image of the first line. Lines 4–6 deepen the mystery by imposing a sense of power, a feeling of apprehension and the awareness of an imminent event. Look at the variety of means by which Hugo creates the suspense. How would you define the atmosphere of this first stanza?

Stanza 2. The second stanza extends and elucidates the enigmatic self-definition: the 'je' is now seen clearly to be the poet. But a strong contrast is drawn between the common notion and mere title of 'poet' and his own conviction of the depth and mystery of his function. How does the style give colouring to this contrast in lines 7–9? The somewhat baffling details of the first line of the poem ('...d'ombre et de marbre') become clearer with the words 'L'escalier mystérieux' ('l'escalier', in French, meaning more than just the actual stairs). What, in your opinion, is the significance of this central metaphor of the poet as a stairway? Notice how the description is both forcefully egocentric ('Moi qu'on nomme...Je suis...Je suis...') and strangely impersonal. The unusual form of 'Je suis l'escalier Ténèbres' also lends a legendary or allegorical quality to the poet's rôle.

The idea of darkness, dominant in the first stanza ('ombre...noirs...nuit'), is now horrifically personified. The eyes of a watchful presence, whose intentions cannot be read (cf. '...ses *vagues* yeux' with '...la nuit *muette*'), seem to lurk in every coil of the spiral staircase, that is to say, within every obscure fold of the poet's tortuous being. What do sound and rhythm contribute to the dramatic effect of line 12? Look closely at the way in which the boundaries between animate and inanimate, human and inhuman, substantial and unsubstantial are blurred, and darkness, at one time enveloping the stairway, at another seems contained within it.

Stanza 3. The third stanza strikes a firm prophetic note. What are the implications of the anticipated transformation of 'flambeaux', festive torches, into 'cierges'? Note how flame dwindling into a small flickering light suggests a descent into a dank, airless atmosphere (cf. later references to 'spectres' and 'tombe morte'). Here the poet's alienation from the superficial pursuits of life is confirmed: his ascetic purity ('mes degrés vierges'), his superior destiny ('Mes marches ne sont pas faites...'), his devotion to things more permanent ('Passez, les joyeux du jour!'). In this distinction between two incompatible worlds, how appropriate are the expressions '...pieds ailés des fêtes', '...pieds nus de l'amour'? These six lines are a good example of emphasis achieved by phonetic and syntactical repetition (the double imperative, the repeated consonants, the rich rhymes, the parallel structures). They are symptomatic of the very close-knit phonetic patterns throughout the poem which ensure its unity and density.

Stanza 4. Abandoning 'les joyeux du jour' to their frivolities in the daylight world above, the poet reasserts his own eerie depth, which combines darkness and a ghastly pallor. What does the adjective 'blême' suggest here? How effective, in the general context, is the double implication of the words 'Tout tremble'? Like the darkness which was earlier given vaguely human features, now the spectres, usually thought of as unsubstantial and frightening, are described in emphatic physical terms and are themselves fear-stricken. One should point out here the value of the choice of the imparisyllabic line. Verlaine has described the *vers impair* as 'Plus vague et plus soluble dans l'air, / Sans rien en lui qui pèse ou qui pose'. Does the use of it in this poem help to create any effect akin to that suggested by Verlaine?

Lines 22–4 not only advertise the poet's position beyond the confines of life, but also stress the immense span of his domain and influence ('Je viens de... J'aboutis à...'), just as in the first stanza he could, even from the nethermost depths, silence and restrain the thunder in the sky. The final picture, in contrast to the previous murkiness and vagueness of outline, focuses one's attention very pointedly on the significance of the door (note the demonstrative adjective in 'J'aboutis à *cette* porte...') and on a thin line of light, the boundary between two worlds.

Stanza 5. Developing the reference to the chink of light and the door, this stanza turns momentarily to describe the lavish scene on the other side. Individual details of the third stanza, which was a stanza of authoritative forewarning, now recur in a richer descriptive setting. There is a spirit of insouciance in the festivities, as if the revellers were oblivious of the warning, 'Les flambeaux deviendront cierges'. What do 'les maîtres' and the banquet represent? Do you see similarities between this scene and the Biblical story of Belshazzar's feast (cf. Daniel 5)?

Analyse Hugo's use of effects of contrast here (e.g. between the poet's life of dark contemplation and this gaudy show of carnality), looking back at phrases elsewhere in the poem which throw into relief the noisy gaiety, the colour of blood, the sullied throne, the wanton self-offerings of the courtesans, and the fact that everything bows in awe before these figures of power. Notice how the abruptness of the verb 'rit' is intensified by the two consecutive stresses (cf. the similar accentuation in line 12) and how, for the first time in the poem, the initial rhymes are not closed by a consonant (in contrast with 'marbre...l'arbre', 'cierges...vierges', etc.) and suggest a sudden lack of restraint.

Stanza 6. Having drawn back the corner of the curtain on the superficial orgy of life, the poet retires again into the nether world where the essential purposes are being worked out, sure in the knowledge of his own function. The first line, 'Laissez la clef et le pène' is a warning that there are certain territories over which kings of the world have no dominion, and certain forces which cannot be hurried. 'L'heure viendra' reintroduces the prophetic note, underlining the inevitability and menace of some fateful event. Compare the sense of anticipation here with that created in lines 5–6 and line 13. One imagines, from the phrase 'la peine / Médite', that somewhere in a realm unknown to those revelling in thoughtless merriments and plunged in their orgies, a spirit of suffering and purgation, strongly aware of the presence of death, is pursuing its meditation. The end of this meditation will coincide with the moment of reckoning. How does Hugo intensify the mood or atmosphere by his use of verse-form in lines 31–3 (cf. a similar handling in lines 4–6)?

The poem ends as enigmatically as it began (the indeterminate 'Quelqu'un...' and the equally unspecific corresponding '...quelqu'un', the emphasis on darkness, the ambiguity of the plural '...les ombres' which might mean shadows or spirits of the dead), but with an absolute certainty of tone, the certainty that the event will be. What force does the positioning of the two future tenses 'Montera...descendra' lend to this finale? The last three lines bring to fruition the metaphor of the poet as 'l'escalier': he is the place of exchange and passage, an essential link between the mystery of the beyond and the empty pomp of human life. He is also the servant of a greater power (contrast with 'Tout les sert...'), whose destiny will be fulfilled (cf. the suggestion of predestination in line 16) at this fatal hour.

The overall structural pattern of the poem is particularly evocative: the way in which the splash of colour of the fifth stanza is surrounded by an ominous dark (or one might say caught within the grasp of an infinite subterranean power), and the more obvious metaphor of the banquet contained within the more suggestive one of the stairway, which dominates the poem and cannot be readily reduced to the language of reason.

Gérard de Nerval

(1808–1855)

Myrtho

Je pense à toi, Myrtho, divine enchanteresse,
Au Pausilippe altier, de mille feux brillant,
A ton front inondé des clartés d'Orient,
Aux raisins noirs mêlés avec l'or de ta tresse.   4

C'est dans ta coupe aussi que j'avais bu l'ivresse,
Et dans l'éclair furtif de ton œil souriant,
Quand aux pieds d'Iacchus on me voyait priant,
Car la Muse m'a fait l'un des fils de la Grèce.   8

Je sais pourquoi là-bas le volcan s'est rouvert...
C'est qu'hier tu l'avais touché d'un pied agile,
Et de cendres soudain l'horizon s'est couvert.   11

Depuis qu'un duc normand brisa tes dieux d'argile,
Toujours, sous les rameaux du laurier de Virgile,
Le pâle Hortensia s'unit au Myrthe vert!   14

Myrtho

Lines 1–4. Nerval's poetry is notoriously obscure and allusive; without access to the encyclopedia, many of his poems would remain abstruse. But once penetrated, the work is impressively rich. The density of *Myrtho* is typical: there are references to mythological, classical and more modern figures, some of whom cannot be identified; to exotic places and mysterious events from the poet's past; to flowers whose capital letters seem to give them some symbolic significance. And the unpredictable tenses imply a progression which is perfectly valid in the poet's mental time-scale but which is at first disconcerting for the reader. Yet the whole sonnet eventually justifies the probings of exegesis.

The first question concerns the identity of Myrtho, for she is no known goddess even if she is described as 'divine', and even if the strangeness of her name suggests a mythic figure. She is more likely a poetic creation, a girl who graces the Mediterranean landscape (cf. Dafné in *Delfica*) and has initiated the poet to a world of intoxicating light and an age of ancient splendour. The implication of the opening address is one of imaginative presence and actual absence: Myrtho is in the poet's thoughts, not in his company. The scene on Posilipo, the site of Vergil's tomb and a part of the volcanic landscape around Naples, is similarly distant. But such is the force with which they have imprinted themselves that they can be recalled with the utmost ease and clarity: firstly the girl, then the place, then girl and place together, complementing each other perfectly. Study the parallelism of the phrases dependent on 'Je pense' (reinforcing each other by their similar structure, suggesting by their repetition an eager mind's eye conjuring up successive waves of reminiscent vision, alternating between 'à toi...Au Pausilippe...A ton front...Aux raisins' and thus helping to interlace ideas of a personal and a natural richness, and culminating in references to luminosity). Note the qualities of light which give the description a splendour (fire and brilliance, light and liquid abundance, the multiplicity of 'mille feux' and the symbolic singularity of 'l'or'); the complex appeal of the woman (is there a suggestion of a duality in her nature?); the way in which the 'raisins noirs' evoke the image of a Bacchante and foreshadow the idea of intoxication in the second quatrain and explain perhaps the 'aussi' of line 5.

Lines 5–8. The second stanza recalls a kind of ritual incident in which Myrtho was a central influence. The poet had been made drunk by her brilliant enchantment, and was inspired through her, it seems, to worship at the feet of Iacchus (another name for Bacchus, the god of wine). That he can commune with the ancient divinities is because the poetic Muse, in this land of Vergil, has taken him as an adopted son into the Classical spirit of the Mediterranean; the fact that Vergil was a Latin poet, Iacchus a Roman god, while he describes himself as a son of Greece, does not matter since both Classical cultures represent for him the harmony of the Golden Age, so regretted in *Delfica*. In this picture of a 'vie antérieure', the luminosity of the first quatrain is still present (note the phonetic bond between '*cl*artés...ave*c* l'or...é*cl*air') but the adjective 'furtif' introduces a disturbing notion of evanescence, stealth and possible duplicity. The metaphor of lines 5–6 fuses light ('éclair'), liquid ('bu') and a part of the human body ('œil') in a combination such as that which also animated line 3; and the enchantment is exercised simultaneously as a physical inebriation, a luminous hypnotism and a spiritual mystery. Notice, however, that Myrtho is no longer the passive recipient ('inondé') but the active source ('souriant') or agent of light. It is as if she has been imbued with the light of wisdom ('clartés d'Orient' may suggest Eastern spiritual illumination as well as brilliant sun) with which she now illumines the poet. Would you say that the intoxication experienced by Nerval is one of human love or mystical ecstasy? What effect does the rapidly changing sequence of tenses and the *passé composé* of line 8 have? In what tone might this last line be spoken? What might be the relationship between Myrtho and 'la Muse'?

Lines 9–11. The sestet begins a new movement on a note of discreet self-satisfaction and assurance: the poet's experience has endowed him with a secret knowledge. His mind moves as easily in space as in time, and as 'un des fils de la Grèce', he can understand events in the distant Mediterranean ('là-bas') even when he is not there. (The 'là-bas' here is vague enough to be Posilipo, Greece or some obscure region of inner experience.) The dormant volcano, once full of fire and energy, has erupted again (notice the prefix of 'rouvert'). This volcano may well be a symbol of the poet's enthusiasm for a past age rekindled by the light, fire and beauty of Myrtho and Posilipo. It may be also a sign, as in ancient beliefs, of a deep disturbance in the order of the gods. The girl's magical power, associated from the outset with both the gods' fire and the lushness of the vegetal world, extends beyond the human and deep into the body of nature. As if with the deftest touch of a wand (cf. the fleeting contact suggested by 'touché d'un pied agile' with similar suggestions in 'l'éclair furtif'), she has unleashed the violence of a volcanic eruption. How does Nerval give rhythmical emphasis to the explanation of this happening? The final line of the tercet has ambiguous connotations: on the one hand, it confirms the vast, lightning-swift power of Myrtho; on the other, it links it with obliteration and darkness, casts the mind back to those unsettling adjectives 'noirs' and 'furtif', and strengthens the idea that, as elsewhere in Nerval's work, woman represents an attractive but dangerous ideal. It is not clear either whether the horizon is that of the Mediterranean or that of the poet who, from a distant country, sees his wishful mental skyline veiled by 'cendres', a traditional symbol of grief and mourning. Could the fire and the ash be passion and sadness? Compare the use of the Pluperfect and *passé composé* in lines 9–11 with their use in lines 5–8; in what way does the implied sequence of events in both stanzas reinforce the analogy between the poet and the volcano and the idea that the eruption or force of reawakening is within the poet himself? Note that, just as he was at the foot of Bacchus and kindled to a drunken exaltation, so the volcano is touched to life by the fleeting foot of a divinity.

Lines 12–14. The theme of violence opens the second tercet. The 'duc normand' can remain unidentified, for his importance is as a symbol of military strength and new civilizations which have destroyed ancient deities (those for whom Myrtho is a spirit of inspiration). But significantly, the act of past destruction ('brisa'), conclusively over from an historical point of view, is linked in a causal relationship with something which has come together from that moment on, and continues to live on in the present ('s'unit'), as a symbolic unity. The hydrangea can be taken as a symbol of non-Classical civilizations (it is a relatively recent immigrant to Europe from the Far East), while the myrtle is the plant sacred to Venus, goddess of love. The last stanza thus proposes a reconciliation between modern and ancient, between the pallor of present civilization, the late Christian era, and the pagan vigour of earlier gods (the evergreen myrtle suggests that they still live on). The spirit which oversees this union is Vergil's, a triumphant poetic spirit (cf. 'laurier') which can span all ages and cultures; and one could well see Myrtho as his accomplice, a divine agent who has initiated Nerval in the mystic rites of poetry and love (note her connection with Venus evoked in the last line). On the other hand, the ending may be a negative one: for the tercets strike a note of violence which breaks the rich reigning harmony of the first eight lines; the brilliant play of light (and all that it may have represented) has receded into the background, as, too, has the suggestion of body and spirit united in the same ecstasy; the elements of light, air and water are superseded by earth; and the interlacing of paleness and green is only a weak and fragile, though poetically delicate, echo of the lush grape-black and regal gold. The poem has no clear interpretative pattern, only tenuous echoes of certain themes: light, intoxication, worship, reawakening, violence, communion and harmony. But it is given some sort of poetic stability by the last two lines: the 'Toujours' fuses all the various tenses into an eternal present; the close echo of 'Myrtho' in 'Myrthe' gives the poem an aura of unity; the final reconciliation of contrasts (note the central position of 's'unit') provides a satisfying and balanced ending, so that one has the impression that some tension has been resolved. Could one also see the intertwining of the plants as a *correspondance* of the meeting between the poet and Myrtho?

Do you feel satisfied by this allusive type of poem? Do the disparate elements make up a sufficiently composite picture for the reader to recognize the poem as a carefully worked piece of art? Are there any aspects of *Myrtho* which might explain in part the Surrealists' enthusiasm for Nerval?

Vers dorés

Eh quoi! tout est sensible!

PYTHAGORE

Homme, libre penseur! te crois-tu seul pensant
Dans ce monde où la vie éclate en toute chose?
Des forces que tu tiens ta liberté dispose,
Mais de tous tes conseils l'univers est absent.   4

Respecte dans la bête un esprit agissant:
Chaque fleur est une âme à la Nature éclose;
Un mystère d'amour dans le métal repose;
'Tout est sensible!' Et tout sur ton être est puissant.   8

Crains, dans le mur aveugle, un regard qui t'épie:
A la matière même un verbe est attaché...
Ne la fais pas servir à quelque usage impie!   11

Souvent dans l'être obscur habite un Dieu caché;
Et comme un œil naissant couvert par ses paupières,
Un pur esprit s'accroît sous l'écorce des pierres!   14

Vers dorés

Lines 1–4. The idea that what Man chooses to dismiss as brute nature is in fact pulsating with hidden thought and feeling is by no means new to the nineteenth century but, as Nerval's epigraph is meant to indicate, can be found in the classical writings of ancient philosophy (the idea is also at the basis of many primitive religions). This sonnet is a reminder and a warning to a European civilization which, in Nerval's eyes, was in danger of becoming too complacent and too easily satisfied by a superficial materialism. In an effort to reveal the obscured harmony of creation, the poet hints strongly that Man's alienation from the universe has come about through his own homocentric vision; the world needs to be looked at afresh through the eyes of a poet. The two opening lines set the tone of admonition with their ironic address which defines Man in terms later to be devalued, and with their shaming question uttered in disbelief. How effective is this as an opening? Note how Nerval directs attention to the word 'seul' which echoes the last syllable of 'penseur', and how this sense of Man's uniqueness is then questioned by the emphasis on 'toute' in the second line. Nerval argues his point with a poetic concentration: it is worth remarking how the rhetorical lure ('Homme, libre penseur!') and counterthrust ('te crois-tu seul pensant...') is paralleled by the movement (signalled by 'Mais...') from a line of relative praise (line 3) to a line of condemnation (line 4) which renders the former ironic. The poet provokes reaction by deliberate juxtaposition of concession and reprimand. Man has freedom to exert power within a certain limited scope ('Des forces que tu tiens...') but the exercise of this power disregards the sensitivity of the universe. Which of these first four lines is the most vibrant with meaning?

Lines 5–8. The second stanza, as the first, opens with a line of firm sonority ('*Réspecte...bête...esprit*') which demands the listener's attention. Nerval is about to offer advice from which the universe is decidedly not absent. The references to the animal, vegetable and mineral realms are carefully juxtaposed, so that one has the impression that the 'toute chose' of line 2 is being studiously broken down by the poet's explanatory rhetoric before it is eventually recomposed by the 'tout' of line 8. In so far as each animal has a mind, Man is not the only thinking being on earth; and in so far as the mind is 'agissant', Man cannot discount animals as passive irrelevancies. Each flower exhales not only its scent but a spiritual essence (cf. Baudelaire's *Harmonie du soir*) which fuses it subtly with the whole of Nature; its trusting innocence ('à la Nature éclose') is an example to Man who is locked in his own self-regard. Note how the vigorous echo 'éclate' / 'éclose' reinforces the idea of an expansive, living universe which one cannot ignore. Even the mute, immobile world of minerals is more mysterious than Man thinks. Hidden in the unyielding hardness of metal lie vague, ethereal emotions. Whilst Man can and often does attribute in a rather stylized way feelings and attitudes to animals and plants, the mineral world is more often regarded as totally impassive and dead. For this reason, line 7 provides the most surprising assertion of the stanza. How satisfactory is the Pythagorean dictum 'Tout est sensible' as a summary of lines 5–7? Why does the poet stress 'tout'? What important change of tone takes place in line 8 and how does the ending of this stanza compare with the ending of the first quatrain?

Lines 9–11. The steady devaluation of Man's importance continues into the first tercet; the respect which exists between compeers is momentarily replaced by a fear generated by presences which lurk unsuspected in the stone-work of a wall. This chilling intuition of an inescapable judging eye unnerves the reader and gives a concreteness (in every sense) to the abstract generality 'Et tout sur ton être est puissant'. In what way does the apparent contradiction of 'aveugle' and 'qui t'épie' add to the effect of the line? Three ideas have become clear: firstly, that Nature is as active as Man (lines 2, 5–9); secondly, that Nature does not exist in indifferent isolation but possesses a definite relationship with Man (lines 8 and 9); and thirdly, that the division often made between matter and spirit is, according to Nerval, invalid (see especially lines 6–7). These three strands are brought together in the ambiguity of 'un verbe' in line 10. If one takes its simple grammatical meaning, it stresses the *active* rôle of matter (matter can be the active subject of a sentence). If one takes 'un verbe' to mean expression in general, then the line implies that Nature can speak to Man, using the 'confuses paroles' which Baudelaire mentions in his poem, *Correspondances*. If one develops the theological associations of 'un verbe', one can infer that, just as in Christian doctrine Christ is the incarnation of the Word of God ('le Verbe'), matter also is imbued with divine spirit and is therefore sacred (this explains the use of the adjective 'impie' in line 11). The third imperative ('Ne la fais pas servir à quelque usage impie!') strikes a further note of reprimand but this time with a tinge of reassurance in that at least it does not deny Man's power to use his environment. But more importantly it demands of Man, this 'libre penseur' with his pretentious reason and notions of superiority, that he respect the spirituality of the non-human world.

Lines 12–14. How does the opening line of this tercet link up with the preceding stanza? What does Nerval include under the rather vague term 'l'être obscur'? Where else in Nerval's poetry does one find the idea of 'un Dieu caché' and an ancient harmony waiting to be rediscovered and reborn? The final two lines strengthen the impression (already given by 'éclate' and 'éclose') that the earth is bursting with life in all its forms and that even the hardest of objects contain a spiritual embryo which will eventually be born to gaze on Mankind, offering the possibility of visual exchange and communion (cf. the image of the 'symboles' in Baudelaire's *Correspondances*, the 'pierreries' in Rimbaud's *Aube* and the 'mille regards pareils' in Eluard's *Sans âge*). Nerval has closed his sonnet with due regard for its organic unity by picking up echoes of earlier images: trace the theme of the eye and the gradual interpenetration of the animal, vegetable, mineral and spiritual realms to suggest something akin to Baudelaire's 'ténébreuse et profonde unité'. The conclusion leaves one with a sense of unease and excitement: unease caused by the fact that the 'Dieu caché' may be an awesome, vengeful deity, excitement by the vision of an Edenic state in which matter and pure spirit are in union not opposition. The terse oracular tone (notice the twelve main verbs in the first twelve lines and the aura of high seriousness created by the frequent use of literary inversion) is continued to the end, although the slightly more expansive movement in lines 13–14 allows a resonant finale to the poem (supported by the strongly alliterative last line).

At first sight, Nerval seems to be a nineteenth-century environmentalist; but what features of his thought distinguish him from his modern counterpart? Make a detailed comparison between this sonnet and Baudelaire's *Correspondances*.

Charles Baudelaire

(1821–1867)

Harmonie du soir

Voici venir les temps où vibrant sur sa tige
Chaque fleur s'évapore ainsi qu'un encensoir;
Les sons et les parfums tournent dans l'air du soir;
Valse mélancolique et langoureux vertige!   4

Chaque fleur s'évapore ainsi qu'un encensoir;
Le violon frémit comme un cœur qu'on afflige;
Valse mélancolique et langoureux vertige!
Le ciel est triste et beau comme un grand reposoir.   8

Le violon frémit comme un cœur qu'on afflige,
Un cœur tendre, qui hait le néant vaste et noir!
Le ciel est triste et beau comme un grand reposoir;
Le soleil s'est noyé dans son sang qui se fige.   12

Un cœur tendre, qui hait le néant vaste et noir,
Du passé lumineux recueille tout vestige!
Le soleil s'est noyé dans son sang qui se fige...
Ton souvenir en moi luit comme un ostensoir!   16

Harmonie du soir

Lines 1–4. Consider the title of the poem: the harmony of evening is a poetic one, a brief moment of interplay and balance between day and night. In the broadest sense the poem is descriptive of a twilight; but the scene is indistinguishable from the sensual and emotional responses which it evokes, with the result that there is neither clear visual image nor clearly identifiable sensation.

Objects of nature lose their materiality and become diffused as in a vapour. As evening descends, the flowers seem to give themselves up in offering. There is a movement of arrival ('Voici venir les temps...') and one of departure ('Chaque fleur s'évapore...'), and, somewhere in the air, an exchange between this special moment in time and the perfume, the exhaled essence, of each flower. Baudelaire has described *le surnaturel* (those privileged moments when the imagination is alive to analogies and the secret harmonics of beauty, and when senses combine in a richness of experience which goes beyond mere sense-perception) as 'intensité, sonorité, limpidité, vibrativité, profondeur et retentissement dans l'espace et dans le temps'. Are any of these words appropriate to the 'atmospheric' description he creates in the first stanza?

Notice the balance between the precise ('vibrant sur sa tige...' and 'Chaque fleur...') and the imprecise or impalpable ('s'évapore... les sons et les parfums tournent dans l'air'); between the almost ecstatic ('langoureux vertige') and the slightly bittersweet ('mélancolique'). What factors contribute to the headiness of the fourth line? Study the suggestive way in which various senses (a responsiveness to shape, scent, sound, rhythm) are brought together in the creation of a rich, complex mood.

Lines 5–8. This is the place to notice the workings of the verse-form known as the *pantoum*. This is a somewhat rigid and rigorous verse-form, made all the more so here by Baudelaire's use of only two rhymes throughout: structurally, the second and fourth lines of a stanza become the first and third lines of the following stanza. It is also a verse-form with an unusual double effect: on the one hand, its strict repetitive architecture slows down the progress of the poem and makes it seem comparatively static; but on the other hand, its elements change places and make one conscious of an incessant internal movement. In this way certain lines are retained, but set in a changed context, subject to new relationships and carrying a different emphasis (a second line in its more subordinate position becomes the first line in the following stanza, initiating the next movement with a greater boldness; while a fourth line, setting the seal on a stanza in an emphatic terminal position, becomes the less conclusive third line of the following one). This technical means is strangely appropriate to a description of evening such as we have here, if one thinks of twilight as a lingering time of day, loath to depart, but a time when change can be best observed; or of the way in which twilight slowly changes its hue in an otherwise unchanging scene. One might add that, with its stylized repetitions, this is an almost ritualistic verse-form, well attuned to a poem which gives such stress to religious ceremonial.

Notice how the delicately poised harmony of the first stanza begins to be dispersed and, as nightfall descends, the mood becomes progressively more sombre. Look at the repeated line 'Chaque fleur s'évapore...', which now begins a stanza in its own right and is no longer a sequel to '...vibrant sur sa tige', so that the emphasis is on departure and loss rather than suspense and exchange. What effect does the use of the verb 'frémir' as opposed to 'vibrer' have on the mood of this stanza? How are the words 'Valse mélancolique...', although repeated exactly, given deeper sadness in their new context? Compare the qualities of the earlier phrase 'mélancolique et langoureux' with the present 'triste et beau' (the disappearance of the lingering multisyllabic adjectives and of the rich internal rhyme).

Lines 9–12. In this third stanza bittersweet mood and ambiguity move closer to opposition and conflict, as 'le ciel' and 'le néant' are forcefully juxtaposed. One is suddenly made to realize that, whereas in the first stanza the idea of melancholy was only faintly traced at the last moment into a dominantly beautiful poetic experience, now it is the word 'beau' which is the isolated element, outweighed in its context by such negative connotations as '...un cœur qu'on afflige', '...le néant vaste et noir' and '...s'est noyé dans son sang'. The emphasis is on darkness and death, even though Baudelaire maintains a firm line of Christian imagery. What do you think are the implications of the references to Christian ritual?

Study again in this stanza the way in which the recurrent lines change their value. Consider how the image of the sun drowning in its own blood, which may appear brutal and somewhat melodramatic, is nevertheless relevant both to the description of the time of day and to the image of a wounded heart. The change of tense in the final line is especially significant: something has been concluded, an all-enveloping sensation becomes an almost static scene, the pliability of turning perfumes and languid vertigo are frozen in the verb 'se fige', and the sense of timelessness is contracted into an awareness of past time.

Lines 13–16. It is in this way that the theme of memory emerges and fulfils the poem in the final stanza.

As the light of the world is snuffed and becomes a death, the poet falls back on the reliability of a quasi-divine inner light ('...lumineux ...luit comme un ostensoir'). This image of the monstrance emphasizes Baudelaire's religious view of memory as the human replica of eternity which resists the incessant invasion of nothingness and from which nothing of value is lost, the sacred container which guards the essence of passing experiences. It is noticeable that, with the theme of memory, there comes a more affirmative emphasis on the poetic self (e.g. the act of will and self-possession implicit in the verb '...recueille', and the stress on the words '...en moi'). Trace the unobtrusive way in which Baudelaire develops the personal element in the poem. There has been a movement from what promised, in the first stanza, to be heady self-abandonment to the poetic harmony of the outside world; to a growing revulsion against oncoming darkness and void; and finally to a retreat by the poet into his own internal world. 'Ton souvenir' would seem to refer to a feminine second person and the value of love (cf. 'Un cœur tendre...') as a guarantee against the threat of 'le néant'.

The progression of the religious imagery gives the poem a dramatic and triumphant ending. 'Encensoir' is an incense-holder, swung on a chain to spread its fragrant smoke. 'Reposoir' is a 'station of the Cross', an altar on the route of a religious procession. 'Ostensoir' is the monstrance, the receptacle in which the sacraments are placed and offered before the altar. The three devotional words are signs (by what techniques is their affinity accentuated?) which appear to mark the stages of a religious approach. But as darkness falls, a communion is made, not with the transient invitations of the physical world, but with that sacramental part of the poet's inner self which is made to transcend time. As the blood of the world is symbolically spilled (notice the close interrelation of the last two lines and the meaningful pause), a resurrection takes place in the poet's own spirituality.

Spleen

Pluviôse, irrité contre la ville entière,
De son urne à grands flots verse un froid ténébreux
Aux pâles habitants du voisin cimetière
Et la mortalité sur les faubourgs brumeux.　　　　4

Mon chat sur le carreau cherchant une litière
Agite sans repos son corps maigre et galeux;
L'âme d'un vieux poëte erre dans la gouttière
Avec la triste voix d'un fantôme frileux.　　　　8

Le bourdon se lamente, et la bûche enfumée
Accompagne en fausset la pendule enrhumée,
Cependant qu'en un jeu plein de sales parfums,　　　11

Héritage fatal d'une vieille hydropique,
Le beau valet de cœur et la dame de pique
Causent sinistrement de leurs amours défunts.   14

Spleen

Lines 1–4. 'Pluviôse' was the name given in the Revolutionary calendar to the period from 21st January to 21st February. The unfamiliarity of the word, compared with 'février', lends itself to a mysterious personification, while the Latinate form adds a mythical quality (cf. '...de son urne'). The word has an in-built descriptive value not present in the conventional names of months, as well as an unhealthy, lugubrious sound, stemming partly from its associations with words with a similar ending (cf. 'chlorose', 'sclérose', 'morose'). Perhaps it is also appropriate that a Revolutionary month should be chosen in this poem depicting a period of radical disturbance and restlessness.

'Pluviôse' assumes the character of a perverse host, whose mere niggling annoyance can bring down such insidious disease over the whole expanse of a city. The word 'urne' has a double connotation in this context. It is both a serving vessel and a receptacle for the ashes of the dead. In the first sense, the form of 'verse...Aux pâles habitants' makes the occupants of the cemetery seem his guests; in the second sense, the populous quarters of the city are seen to be wreathed in a kind of grey death. 'Pluviôse', it appears, is dispensing a noxious sustenance to the dead, and death to the living.

How does the long continuous sentence suit the mood? Note the strength of the position of '...verse'. What is the value of the epithet 'voisin'? Notice how, although darkness, cold and mist are specifically mentioned, the idea of rain is only suggested.

Lines 5–8. This stanza moves closer by implication to the poet's own world. The first movements described are those of his cat, cats being notoriously sensitive to changes in atmosphere, while the poet himself remains vaguely in the background. The description of the first two lines is especially evocative. We are given no detailed picture of the room, but 'le carreau', a cold, hard floor, speaks of the bareness of the poet's quarters. That the cat seeks the comfort of any meagre 'litière' (normally the lowliest bed of straw) and fails to find it confirms the inhospitable poverty of the surroundings. The words 'Maigre et galeux' depict a bony, undernourished cat, the very antithesis of the sensuous, luxurious animal found in other poems by Baudelaire. The jutting bones on the hard tile are the epitome of discomfort, while the itchiness of his mange seems to be a contagion caught from the irritation of 'Pluviôse' himself (subtly suggested by the particularly strong sound-link between 'irrité' and '...litière / Agite').

From the image of the cat, one passes to another disturbing presence which, though reflecting a human plight, does not quite belong to the world of human beings. The two are linked by the fact that they are both restless spirits in wretched surroundings. One's first interpretation of 'L'âme d'un vieux poëte...' is that this is the dissatisfied soul of some poet, a former occupant of the garret, who has not gone to rest quietly in the 'voisin cimetière'. On the other hand, since mortality is creeping its way through the world of the living, this could be the writer seeing *himself* already as a lamenting ghost, a poor shadow of himself. Perhaps a mere sound-impression (e.g. the relentless drone of rain in the guttering) has been enough to provoke the idea of a suffering voice. But one can easily imagine in this context that the writer is responsive by some sixth sense, just as a cat is aware of something amiss, to the fact that an uneasy kindred spirit is abroad.

Examine the variety of sound-effects in this stanza: not just the alliteration or internal rhyme in themselves, but the point at which they occur to create a link or provide stress.

Lines 9–11. 'Le bourdon' can mean both the low resonances of organ-music and the tolling of a great bell. Although not so explicitly funereal as 'le glas', it throws one's attention back inevitably to the reference to '...voisin cimetière'. Particularly remarkable is the way in which Baudelaire has assorted the various instruments in this macabre and grotesque concert, using this first rhyming couplet in the poem to highlight the pairing of 'la bûche' and 'la pendule' in an eccentric duo, and exploiting the richly onomatopoeic quality of the language. As well as the idea of shrillness, the phrase '...en fausset' contains that of discord: consider the various images in the poem suggesting beings and objects out of harmony. Trace the way in which the suggestion of pervasive damp and things choking in a malignant atmosphere is further developed in these lines.

After the cohesive quality of the couplet, the unattached last line 'Cependant qu'en...' sketches an unwholesome setting for the final image before we know anything of the protagonists, and creates an element of suspense. For the moment it is by no means certain what kind of game is implied by '...un jeu plein de sales parfums'.

Lines 12–14. Line 12, in postponing the appearance of the two figures, sustains the dramatic anticipation. It reinforces the sense of fatality, and brings together, in the most emphatic form, the ideas of disease and water, the word 'hydropique' corroborating the other images of a creeping wetness affecting the insides of things. The full suggestiveness of '...sales parfums' now emerges: the mustiness of age, the dankness of the surroundings, the odour of ill health, and the unsavoury perfumes of an old woman trying to preserve a remnant of youth all come together as possibilities. The words 'Héritage fatal' stress that a deterministic force from the past hangs over the poet's life, so that this is a dreary, dank imprisonment both in time and space; and the mention of the old woman, revealing that two dead spirits, one male, one female ('vieux poëte...vieille hydropique'), lurk in the atmosphere of his lodgings, makes one first aware of a potential love-theme.

The pack of cards, with its associations of fortune-telling, necromancy and inescapable patterns of destiny, brings everything to a final focus. The sinister conversation pursued by the Jack of Hearts and Queen of Spades makes them suspect figures. What traditional value do these cards have which adds to the negative mood of this concluding section? Their talk of former loves suggests that they might be the symbolic reflection of a love-relationship between the 'vieux poëte' and the 'vieille hydropique', an artistic portrayal outlasting what has now passed from the land of the living. Like a death-knell at the end (note the abruptness of the final masculine rhyme), the words 'amours défunts' give unanswerable weight to the idea of lost love, and possibly of lost grandeur. One might see 'le valet' and 'la dame' as decaying aristocrats, lying redundant with no game to play – a suggestion which would add new relevance to the choice of a Revolutionary month in line 1, and to the sound-link between the lines 'Pluviôse, irrité...' and 'Causent sinistrement...' which put a firm phonetic clasp around the poem. The theme of lost status, perhaps even of a fall from grace, was already apparent in the detail of the fate of the poet, a superior spirit doomed to wander in the gutterings. The final word 'défunts', effectively joined with 'parfums', leaves the ultimate smell of mortality and a totally fatalistic emphasis on death.

Study the structure of the poem (the transition from townscape to interior scene, from beings to objects, from a grey and depressive general atmosphere to a more precise and challenging final visual image).

Could one look on the state of *spleen*, for Baudelaire, as the negative or reverse experience of those moments, described in *Correspondances*, when 'Les parfums, les couleurs et les sons se répondent'? Does it seem adequate, on the evidence here, to describe it as 'tedium' or 'mortal weariness'? In what way does the other poem in the selection entitled *Spleen* enlarge one's picture? Contrast the range of feelings, mood, imagery and style in these two poems with those, for example, in *La Chevelure*.

Stéphane Mallarmé

(1842–1898)

Autre éventail

O rêveuse, pour que je plonge
Au pur délice sans chemin,
Sache, par un subtil mensonge,
Garder mon aile dans ta main.   4

Une fraîcheur de crépuscule
Te vient à chaque battement
Dont le coup prisonnier recule
L'horizon délicatement.   8

Vertige! voici que frissonne
L'espace comme un grand baiser
Qui, fou de naître pour personne,
Ne peut jaillir ni s'apaiser.   12

Sens-tu le paradis farouche
Ainsi qu'un rire enseveli
Se couler du coin de ta bouche
Au fond de l'unanime pli!   16

Le sceptre des rivages roses
Stagnants sur les soirs d'or, ce l'est,
Ce blanc vol fermé que tu poses
Contre le feu d'un bracelet.   20

Autre éventail

Stanza 1. In approaching this poem, one should remember that Mallarmé was dedicated, not to things in themselves, but to the nebulous pursuit of 'l'âme des choses'. Nor was he concerned with depicting his own emotions, but with creating a superior anonymous poetry, situated in a spiritual realm, purified from the trivia of personal feelings. It is an art of the ethereal, volatilizing objects of physical experience into a state of 'presque disparition vibratoire', so that all that remains is their aura, their spirit, their suggestive charge or symbolic life.

Stated over-simply, the inspiration of this poem is the beauty of a woman and her fan (in fact, Mlle Mallarmé). But, except in the title, the words 'woman' and 'fan' are never used: there is simply a vague feminine quality ('O rêveuse') and a metaphor, a wing held in the hand; and Mallarmé's aim is to bring to life on the page something almost impalpable: a silent language of movement and rhythm, intricately related to the obscure principle of beauty which governs its patterns in the air. One of the difficulties of the poem is knowing who is the speaker: it might be the poet, aspiring to be plunged into the same kind of ecstatic flight as that experienced by the fan, or it might be the fan itself, calling to be opened and set in motion by its mistress. But it is perhaps most rewarding to leave the question unresolved, so closely identified in the imagination is the one with the other, and in this way to preserve the margin of ambiguity and doubt subtly exploited by Mallarmé. Explore the possibilities of the fan as the symbol of poetry: what might the 'rêveuse', as the prime mover, represent (note that she is epitomized by this adjectival noun alone); what seems to be the ultimate aim (note that the coveted state of 'pur délice sans chemin' virtually defies intellectual apprehension); why should the continued holding of the 'wing' be a 'subtil mensonge', something of a carefully calculated illusion, and how is this relevant to art and the poet's position; does it say anything about the idea of poetry as the free flight of inspiration? Study the way in which Mallarmé has made this first stanza imitative of the airy movements of a fan: the dramatic positioning of 'plonge', the evocative play of alliterations, and above all the interweaving development of the syntax.

Stanza 2. After the opening invocation, the second stanza settles into a more gentle and measured invitation: 'battement' represents a more modest motion in the air than that suggested by 'plonge', 'une fraîcheur' is as yet only a faint harbinger of the coveted 'pur délice', and the rhythm of the stanza follows its course without interruption or violent variation. This stanza gives the semblance of a setting, but a setting too indefinite to fall firmly into reality: it is perhaps twilight, that 'in-between' time, much loved by Verlaine, which is neither light nor dark; and there is a horizon, that 'in-between' place which is the very fringe of absence and the theatre of sunset. The theme of the interdependence between 'rêveuse' and 'aile' now expands to embrace the idea of an exchange between the 'rêveuse' and 'l'horizon', through the intermediary of the fan: its fluttering motions set up an invisible ripple in space which extends to the horizon, causing it to furl back almost imperceptibly, while she in turn receives an incoming breath from the distant air. In what way might this image further the view of the fan as a symbol of the function of poetry? (Note that the emphasis is still on its imprisoned status as an ethereal agent, and on the strange balance of limitless flight and restraint.) What contribution is made to the poetic quality of this stanza by the *enjambement* into the final line, by the tiny trapped mute 'e' in '. . . recule/L'horizon', and by the almost unaccentuated '. . . délicatement' at the end?

Stanza 3. After the delicacy, calm and poise, the third stanza introduces a suddenly changed mood, anticipating a vibrant 'pur délice'. How does Mallarmé provoke a sense of expectation and energy? It is here that the communication between 'rêveuse' and 'horizon' develops into something more passionate, and that what has already been seen as the evocation of the hidden vitality of a fan and a suggestive symbol of poetry shows itself, equally, to be a love-poem. These lines are a gracious tribute to the beauty or spiritual charm of the lady of the fan. The image 'L'espace comme un grand baiser' suggests that, through her wordless and anonymous language, she has entranced and won the love of a silent suitor, Space; that the passes of her fan, reaching deep into the senses of the air and gently repulsing it, have excited its ardour, so that it now gathers itself in an impassioned offering. But it cannot reach her. What has been summoned by the fan can be as easily dismissed by it, and space is held there, as if frustrated, 'fou de naître pour personne', unable to make the final passage beyond the fan itself. The breath of *l'azur* is caught in a kind of suspended animation ('Ne peut jaillir ni s'apaiser', a phrase which harks back to 'délice *sans chemin*'), unwilling to return whence it came, unable to fuse with its human goal and fulfil itself absolutely. It has its relationship with the instrument but not, apart from the slight wafting breath, with the instrumentalist. What does this add to the pattern of symbolism already shaped? Notice how Mallarmé in this stanza has ensured a constantly rising intonation, a 'stretching upwards' of the syntax (cf. the beginning of *Petit air*), leading to the poise of the two final verbs, stilled between advance and retreat, upsurge and relapse.

Stanza 4. Having described the loving awakening of space, the voice (fan–poet?) proceeds to ask its feminine captor if she does not feel the promise of a response (the word 'farouche' here contains the hint of *effarouché*, a timid and startled excitement), a kiss of her own, slipping from her own lips to meet the unsubstantial one which is halted there. But there is to be no direct encounter: the human surge of love is seen to slip disengagingly from the corner of her lips like a barely uttered or repressed laugh and disappears to be entombed in the artistic hollow of the fan, which acts as intermediary and meeting point. What is the value of the indirect, evasive and precious language in this stanza? Is one justified in looking upon the phrases 'le paradis farouche' and 'l'unanime pli' as ornamental synonyms for a kiss and the fan (why 'unanime'? because it is in perfect accord with her will or with her smile? because it is a fold or series of folds which becomes as one mind and transforms itself into a single arc or, in closing, into a single thin line?)? Study the way in which, in contrast to the long upward sweep of the previous stanza, this one follows a fluid downward course: note that the terminal 'e' mutes can be elided into the following vowels ('. . . farouche Ainsi' and '. . . bouche Au fond'), while the words 'enseveli' and 'Au fond' are the counterweight to 'naître' and 'jaillir'. In this way the fine balance in the poem between suggestions of invitation and repulsion, promise and retreat, is maintained. Note, too, how the stanza wavers between interrogation and exclamation, reflecting the voice's hesitant interpretation of the woman's feelings.

Stanza 5. In the final stanza, the movements of the fan come to rest. How does Mallarmé now emphasize immobility? The wing, which has called for liberty of ecstatic flight, elicited the kiss of space and absorbed the tentative, half-smiled response of the 'rêveuse', becomes 'blanc vol fermé'. Leaving the realm of the ideal (or the sublime illusion), it settles again as an ornament, lying flatly alongside a bracelet on a woman's wrist. Yet even closed and at rest, it is no mere fan: it is 'blanc vol fermé' (a fine definition of poetry as seen by Mallarmé, pure flight in potential, all the unsubstantial joy which the white page holds in prospect) and 'sceptre' (the outward and visible sign of a supreme power). In what way are these last lines a tribute, not simply to the art of the fan, but more especially to the supremacy of the artist? How is the aesthetic triumph of artifice over the natural evoked?

How appropriately can one see the five stanzas of the poem as the five brief acts of a play, each with its own mood, pace and function? Can one also see in them (suggested in the rhythm, alliterations, upward and downward sweeps, variations of movement) five different motions or expressions of a fan? Compare the imagery of this piece with the 'plumage instrumental' of *Sainte*, with the imprisonment of the wing in *Le vierge, le vivace*. . ., and with the flight beyond all reach and all known horizons of *Petit air*. Compare the fan as a symbol of poetry with the cigar in *Toute l'âme résumée*...: which gives the richer pattern of suggestions?

Au seul souci de voyager...

Au seul souci de voyager
Outre une Inde splendide et trouble
– Ce salut soit le messager
Du temps, cap que ta poupe double   4

Comme sur quelque vergue bas
Plongeante avec la caravelle
Écumait toujours en ébats
Un oiseau d'annonce nouvelle   8

Qui criait monotonement
Sans que la barre ne varie
Un inutile gisement
Nuit, désespoir et pierrerie   12

Par son chant reflété jusqu'au
Sourire du pâle Vasco.   14

Au seul souci de voyager...

Lines 1–4. Some critics have tried to make Mallarmé's difficult poems more accessible by reconstructing the syntax into its more immediately recognizable grammatical form: that is, for the sake of expediency, turning one of the chief sources of poetry into its prose 'equivalent', and sacrificing multiple possibilities for a firmer grasp of meaning. Helpful as this may be, one senses that it goes against the grain of Mallarmé's intentions and his whole concept of poetic language, which takes words out of their directly communicative function to give them a kind of creative or suggestive independence. It also goes against the grain of that 'seul souci de voyager' which is the presiding wish or toast of this poem: the desire to embark on an adventure in language, not knowing one's destination.

The first two lines of the sonnet, a strangely detached adverbial phrase, promote a sense of direction before any idea of its wider links or purpose begins to emerge. In this partial vacuum, each word seems to invite closer scrutiny and takes on a stronger suggestive edge: 'voyager', the call to adventure and the far-off quest; 'souci', a serious preoccupation and not exotic levity; 'seul', a single-minded pursuit which admits no lesser distractions. Mallarmé is clearly referring to the voyage of poetry, the most consuming spiritual voyage, which takes one beyond known boundaries and geographical climates, however magnificent or evocative. The words 'Ce salut soit...' ('May this salute be...'), preceded by the emphatic dash, then reveal that these two lines are indeed complete in themselves, acting as a kind of salute or opening toast to the spirit of adventure, and that all that follows is a complex extended image (pushing boldly from metaphor to metaphor to highly detailed simile) which expands and illuminates the initial invocation or call to the omens. The poet wishes his salute to be time's messenger, travelling through the centuries (whether carrying Mallarmé's present message to the future reader or summoning inspiration from the distant past is not sure), a conquest in time immediately translated into graphic spatial terms as a cape or headland rounded by the stately poop or afterdeck of a sailing ship. The two superimposed images, one temporal and one spatial, stress the idea of transition: a penetration of the barriers of time, and the rounding of an apparently immovable obstacle which yields to open up unlimited vistas and give new freedom of access. Such is the magical influence the poet hopes his words will have. Travel, the beyond, ventures in time and space: these form the thematic texture of the first stanza. What value has Mallarmé drawn from the *enjambements* of '...voyager/Outre' and 'messager/Du temps' and, subsequently, from the run-on effect between the first and second quatrains? Does the two-toned description 'splendide et trouble' have any repercussions deeper in the poem? Is there evidence that the poet has been attentive here to his sound-patterning, as well as to his architectural arrangement?

Lines 5–8. The second quatrain introduces the elaborate simile, which proceeds to journey richly and tortuously in one continuous movement from the metaphor of the rounding of the cape to the ultimate word of the poem. The image of the bird recalls lines from *Brise marine*: 'Je sens que des oiseaux sont ivres / D'être parmi l'écume inconnue et les cieux'. The same intoxication is implicit in the agile flitting movements of 'en ébats', and there is the same identification with sea-foam, made all the more forceful here by the use of 'Ecumait' as a verb, attributed to the bird itself. (By giving this verb no object, Mallarmé has left its meaning open: there is a suggestion of 'roamed the seas', as in 'écumer les mers', to live a pirate's life; or it could mean 'skimmed the waves'; alternatively, in its intransitive sense, it could be translated as 'burst into foam', 'frothed', 'glinted with foam', all of which give dynamic impressions of the bird and the sea interlaced as one; finally there is a possibility that this may be seen as a foaming with frenzy or wildness, which would give a link with the bird in the poem *Petit air* and perhaps, remotely, with the idea of an oracle.) In the same context, the wing of *Autre éventail* comes to mind, plunging 'Au pur délice sans chemin' and acting as an intermediary between the dreamer and the distant horizon. Here the bird, dipping as the boat keels and the yard-arm plunges low to the water, is itself a messenger ('Un oiseau d'annonce nouvelle'), so revitalizing the original metaphor of words in flight as 'le messager du temps'. Show how Mallarmé in this stanza has tried to make his sentence-structure imitative of the rhythm and movement of the boat. Why is the switch into the Imperfect tense so appropriate?

Lines 9–12. Just as the passage from the first to the second quatrain might resemble the rounding of a headland, leaving behind the constricted metaphors and expanding into new vistas of scenic and motive description, so the end of the second quatrain is another turning-point. It marks a deepening of the theme of the voyage, showing not only its splendour but its frustration. The promise implicit in the terminal words '...d'annonce nouvelle' is counterbalanced, though not annulled, by the prospect of 'Un inutile gisement'; and the bird, so far representing nothing but speed and excited mobility, assumes the rôle of prophet of disappointment. The word 'gisement' has two chief meanings: a navigational bearing taken on magnetic North; or a mineral-rich seam in the earth. Mallarmé has left the ambiguity. In the nautical context of ancient sailing ships taking their night bearings on the pole star, the first meaning exerts the stronger pull: it is supported by the image of the helmsman holding his course, and in this pattern 'Nuit, désespoir et pierrerie' evokes the night sky, studded with stars like precious stones, but inhuman and offering no authentic guidance to an ultimate goal (cf. the 'guirlandes célèbres' in the sonnet *Quand l'ombre menaça...*). On the other hand the close juxtaposition of 'gisement' and 'pierrerie' is tempting, causing one's own direction to waver a little: in this case the words 'Nuit, désespoir et pierrerie' might suggest that, in spite of glittering finds, there is no Eldorado, no discovery of the seam to quench all desires, and no ultimate alleviation of man's despairing quest. But whatever one's precise interpretation, there is a striking contrast of splendour and despair; and the point is that, despite the persistent forewarning voice, the helm holds its direction and does not deviate one degree. It is these words, 'Sans que la barre ne varie', which prepare for the introduction of the prestigious figure dramatized in the final couplet. Notice the way in which Mallarmé has brought a new dominant sound into this stanza to convey the insistent cry of the bird. Why does the word 'Nuit' strike home so emphatically? Could one momentarily associate it with the verb 'nuire'? What is the effect of the use of the present tense for '...ne varie'?

Lines 13–14. This isolated couplet transfers the focus from boat, sea and bird to a human figure; from the surrounding agitation, energy or abstraction to the quiet composure and particularity of one man, albeit a symbolic one. Mallarmé has already played on ambiguity in the poem to increase its suggestive field and make it an act of exploration for the reader: ambiguity of vocabulary ('Ecumait', 'gisement', 'pierrerie', 'Nuit') and of structure (is 'cap' in apposition to 'salut', 'messager' or 'temps', and to what does the loosely joined 'Comme' refer?). Once again, as the transition is made, more than one possible relationship is opened up: is it the 'inutile gisement' reflected in the expression on Vasco's face, or the bird itself and all that it represents? Whatever the answer, Vasco's smile is steady and somehow luminous (as the verb 'reflété' suggests); and though his *pâleur* bears witness to the arduousness of the seemingly impossible venture and confirms both the solitude and the '*souci* de voyager', his quiet radiance of purpose is not dimmed by the prospect of 'Nuit' and 'désespoir'. Da Gama it was who discovered the route to India via the Cape of Good Hope: this realization throws one's attention back to the words 'Inde', 'cap' and 'désespoir'. What is the significance of the fact that, in invoking the example of this explorer whose name stands out like a beacon as the last word, the poet is raising his salute to the urge to travel '*Outre* une Inde splendide et trouble'? One notices that the two key figures in the lavish simile, the bird and Vasco, are woven closely to the earlier metaphors of 'messager' and 'cap' respectively. One also becomes aware that, on the wings of that first wish, one has been carried on a journey through time, back to the fifteenth century, finally to join with that spirit which will now carry humanity forward into the future.

One should compare this poem in detail with *Brise marine*: not only do they share the theme of the journey and the possible shipwreck, but they follow roughly the same course (from the wishful call to depart, to the vision of birds and foam, to the suggestion of a doomed journey, to the final exaltation of the magical spell of the mariner). There have obviously been great changes in technique, however, by the time of this later poem: a movement from the lyrical to the impersonal, from separate grammatical units to one mysteriously articulated continuous sentence, from the punctuated to the unpunctuated; the choice of the sonnet form which, as Valéry says, 'condamne le poète à la perfection', and a much tighter cohesion of imagery. What do you find distinctive about Mallarmé's imagination and artistry, compared with those of Baudelaire and Rimbaud in their poems on the theme of the journey?

Charles Cros

(1842–1888)

Conquérant

J'ai balayé tout le pays
En une fière cavalcade;
Partout les gens se sont soumis,
Ils viennent me chanter l'aubade.   4

Ce cérémonial est fade;
Aux murs mes ordres sont écrits.
Amenez-moi (mais pas de cris)
Des filles pour la rigolade.   8

L'une sanglote, l'autre a peur,
La troisième a le sein trompeur
Et l'autre s'habille en insecte.   11

Mais la plus belle ne dit rien;
Elle a le rire aérien
Et ne craint pas qu'on la respecte.   14

Conquérant

Lines 1–4. Cros makes a special place in his work for refined and filmy fantasies, spiced with extravagance, sensuality and a touch of sadism, which could have sprung from the atmosphere of the *Arabian Nights*. *Conquérant* is such a piece of delicate myth-making.

As if celebrating some Genghis Khan, it evokes from the outset an offhand power and arrogance which knows no obstacles and brooks no argument. The verb 'j'ai balayé' implies a contemptuously easy action. It might mean that the poet, in his adopted rôle, has swept over the vast countryside in his conquering travels or that he has swept *aside* the whole country. One is struck by the disproportion between the facility of his victory and the immensity of 'tout le pays'. Similarly, though only a single 'je', he appears to form a cavalcade in his own right: the conqueror may well have been flanked by horsemen, but the syntax of 'J'ai balayé...*en* une fière cavalcade' suggests that, in this imaginative vision, he himself constituted monarch and retinue. (What effect does the initial use of the *passé composé* have, especially accompanied as it is by a rapid and taut succession of similar sounds?)

'Partout', echoing 'tout le pays', confirms the absolute nature of his sway, the words '...*se* sont soumis' indicating a populace, not so much held in submission by external force as bowing down of their own accord in recognition of the unmistakable signs of authority. They flatter his whims and do all for his pleasure. The verb 'Ils viennent...', in the habitual present, seems flat and trivial after the positive accomplishment of 'J'ai balayé...'; and the rhythm of this line, describing the people's response, is less clear-cut than that of the first two lines, with their energetically stressed 4 + 4 pattern.

Lines 5–8. But tyrants soon tire of fawning subjects, empty gestures and musical niceties, and their appetite for power and action finds little satisfaction in ceremony. '*Ce* cérémonial' might indeed refer both to 'l'aubade', the people's morning song of praise, and to the 'fière cavalcade' which he himself led. The first two lines subtly illustrate the gulf between the insipid, compliant world of his underlings and his own intransigence (on the one hand, the almost sickly alliteration and barely accented six syllables of 'Ce cérémonial...'; on the other, the brusque dismissal implicit in the word 'fade' and the monosyllabic rigidity of 'Aux murs mes ordres...'). That his commands are written on walls impresses not only that they are unyielding (note the value of the inversion here), but that private wish is immediately public decree. The imperatives, the possessive adjective ('...mes ordres'), the personal pronoun ('Amenez-moi...'), combine to show a man bent on self-satisfaction; while the colloquial 'rigolade' and the somewhat disparaging 'filles' sum up the frankness of his appetites, unembroidered and unselfconscious. What is the effect of the parenthesis in line 7: in what tone are these words uttered and how would you interpret them? Study the feminine rhymes of the octet, especially the changing tone as one progresses from 'cavalcade' and 'aubade' to 'fade' and 'rigolade' (what literary atmosphere, for instance, normally accompanies a word like 'aubade'?).

It is difficult to estimate the effect of a given verse-form and rhyme-scheme. But it is fair to say that the octosyllabic line is often used to create a brisk narrative style in poems concerned with telling a story or relating a kind of fable (e.g. consider Rimbaud's *Les Effarés*, Apollinaire's *La Tzigane* or Supervielle's *Haute mer*). Here it certainly gives a dramatic crispness and tension to the overlord's actions: his dismissive disgust, his incontrovertible commands. In the case of rhyme-scheme, one wonders why Cros has chosen to switch from *rimes croisées* to *rimes embrassées* in the second stanza: one could suggest that, by this means, the rhyme 'fade' appears unexpectedly quickly after 'aubade' and accelerates the sense of anticlimax; that the contrast between 'aubade' and 'rigolade' is made stronger by their parallel position at the end of a stanza; while the central couplet acquires greater cohesion, to coincide with the theme of rigid authority.

Lines 9–11. The clearly divided use of the sestet stands out: in what way do its subject-matter and mood differ from those of the octet?

Line 9 introduces a fairly stereotyped vision of slaves brought for a ruler's pleasure: one sobs, one is fear-stricken, while he himself remains callous and unmoved, as the perfunctory inventorial form ('L'une...l'autre...la troisième ...') indicates. But the next two lines have a greater sophistication, less easy to interpret: '...a le sein trompeur' suggests some sexual guile or deceptiveness, and '...s'habille en insecte' refers no doubt to the art of decoration or travesty which appetizes perverse taste and, whether the insect is flimsy butterfly or a more repulsive creature, appeals to the bestial or sadistic pleasure of crushing or dominating. These odd details, showing how far courtesans will go in their perversions to satisfy the sexual or artistic eccentricities of a potentate, are accompanied by slight rhythmical variations (3 + 3 + 2 and 2 + 3 + 3) which contrast with the bolder pattern of the lines describing the conqueror's victorious advance.

Lines 12–14. The last tercet, the most enigmatic stanza of the poem, is the clear climax. It is devoted to one figure, the most beautiful and least submissive. (Notice the neat change of focus from '...tout le pays', 'Partout les gens...' to 'L'une...l'autre...La troisième', and finally to '...la plus belle'.) The conjunction 'Mais...' arouses one's anticipation of a contrast: she is not the same cheap performer in a court spectacle. Her mutism is part of her attraction: although fulfilling his prescription ('mais pas de cris'), her inexpressiveness is not a sign of submission but a compelling feature, the reflection of an indifference, a spirit of challenge or serene superiority. What is the value of the adjective 'aérien' in setting her apart from the 'fadeur' of conventional ceremony, from the emotional reactions or sensual offerings of the other women, and from the appetites of the conqueror himself? What is the effect of the enhanced musicality of lines 12 and 13? Do the sounds here work more evocatively on one's sensitivity than any precise meaning?

Cros saves his most ambiguous line till last. After the ethereal line 13, it has a boldness of tone and implies an unwavering personality. Does it mean that she has no fears in the matter of respect or disrespect; that she is so used to adoration that she is not afraid of being held in awe; or that she knows, so sure is she of her irresistibility, that no man, even a 'conquérant', has the strength to stand at a respectful distance and that all must succumb to her charm? Whatever one's conclusion, she is confident of her own power in a way which the 'conquérant' in his 'fière cavalcade', and dogged by the need for new satisfactions, will never be. She is the Circe, fascinating and destructive, who haunts so much of Cros's work; while he is only the self-compensating poet, the myth-maker.

When one studies this poem alongside others by Cros, does it take on a more subtle imaginative quality and a deeper element of personal revelation than might at first be apparent from its narrative form? How does it compare with Baudelaire's works of exotic imagination?

Hiéroglyphe

J'ai trois fenêtres à ma chambre:
    L'amour, la mer, la mort,
Sang vif, vert calme, violet.

O femme, doux et lourd trésor!   4

Froids vitraux, cloches, odeurs d'ambre.
    La mer, la mort, l'amour,
Ne sentir que ce qui me plaît ...

Femme, plus claire que le jour!   8

Par ce soir doré de septembre,
    La mort, l'amour, la mer,
Me noyer dans l'oubli complet.

Femme! femme! cercueil de chair!   12

Hiéroglyphe

Lines 1–3. The mysterious flavour of the title leads one to expect a poetic puzzle, a language to be deciphered. But the first line is deceptively elementary and unmysterious in form.

It becomes clear, however, that the words 'fenêtres' and 'chambre' do not refer to mere physical surroundings but to a symbolic setting. The windows could represent various escapes from the enclosure of the poet's life, three crucial objects of contemplation in man's existence, or different intuitions of infinity. The cryptic form of the second line is dramatic: this six-syllable line gives a new density at this point, with each element in the trio commanding two syllables and receiving equal emphasis. The exceptional resemblance of sound suggests an occult similarity between love, the sea and death, and facilitates, in the development of the poem, the interchange of the components in this secretive formula. Although the shorter form of this line gives it a greater concentration, it may well be read in a more lingering way (thanks largely to the lengthened vowels of amuːr, mɛːr and mɔːr) which would add to its mystery.

The imaginative link between windows and the three suggestive concepts is then given an even deeper provocation in the third line, in which the essence of these 'fenêtres' is crystallized in a set of colour-impressions.

There is a neat structural parallelism which obviously connects 'l'amour' with the idea of 'Sang vif', 'la mer' with 'vert calme', and 'la mort' with 'violet'. How do you think Cros has arrived at these correspondences? The reciprocal quality of the two lines is enriched by the echoing pattern of the alliterations: 'L'amour, la mer, la mort' set against '...vif, vert...violet'. It is interesting that red and violet are at the two edges of the spectrum, while green is found at the centre. This leads one to juxtapose in one's imagination a visual spectrum and a more subtle poetic one, in which love and death are the opposite extremes.

Although there seems to be this answering relationship between each element and its partner, one should beware of turning a suggestive poetic formula into an easy equation. For instance, the somewhat brutal positioning of 'Sang vif' immediately after 'mort' suggests that they, too, have a connection. Violet has been identified by Baudelaire with 'l'amour contenu, mystérieux, voilé', and Cros's mind might respond equally to an affinity of this kind. Similarly, Baudelaire speaks of 'le vert paradis des amours enfantines'. So there is no reason why the idea of love here, though apparently paired with 'Sang vif', should not also stir associations of green and violet. This is a reminder that, in a poem such as this, one cannot over-categorize the subtleties of the artist's imagination.

Line 4. This forceful line introduces a host of effects. It is isolated, both typographically and logically: one has passed from an interplay of three abstract concepts (one cannot help thinking of the sea, in this setting, as an abstraction) to a single human subject, but it is not clear what has prompted this transition. It is this line which first makes one aware of two different moods within the poem: on the one hand, the workings of the cryptic combinations, and on the other, the brief lyrical interventions of the poet himself (evident in the emphatic invocation and exclamatory form).

The woman (in view of the physical suggestions of 'ma chambre', 'odeurs d'ambre' and the particularity of '*ce* soir doré de septembre') may be the poet's mistress, contemplated in the intimacy of his own room. But she is more than this. Summed up, in each of the three lines devoted to her, in the figurative language of a single image, and bound by analogy to the three concepts 'amour', 'mer', 'mort', she takes on a universal significance. The word 'femme' naturally evokes the idea of love, an evocation supported in the rest of the line by the suggestion of sweetness, the possible note of endearment in 'trésor', and the internal rhyme which loops one's attention back from 'lourd' to 'amour'. But, at the same time, there is a bond between the two words 'calme' and 'doux', and so indirectly between woman and the sea: even 'trésor', in this context, may turn one's mind to the treasures of the deep. Finally, this line is made to rhyme with 'la mort': a most meaningful link, since the first three lines as a unit have no rhyme and seem to be anticipating one. It is noticeable that the sound of 'femme' echoes equally those of 'L'*am*our, la *m*er, la *m*ort': one cannot tell to which she owes the greatest attachment.

Do you think that one can define the emotional quality implicit in the exclamation 'O'? Is there an element of ambiguity and perhaps a negative undertone in the use of the adjective 'lourd'?

Lines 5–7. We come back to the mysterious ternary structure. But this is not a static, predictable device, since its components are mobile and in a constant interchange. There is now, for instance, a change of order, so that the poetic images (which in the previous stanza followed in apposition to 'L'amour, la mer, la mort') here *precede*, bringing one's imagination into play before one knows anything of the associations to be made. Indeed the first line is sealed by a full-stop, which obliges one, initially, to consider it as a provocative entity in its own right. 'Froids vitraux' is a parallel, both in its position and its sounds, to 'J'ai trois fenêtres...'. The image of stained glass windows gives new depth to this stanza in that it brings together what were introduced as separate ideas in the first three lines: 'fenêtres' and variety of colour. The words 'vitraux' and 'cloches' have a solemn quality and remind one of a church setting. Whether this would be for a wedding or funeral ceremony, 'l'amour' or 'la mort', one cannot say, but 'Froids' as the first note conditions one to the idea of death. On the other hand, the phrase '...odeurs d'ambre' (cf. Baudelaire's *L'Invitation au voyage*) evokes feminine perfumes and therefore, indirectly, love. This opening line of the stanza preludes a deeper sensual involvement, passing from what is predominantly a colour-impression in line 3 to a richer blending of touch, sight, sound and scent. How well do 'Froids vitraux' and 'odeurs d'ambre' counterbalance each other? What different associations lie in the word 'ambre'? Notice how Cros has now slipped into plural images, implying the increased complexity of his vision.

But having first allowed line 5 to work creatively on the imagination, one has to reconsider it in conjunction with line 6. The relation indicated by the positional pairing of 'Froids vitraux' and 'mer' may be explained by the glassy surface of the sea, its coldness and elaborate colour-variations; that between 'cloches' and 'mort' by the funereal tolling of bells; that between 'odeurs d'ambre' and 'amour' by the sensual attraction of body-perfumes. But in making these links one can hardly help enquiring into other, more distant associations between 'Sang vif' and 'odeurs d'ambre' (brightness of colour, warmth, physical intimacy); between 'vert calme' and 'Froids vitraux' (an almost transparent coolness, an impassiveness); and between 'violet' and 'cloches' (an element of ceremony or solemnity). Such poetic soundings can only be speculative, but they show again how intricate the network of associations is in this poem, and the way in which one's mind wavers between different possibilities and correspondences.

The ideas of love, sea and death appear in a new order, which throws 'l'amour' into prominence at the end of the line. Followed as it is by the idea of pleasurable sensation to the exclusion of all else, this word suggests that the dominant tone of the stanza is that of love. But, once more, Cros has carefully cultivated an element of ambiguity, for not only 'l'amour' but also 'La mer, la mort' form part of the preceding apposition to '. . . ce qui me plaît', so that these, too (even death), are seen as sources of pleasure.

What quality of emotion does the infinitive form help to convey here: would you say that the mood is wishful, or perhaps more determined? Does the use of the dots help one to identify this mood more clearly?

Line 8. The transition from the tercet to the isolated line, which in the previous case was abrupt and challenging, is here effected far more fluently. The punctuation avoids any firm division, so that 'Femme' seems to follow on as a natural consequence of '. . . ce qui me plaît', and thus maintains a close link between her and the three 'absolutes'. This is the least ambiguous of the lines describing the feminine figure: woman is seen as a source of clarity, not filtered through stained glass window or prism, brighter than any individual colour, brighter even than daylight. The rhyme-link between 'l'amour' and 'jour' makes the closest identification between the ideas of love and clarity, and helps one to see these four lines as the most positive in the poem.

Lines 9–11. One notices the way in which the six-syllable line tends, as the poem progresses, to lose the precision of its relationship. In the first tercet it is the strict logical echo to 'trois fenêtres' and is then symmetrically bound to 'Sang vif, vert calme, violet'. In the second tercet, it is severed from the three descriptive images and its link with them is more tenuous. Here, in the third tercet, it is grammatically unrelated to the two lines which flank it and is more a refrain, held there by association with one or two words. This increasing structural vagueness accompanies the suggestion of the dying hour of a dying season and the idea of dissolution and abandon implicit in 'Me noyer'.

The three crucial words re-appear in a new combination for a third and final time. 'La mort' is a natural consequence to 'septembre': study how Cros has, in each tercet, made an equally telling transition from the last word of the first line to the first word of the second. Similarly, 'la mer' is immediately blended with 'Me noyer': study again how, in each tercet, the last word of the middle line is in some way reinforced by the first words of the final line. Is the total oblivion referred to that of death, that of drowning, or that of love?

Line 12. A return to the feminine figure sets the seal on the poem. Notice how the number three has a central and mysterious significance in the poet's occult patterns: there are three three-line stanzas, broken by three isolated lines; there are three parts to the repeated formula, echoed by groupings of three images. In what way does Cros gradually intensify the lines devoted to woman?

This last line brings together in the most startling way love and death (nor is the idea of 'la mer' absent, since it is now the turn of this word to be picked up in the final rhyme). The brevity of the metaphor, with its juxtaposition of the animate and the inanimate, the warmly physical and the coldly impersonal, is brutal. These three words are sufficient to lock together all the associated evocations of love and death scattered elsewhere in the poem. 'Sang vif' was an ambiguous image: it might have represented live-blooded passion or violent death (intriguingly, red and violet, although at opposite edges of the spectrum, are the most closely related of its colours). There were antitheses between a warmth of sensual impression and a church-like cold, between golden light and a sombre autumnal mood, between the appetite for physical pleasure and a death-wish. What in the previous tercet was only the threshold of death (evening, autumn) or a wishful premonition of it, and what throughout the poem has been only veiled or abstract reference to 'la mort', becomes harshly concrete in the image of the coffin. Similarly, a nebulous suggestion of sensuality is condensed into the final note of carnality. So, flesh and death are seen as synonymous, and woman as a tomb, more fatal than that of the sea, in which man seeks to bury himself. In this way the poem passes from the promise of escape ('J'ai trois fenêtres') to the fatality of imprisonment ('... cercueil').

We come back to the title *Hiéroglyphe*. The words of the poem have been terse, a puzzling code opening up unsuspected levels of poetic interpretation. But in its form, too, it is a hieroglyphic, one key to which might lie in the ability to read the most cryptic line in different directions. One can follow the succession of the three elements 'amour', 'mer' and 'mort' in three horizontal lines, three vertical lines, or in a diagonal pattern. If one does so, one finds that, whichever direction one chooses, all three will be present, in some combination or other, so that no single one dominates. However, there is one exception: if one traces the diagonal line from right to left through the poem, the cipher is broken and it reads 'la mort...la mort...la mort'. This is the fateful, unambiguous line which scores through the poem and finally wins this game of poetic noughts and crosses, played with three of the essential counters of human life.

Paul Verlaine

(1844–1896)

Chanson d'automne

Les sanglots longs
Des violons
   De l'automne
Blessent mon cœur
D'une langueur
   Monotone.

6

Tout suffocant
Et blême, quand
   Sonne l'heure,
Je me souviens
Des jours anciens
   Et je pleure;

12

Et je m'en vais
Au vent mauvais
   Qui m'emporte
Deçà, delà,
Pareil à la
   Feuille morte.

18

Chanson d'automne

Stanza 1. The choice of title, which already brings into play the first rhymes of the poem, gives a foretaste of Verlaine's affection for the musical qualities of verse and the suggestiveness of the autumnal mood. These features are then richly illustrated in the first three lines. How has Verlaine ensured that a musical effect comes over so strongly, before one even has a clear apprehension of the meaning? One notices the subtle blending of the three elements ('sanglots... violons...automne') in the initial image: the way in which the human emotions seem to belong simultaneously to a human person, violins and autumn; the use of the long fluent *enjambement*; the close similarity of sounds which envelops the details in a musical monotone. The image of the violins is nebulous, aiding the impression of intermingling. It could be that the plaintive tone of the autumn wind (cf. 'Au vent mauvais...Feuille morte' later in the poem) or the doleful dripping of the rain (cf. 'sanglots' and 'Et je pleure', as well as Verlaine's poem

'Il pleure dans mon cœur/Comme il pleut sur la ville') have provoked, by association, the idea of the suave notes or the plucked strings of a violin (several
times in his work Verlaine links the two ideas of the wind and the rain in the
phrase 'le vent pleure'). Or perhaps it is simply the melancholic mood of a fading
season which invokes a similar melancholia which violin music holds for the
poet. One may even imagine, in spite of the absence of any definite setting,
that there is real violin music in the vicinity and it is this bittersweet tone in the
air which fills his mind with a sense of the autumnal.

What is it in the sounds, stress and position which makes the fourth line so
emphatic? Do you find that it is the acuteness of this dramatic verb 'Blessent'
which remains imprinted in the mind at the end of the stanza, or the vagueness
and pallor of 'langueur' and the flat, expressionless last word?

Stanza 2. A new development of mood marks this stanza. Look at the factors
contributing to this: the less fluent poetic form, with its punctuation and less
direct syntax; the emphasis on the personal physical symptoms 'suffocant...
blême', as opposed to the vaguer and more romanticized 'Blessent mon cœur';
the coming into prominence of the poet himself ('Je me souviens...Et je pleure');
the unduly conspicuous and harsh-sounding rhyme of 'suffocant...quand',
which contrasts with the rich and easy liquid quality of lines 1–3. How would
you define the different moods of these successive verses? The consonantal sounds
of the key line in stanza 1 ('Blessent mon cœur') are now picked out and brought
into prominence at the head of the second stanza ('Tout *su*ffo*c*ant/Et *blê*me,
*qu*and') drawing subtle attention to the theme of emotional pain. Notice how
two of the rhymes of the first stanza are also condensed in the single line 'Sonne
l'heure', contributing to the close-knit phonetic texture of the poem.

The theme of the passage of time, hardly more than suggested in the first
stanza by the reference to autumn, now occupies the central position (the initial
stress of 'Sonne l'heure' intensified by the inversion), and takes on an open lyrical
expression ('Je me souviens/Des jours anciens'). The 'sanglots' which came to
him apparently as sounds or a mood from the outside now become his own
tears ('Et je pleure'). The poet has seemed particularly vulnerable to sensations,
especially sounds ('violons' or a clock striking), and these, aided by memory,
have penetrated and affected his sensitivity. The 'Et' of the last line, which is
much more meaningful in content than the last line in the first stanza which
contains only the adjective 'Monotone', switches from cause to effect and gives
a sudden impression of finality.

Stanza 3. Beginning the last stanza with the unemphatic conjunction 'Et...'
makes it, not a new positive movement in its own right, but a rather limp continu-
ation of the previous stanza. The sense of relapse implicit in the poet's tears
develops into helpless self-abandonment. His spirit seems to be dispersed and
tossed about on the wind.

What effect does the extraordinary juggling of sounds have in the first two
lines? Does the use of *enjambement* in lines 15–16 seem to you to be expressive
(where would you make your pauses in your reading of the first two stanzas, as
compared with this one)? The words 'Deçà, delà', are very evocative of a passive,
wayward movement to and fro. As with '...quand/Sonne l'heure', Verlaine
again suspends his moment of dramatic emphasis, leaving the most insignificant
words (the conjunction 'quand', the article 'la') poised in the rhyming position,
a technique which, coupled with the intonation, helps to conjure up a representation of the air-blown leaf.

Verlaine's particularly expert handling of rhythmical accentuation is noticeable throughout the poem. In the first stanza, the line 'Blessent mon cœur' (with its two forceful stresses) stands out from its musically vague background. In the second stanza, it is the crucial line 'Sonne l'heure' which contains two main stresses, but this time concentrated into three syllables and made even more emphatic, so that it rings like a death-knell for the nostalgic poet. In the final stanza, which depicts the decomposition of the poet's spirit and will, this double stress is withheld till the very last line: this removes the firm rhythmical centre-pin which supported the two previous stanzas and endows the final one with a diffuse, aimless quality; it also underlines the fatalistic mood of the last words (the vowels of which contrast noticeably with the repetitive sound of 'Deçà, delà, Pareil à la . . .'). Following this rhythmical pattern ('Blessent mon cœur . . . Sonne l'heure . . . Feuille morte'), one sees in neat relief the thematic development of the poem: from an emotional wound, to the demoralizing awareness of passing time, to the abandonment of his weak and fragile self to a kind of death.

Compare and contrast this poem, in themes, vocabulary and techniques, with Apollinaire's *Le Pont Mirabeau*.

Colloque sentimental

Dans le vieux parc solitaire et glacé,
Deux formes ont tout à l'heure passé.

Leurs yeux sont morts et leurs lèvres sont molles,
Et l'on entend à peine leurs paroles.   4

Dans le vieux parc solitaire et glacé,
Deux spectres ont évoqué le passé.

–Te souvient-il de notre extase ancienne?
–Pourquoi voulez-vous donc qu'il m'en souvienne?   8

–Ton cœur bat-il toujours à mon seul nom?
Toujours vois-tu mon âme en rêve?–Non.

–Ah! les beaux jours de bonheur indicible
Où nous joignions nos bouches!–C'est possible.   12

–Qu'il était bleu, le ciel, et grand, l'espoir!
–L'espoir a fui, vaincu, vers le ciel noir.

Tels ils marchaient dans les avoines folles,
Et la nuit seule entendit leurs paroles.   16

Colloque sentimental

Lines 1–6. In several ways this is a theatrical poem, a kind of staging for two voices. The first six lines sketch in the setting and act as a prologue.

The setting itself is both stylized décor, with connotations of the luxurious and aristocratic (one imagines the stately grounds of an eighteenth-century manor), and a suggestive context for a romantic drama, with its isolation, chill of mystery and encounter between shadowy figures. The mood is strangely cold and impersonal. The spectator seems at a distance from the characters. What contribution does the use of tenses make to the establishing of the atmosphere? What is the effect of the progression from 'Deux formes' to 'Deux spectres' and how does it modify one's reading of 'Leurs yeux sont morts'? What is it that makes these spectral figures seem absent but present, stark but vague, human but inhuman? Do you notice a certain stiffness in the style of these six lines which prefigures the rigidity of the exchanges which follow? Is the division into couplets a well chosen verse-form?

Lines 7–14. We pass from what were virtually the stage-directions to actual dialogue. But although this dialogue is crisp and precise, one cannot be too sure (in view of the fact that 'L'on entend à peine leurs paroles') of the complete tenor of their conversation. Nor can one be sure whether these words, as nebulous in the air as a frosted breath, belong to the present or to the past. The actual dialogue does little to relieve the impersonality and doubt: there is no way of telling which is the man and which is the woman (although in the context of the *Fêtes galantes* from which this poem is taken and of Verlaine's work as a whole, where the man is so often the pleading figure and woman the evasive one, one imagines the first voice to be that of the male partner). The first couplet impresses the distance between the two persons, and a distinct chill other than that of the icy weather or the spectral associations present in the description of 'le vieux parc solitaire et glacé': the coldness in their emotional relationship. There is a noticeable discrepancy in the form of their address: the 'vous' reply, between people who have presumably been lovers, seems particularly hurtful. There is also a different alliterative note in their voices: the first has a soft sibilant quality ('Te *s*ouvient-il de notre exta*s*e ancienne?'), the second a hard cutting edge ('Pour*qu*oi voulez-vous don*c qu*'il m'en souvienne?'). The insertion of the word 'donc' gives a brusque, challenging and haughty tone to the reply, a reply which offers no satisfaction and is only a question countering a question. One notices, finally, the use of the impersonal form 'Te souvient-il' and its repetition in the subjunctive, which adds a stilted and formal note to the exchange.

What change of structure is there in the dialogue of lines 9–12 and what effects does this create? Is there any new variation of tone in either of the voices? How effective is the incongruity of such phrases as 'Ton cœur bat-il toujours...', 'Toujours vois-tu...' and 'nous joignions nos bouches'? Do you think that Verlaine has succeeded in creating two well differentiated characters, both subtly drawn in their own right (look particularly at the vocabulary favoured by the first voice and the rather lavish phonetic quality of its expression)?

Lines 13–14 are a most emphatic finale to this dialogue, a dialogue briefly overheard before the characters leave the stage and fade into the distance. The first voice is heard at its most urgent and exclamatory. The fragmentary simplicity of the syntax ('bleu, le ciel, et grand, l'espoir') implies an almost childlike, desperate need to convince. The broken, rudimentary style seems a somewhat pathetic last attempt to put words to, and hold together, what was previously beyond words, 'bonheur indicible'. But the responding voice, already negative or non-committal, now answers in the most fateful way, perversely taking the same vocabulary and throwing it back with demoralizing brutality. What is the effect of the reversal of the order of 'l'espoir' and 'ciel'; of the position of 'vaincu'; of the prominent acute vowels in 'fui' and 'vaincu'; and of the changed epithet attached, now more cohesively, to 'ciel'? (Compare the function of this line with the final stanza of Baudelaire's *Quand le ciel bas et lourd....* It is also interesting to make a link with the final line of Baudelaire's other *Spleen* poem, *Pluviôse...*, which reads: 'Causent sinistrement de leurs amours défunts'.)

Lines 15–16. In this last couplet Verlaine performs a masterful change of scenery. How appropriate is this new décor in view of the nature of the conversation? Does he intend a double meaning in the adjective 'folles'? The poem is now more enigmatic than ever. It is almost impossible to situate these two spirits in time and space. Did their exchanges take place 'Dans le vieux parc' or 'dans les avoines folles'; did the spectres actually pass from one setting to another during their exchanges; or are the two settings in fact one and the same: the neglected grounds of an old manor now running to seed? The time element is equally uncertain: one slips through a range of Present, Perfect, Imperfect and Past Historic tenses. Only the final Past Historic has a conclusive value: after '*Tels* ils marchaient...' which serves to summarize all that has preceded, this tense sets the seal on their drama and makes it very much a past event. After ghostly words in the air scarcely heard, the poem ends with words tantamount to silence and an atmosphere of solitude and dereliction. Actors, speech and audience, to say nothing of love and hope, have all disappeared. And, if no-one heard their words, who could be the narrator?

What are the ironic implications of the title? Why the word 'colloque' as opposed to 'conversation'? How does this compare with the more traditional view of lovers' souls? (One might make a useful comparison with Desnos's view of love, death and relations with the *fantôme* of a loved one.)

Arthur Rimbaud

(1854–1891)

Les Effarés

Noirs dans la neige et dans la brume,
Au grand soupirail qui s'allume,
    Leurs culs en rond,   3

A genoux, cinq petits, – misère! –
Regardent le Boulanger faire
    Le lourd pain blond.   6

Ils voient le fort bras blanc qui tourne
La pâte grise et qui l'enfourne
    Dans un trou clair.   9

Ils écoutent le bon pain cuire.
Le Boulanger au gras sourire
    Grogne un vieil air.   12

Ils sont blottis, pas un ne bouge,
Au souffle du soupirail rouge
    Chaud comme un sein.   15

Quand pour quelque médianoche,
Façonné comme une brioche
    On sort le pain,   18

Quand, sous les poutres enfumées,
Chantent les croûtes parfumées
    Et les grillons,   21

Que ce trou chaud souffle la vie,
Ils ont leur âme si ravie
    Sous leurs haillons,   24

Ils se ressentent si bien vivre,
Les pauvres Jésus pleins de givre,
    Qu'ils sont là tous,   27

Collant leurs petits museaux roses
Au treillage, grognant des choses
    Entre les trous,   30

Tout bêtes, faisant leurs prières
Et repliés vers ces lumières
    Du ciel rouvert,   33

Si fort, qu'ils crèvent leur culotte
Et que leur chemise tremblote
    Au vent d'hiver.   36

Les Effarés

Stanzas 1–2. No French poet of the nineteenth century has attuned himself so infectiously to the spirit of childhood as Rimbaud: to its freshness of sensation, immediacy of emotion, spontaneity of vision. *Les Effarés* is one of his most endearing poems: sympathetic, playful, slightly magical.

One notices the starkly pictorial quality of the opening of the poem: black outlined against the white of the snow, brightness gleaming through the murky fog, and, set in picturesque relief, five round little bottoms. This almost Dickensian scene shows Rimbaud's ability as a cartoonist: he seizes on one or two salient details which, suitably isolated and inflated, tell a whole story.

The story here, as the second stanza goes on to reveal, is that of poverty and social deprivation; and the language which accompanies it is appropriately plebeian and vulgar. Does Rimbaud appear to be self-conscious of the fact that, in depicting poor underprivileged mites out in the winter's snow, he is treating a well-worn, even hackneyed, theme? How effectively does the poet use his verse-form in these two stanzas, and especially the brevity and rhythmical emphasis of the four-syllable line?

Stanzas 3–4. These stanzas give a closer focus on the activities going on inside the bakehouse. From a view of the children watching, we have a view of what they see: instead of 'le Boulanger', there is the detail of 'le fort bras blanc'; instead of the indefinite 'faire', there are the precise actions 'tourne' and 'l'enfourne'; instead of the traditional image of 'pain blond', there is the particular texture and colour of 'pâte grise'. Here the contrast is accentuated between the harshness and brutality of the outside world and the inviting warmth of this interior scene, between the static figures crayonned there and the series of energetic actions of a man at work.

What qualities of personality in the Baker does Rimbaud's description suggest? Note the poet's use of simple, unambitious vocabulary to suit his purpose (a vocabulary far removed from a more ornate or circumlocutory poetic language, and even from Rimbaud's own linguistic eccentricities in *Le Bateau ivre*). How does he create a feeling of vigour?

Stanza 5. We return to the rapt, immobile figures (the punctuated line helps to suggest that they are poised there with bated breath). Their posture ('Ils sont blottis...') implies their need for warmth, comfort and security, and perhaps that this is a haven against fear for these little timorous outcasts away from home (cf. the title *Les Effarés*). The word 'blottis' almost predicts the image 'Chaud comme un sein', which gives the bakery the symbolic quality of a life-giving source, and makes the 'soupirail' the narrow outlet for this nourishment.

We have referred to the forceful *visual* appeal of the poem (note, in this respect, the use of colour); study how Rimbaud also develops the *tactile* qualities of the description. We have noted, too, a particularly energetic use of rhythm; examine how this works in conjunction with a close-knit phonetic texture (look at the patterns of assonance and alliteration which are woven from stanza to stanza).

Stanzas 6–7. The appearance of the simile at the end of the previous stanza, introducing a vaguely symbolic note, seems to spark off a more fanciful description which takes one further away from the sharp realism of the very first scene. The word 'Médianoche', which creates a surprisingly luxurious virtuoso rhyme and gives a touch of foreignness after the familiar and homely vocabulary which has preceded, is particularly well-chosen. Seen as a midnight feast (usually eaten at the end of a fast-day), it re-emphasizes the division between the 'haves' and the 'have-nots' of the world, with their two ways of life summed up in the juxtaposition of 'pain', plain bread, and 'brioche', the more extravagant pastry (contrast the blunt words '...faire/Le lourd pain blond' with the more decorative 'Façonné comme une brioche'). Significantly, it is only in their mind's eye that these urchins imagine the bread as 'brioche'. Seen as a hint of midnight, the witching hour, the word suggests the time when magical transformations take place. The making of bread is the prime example of such a transformation: 'La pâte grise...', formless, stodgy, dull in colour, becomes 'les croûtes parfumées', crisp, shaped and golden. But coinciding with this is a similar transformation in the nature of the poem itself: from something primarily visual and earthy, it becomes endowed with a touch of fantasy and imaginative vision. The whole place seems to come alive: the image of glowing bread fills the room to the very roof; the crickets, those habitual hearth-dwellers, chirp in harmony with the singing crusts of the cooling loaves (note how the combination of sound-echoes and rich rhyme, 'les poutres enfumées' and 'les croûtes parfumées', gives a forceful melodic quality here). There is a play of synaesthesia (cf. Baudelaire, 'Les parfums, les couleurs et les sons se répondent'): vision, scent, sound and a feeling of warmth. Why should it be that just one of the five senses is left out?

Stanzas 8–11. 'Que', which is only a stylistic variant of 'Quand', nevertheless breaks the regularity and gives an indication of a new development. For the children, the oven-door and the grating at which they are huddled now seem one and the same thing (what is it that creates this impression?). The poetic atmosphere becomes more suggestive, strengthened by the growing prominence of religious vocabulary. 'Souffle' becomes the breath of life. They are in a state of transport ('...leur âme si ravie'), are referred to as '...pauvres Jésus', are seen to be praying and are clinging close, not to the mere light of a bakehouse, but to '...ces lumières du ciel rouvert'. Notice how the poem moves only gradually towards a more definite symbolic value: the phrases '...leur âme si ravie' and 'pauvres Jésus' may be little more than clichés, just as '...souffle la vie' may refer to no more than the smell of the bread which is, for these children, the smell of life; but the language of '...faisant leurs prières' and 'Du ciel rouvert' is overtly religious, takes one's attention back to 'A genoux', and invites one to envisage a deeper level of meaning. 'Le Boulanger', with his capital letter, may be a symbol of the Maker, the master-craftsman in his workshop, giving a glimpse of perfect creation and the secret of life (one thinks of the eucharistic meaning of bread). And the 'pauvres Jésus' may be little tatterdemalion sons of God, thrown into the hardship and suffering of the world, but still capable of savouring, if only from a distance, a vision of paradise to be regained.

As if suspicious of his own tendency towards sentimentality or over-rarefied religious symbolism, Rimbaud, while encouraging our flights of fancy, keeps us well grounded in the realities of everyday physical life. Study the way in which he sets up a pattern of incongruous juxtapositions, in most cases extremely well balanced, to achieve this.

Stanza 12. The poet saves the most undermining incongruity till last. He has built up his effect in a long meandering sentence, which holds us in suspense while becoming increasingly emphatic. (The intensification of '...*si* ravie', '...*si* bien vivre', '*Si* fort', etc. and the repetitions help to convey the children's growing excitement and inability to contain themselves.) We reach a high-point of religious suggestion, then suddenly demolished. As the children stretch too eagerly towards the vent (or is it the force of their praying, the impetuosity of their souls?), their trousers split and out pop five shirt-tails. One has the impression that Rimbaud has misled us by directing our attention more and more compulsively towards a symbolic interpretation, only to juxtapose heaven and buttocks ('culotte' here inevitably conjures up the 'culs' of the first stanza) and return the poem to a cartoon image which cannot be taken seriously. Perhaps the last gesture is one of scorn and defiance on Rimbaud's part, aimed at the whole notion of paradise; at those responsible for social deprivation; and at the reader, whose sentiments and conventional poetic expectations have been toyed with.

Look closely at the stages of development in the structure of the poem, and the clever way in which the verse-form (*enjambements*, short lines, rhythmical emphasis, variations in sentence-structure, etc.) has been exploited.

How effectively do you think Rimbaud has combined elements of social realism and fairy-story, superficial cartoon and deeper levels of poetic suggestion, sentimentality and ironic humour, sympathetic involvement with his subject and a mocking detachment? Would you agree with Verlaine who has described this poem as 'gentiment caricatural et (...) si cordial'?

Ma Bohème

(Fantaisie)

Je m'en allais, les poings dans mes poches crevées;
Mon paletot aussi devenait idéal;
J'allais sous le ciel, Muse! et j'étais ton féal;
Oh! là là! que d'amours splendides j'ai rêvées!   4

Mon unique culotte avait un large trou.
– Petit-Poucet rêveur, j'égrenais dans ma course
Des rimes. Mon auberge était à la Grande-Ourse.
– Mes étoiles au ciel avaient un doux frou-frou   8

Et je les écoutais, assis au bord des routes,
Ces bons soirs de septembre où je sentais des gouttes
De rosée à mon front, comme un vin de vigueur;   11

Où, rimant au milieu des ombres fantastiques,
Comme des lyres, je tirais les élastiques
De mes souliers blessés, un pied près de mon cœur!   14

Ma Bohème

Lines 1–4. The poem's title and accompanying description (*fantaisie*) prefigure the characteristics of these first four lines. There is a brief, striking picture of a confirmed bohemian figure, summed up in the two details of worn-out pockets and a threadbare overcoat, as well as in the indefinite verb ('Je m'en allais') which implies habitually setting off to nowhere in particular. His attitude seems forthright and insouciant: 'poings' rather than 'mains' suggests a somewhat bluff, unaccommodating manner. At the same time he can laugh lightheartedly at his circumstances. The words '. . . aussi devenait idéal' imply a playful bantering spirit and contain several suggestions: they indicate that his coat is rapidly going the same way as his worn-out pockets, and the sooner it happens, the more it will suit his idealized image of his tramp-like existence; one could also read the word 'idéal' as meaning that there is so little left of his coat in reality, that it is now only an 'idea' of a coat (one might relate this notion of a coat acquiring a 'spiritual' quality with the phrase '. . . usé jusqu'à l'âme', applied by certain nineteenth-century writers to threadbare clothing); Rimbaud is also gently ridiculing Romantic vocabulary (cf. the more melodramatic title *Spleen et Idéal* by Baudelaire) by setting the word in an incongruous context. As in best bohemian traditions, material poverty is seen here as no impediment to, and even a necessary condition of, peace of mind and freedom of spirit.

The word 'idéal' launches the element of *fantaisie*. 'J'allais sous le ciel' seems to dismiss all other aspects of nature from the picture: the poet and the sky are left on their own, as if there were nothing in the world but them. The abrupt address to the Muse (another traditional poetic detail called up with a touch of tongue-in-cheek humour) is full of youthful gusto; while the archaic word 'féal', meaning a faithful follower, draws together the image of the hobo and the romanticized figure of a knight-errant serving his mistress, and gives a premonition of legendary exploits. But one is led to wonder if such exploits ever materialized. 'Oh! là là! que d'amours splendides j'ai rêvées!' conveys a certain pride and relish in the extravagance of his own dreams, but also the reflectiveness of someone who can now look back and know that they have been dreams (note the change of tense here, which gives a different vantage-point in time, probably that of the slightly older poet who can still share, but good-humouredly mocks, the high-flown aspirations of his younger self). The interjection 'Oh! là là!', which gives such a feeling of exhilaration, impresses his juvenile spontaneity, lack of poetic decorum, and cavalier attitude to poetic expression.

Lines 5–8. What effect does the first line of this stanza create after the mood of the final lines of the previous one? Does the context induce one to read in the double meaning of the adjective 'unique' here?

The description of himself as 'Petit-Poucet rêveur' is a further example of the tendency to see himself as a story-book hero (on this occasion Tom Thumb), but with the difference that he is both adventurer and poet, impish gadabout and casual dreamer. And, as a dreamer, his mode of composing poetry is singularly offhand: where other, more laborious poets sweat in their rooms in the search for the appropriate rhyme, he strolls under the stars tossing off rhymes with a nonchalant facility (the use of the word 'égrener' helps to suggest this). Notice how Rimbaud has used *enjambement* to withhold for a moment an unexpected direct object, and thus give a surprising twist to his metaphor. The *rejet* obviously throws into prominence the words 'Des rimes': linking this with the reference to 'Muse' and his later repetition of 'rimant', what do you think Rimbaud's attitude to his poetry is? 'Mon auberge était à la Grande-

Ourse' continues the vein of linguistic inventiveness already evident in the punning of the second line of the poem: notice how colourfully he has revitalized the image 'dormir à la belle étoile', at the same time giving it a new picturesque value by association with the word 'auberge'. This evocative line is also a neat summary of the way in which his material poverty (the vagrant can afford no other inn for the night) and imaginative richness go hand in hand. Since 'ma course' and 'Grande-Ourse' are forcefully linked as rhymes, and the word 'course' can be used to describe the path of the stars, it may well be that the ethereal dreamer imagines himself momentarily to be, not just 'sous le ciel', but actually up in the heavens himself (which would then evoke yet another way of looking at the image 'Mon auberge...'). The possessive adjective of 'Mes étoiles...' is striking. Not only does it re-emphasize what a buoyantly egocentric poem this is (with 'Je' or 'Mon' at the head of almost every sentence), but it expands the theme of personal belongings: seen in contrast to the similarly constructed clause, 'Mon unique culotte...', it casts the poet, if not as the virtual owner of the heavenly realm, then at least as someone enjoying an unusually intimate relationship with it. The description of the stars as having '...un doux frou-frou' is yet another instance of his joyous disrespect for the conventions of language and poetic vision. It is an almost outrageous sample of synaesthesia: the shimmering of the stars is translated into a rustling sound, no doubt as a humorous parody of the traditional poetic concept, well-worked by many Romantic poets, of the 'harmony of the spheres'. But at the same time one feels a genuine tenderness and affection in this reminiscence, both towards the hospitable night sky and towards the boy who listened to the swishing of the air and felt it to be the voice of the stars.

Lines 9–11. How effective do you find the fluent transition from the octet to the sestet, and the prolonged repetition of the rhyming sounds? In what respects does the mood of this tercet change, to match the image of a lad now sitting by the roadside instead of continuing his jaunty walk? How, particularly, does Rimbaud exploit his sentence-structure to reinforce this change?

'Ces bons soirs de septembre' (the demonstrative 'Ces' brings them closer and makes them more amicable) touches the same note of familiarity with nature which was apparent in '*Mes* étoiles...' and '*doux* frou-frou'. As the more passive 'rêveur' takes over from the active there is an easy intermingling of sensations. The coolness of dew on his forehead has an invigorating inner effect like that of strong wine, a simile clearly linked to the earlier reference to 'auberge'. (One may indeed see a logical progression in the poem from setting off, journeying, covering great distances, to thinking of his inn for the night, finding his halting-place, receiving refreshment and, finally, getting ready for bed.) Once more Rimbaud takes two fairly well-worn poetic images, that of dew as the gentle sustenance from heaven, and that of the poet's brow, traditionally crowned with laurels, graced with divine intuition, or troubled with anguish; and gives them a more plebeian and picturesque twist. In their place we have an image of dew as a rough wine, the heavens as an inn, and poetic inspiration served in a strikingly physical form.

Lines 12–14. But although seemingly one of the heavenly fraternity, the poet is also the servant of the Muse to whom he owes his last respects. So, we return to his rhyming and a serenade to his mistress Muse (inevitably conjured back into the picture by association with 'lyres'). The stage is set with an appropriately dramatic backcloth. Yet one wonders again if Rimbaud is not slyly ridiculing the portentous imagery of a poet such as Hugo (cf. for instance,

Je suis fait d'ombre et de marbre...), a suspicion confirmed by the impudent rhyme 'fantastiques...élastiques' and by the intensely incongruous and deflating image of the last two lines. It shows a fast-moving irony at his own expense: for the only lyre of the latter-day hobo–poet is the twanging sound of the elastic in his shoes as he stretches them for relief. It is also, by juxtaposition of the sublime and the ridiculous, a grand 'debunking' of the Romantic vein in poetry. One could have 'pied blessé', 'cœur blessé', but 'souliers blessés' is an odd pairing indeed, seeming to endow his shoes, now the worse for wear, with a semi-heroic quality. More particularly, Rimbaud has taken two of poetry's favourite emotive words 'blessés' and 'cœur' (cf. Verlaine's use of these words in *Chanson d'automne*), parted them and put them with the clumsiest bed-fellows. This leaves us with a picture of the poet in a grossly improbable and uncomfortable position, a view of poetry which could hardly be more self-mocking, and a strong suspicion that the writer is enjoying his word-play to the very end, with a metrical foot close to his heart!

How would you sum up the spirit of this poem?

Jules Laforgue

(1860–1887)

Complainte de la lune en province

Ah! la belle pleine Lune,
Grosse comme une fortune!

La retraite sonne au loin,
Un passant, monsieur l'adjoint;   4

Un clavecin joue en face,
Un chat traverse la place:

La province qui s'endort!
Plaquant un dernier accord,   8

Le piano clôt sa fenêtre.
Quelle heure peut-il bien être?

Calme Lune, quel exil!
Faut-il dire: ainsi soit-il?   12

Lune, ô dilettante Lune,
A tous les climats commune,

Tu vis hier le Missouri,
Et les remparts de Paris,   16

Les fiords bleus de la Norvège,
Les pôles, les mers, que sais-je?

Lune heureuse! ainsi tu vois,
A cette heure, le convoi   20

De son voyage de noce!
Ils sont partis pour l'Ecosse.

Quel panneau, si, cet hiver,
Elle eût pris au mot mes vers!   24

Lune, vagabonde Lune,
Faisons cause et mœurs communes?

O riches nuits! je me meurs,
La province dans le cœur!   28

Et la lune a, bonne vieille,
Du coton dans les oreilles.

Complainte de la lune en province

Lines 1–2. The *complainte* is the form adopted by Laforgue for his most famous collection of poems. It is, traditionally, a popular song or ballad on some tragic or moral theme, but in his hands it becomes a medium allowing a peculiar balance of songster's ingenuousness and philosophical disenchantment, of simple 'popular' accessibility and evasiveness, of lyrical over-emphasis and anti-lyricism. A lonely poet's tribute to the beauty of the moon: a well-worn theme, Laforgue's treatment of which is suspect, to say the least. The forced emotive opening, the rather too fulsome alliteration magnified by the 'e' mutes, the banality of the epithets are a first hint of travesty. Hint becomes certainty in the following simile, which punctures the semblance of poetic emotion: mercenary imaginings do not mingle well with aesthetic transport, and the image of the moon as a fat money-bag or gold coin shining in the heavens comes perilously close to what in English slang is known as 'pie in the sky'!

Lines 3–12. After the opening celebration, we switch to the uneventful *ennui* of provincial night-life, graphically captured in the few representative details of its local dignitary ('monsieur l'adjoint', the deputy mayor), its home music sessions, its early nights ('la retraite' is the lights-out or curfew signal) and deserted streets. What stylistic means does Laforgue use to convey the unrelieved emptiness and sterility of 'la province'? It is worth pointing out that in *Complainte du soir des comices agricoles* the wretched human spectacle merits a humorous musical accompaniment, and that in *L'Hiver qui vient* (as in Rimbaud's *Après le déluge*) piano-playing is made to epitomize the hollow cultural pretentions of the bourgeoisie. In this case a kind of mock-fanfare is provided as 'life' in the provincial town is snuffed. What is the effect of the run-on lines between the fourth and fifth couplets; what creates the comic vision? Note how the elliptical image of the piano, causing a sudden feeling of conclusion and exclusion, brings the miniature 'slice of life' sequence to an end, and leads quite naturally, as if the observer were thrown back on himself and an awareness of time, to the abrupt self-questioning 'Quelle heure...?' and then once more to the hypnotic moon. The rhetorical address brings into the open a serious theme which was only implicit in the flat descriptions of the small town street: that of exile (not only the poet's exile in this mediocre and spiritless setting, but his more radical exile from the celestial plane in which the moon itself moves, this being no doubt the more influential in prompting his plaintive query as to whether such alienation must be an irremediable fate). Yet even here the jingling rhymes and brisk, staccato phrases which skip through the emotional theme as if it hardly existed make one wonder if it is not an ironically undernourished bit of Romanticism. One detects, too, a touch of borrowing and parody from the flippant atmosphere of Verlaine's *Fêtes galantes* (the offhand buttonholing of 'Hé! bonsoir, la Lune!' in *Sur l'herbe* and the mock ceremony of 'Ainsi soit-il' at the end of *A Clymène*), which does not help to encourage more than a melodramatic tear.

Lines 13–18. A strain of rhetorical exaggeration ('Lune, ô dilettante Lune') brings the next change of focus: a view of the moon's superior cosmopolitanism. In what way are these verses used to contrast with the earlier image of the dormant province (e.g. the different handling of the couplets)? In spite of this, does it seem that these geographical notations of the moon's unperturbed globe-trotting and the previous sparse inventory of provincial nocturnal activities ultimately have the same effect: to confirm the sense of 'exil'? In what way does his final query 'que sais-je?' reveal the same kind of attitude as that apparent in the earlier 'ainsi soit-il'? Is the progression from geographical proper names to the more universal elements ('pôles' and 'mers') in any way relevant to this conclusion? The adjective 'dilettante' is an unusual and suggestive choice: is it that the moon follows the spectacle of life as a casual amateur, owing its allegiance to no particular part of the world, that it possesses the same ironic detachment which Laforgue himself cultivates in his poetry, the 'dandysme lunaire' of a 'viveur lunaire', as described in *Locutions de Pierrots*?

Lines 19–24. After what has been a long circumnavigation, the love theme now makes its appearance (cf. *Complainte à Notre-Dame des Soirs*, where only the last line reveals that an amorous set-back is at the root of his pseudo-devotions to Our Lady of the Moon). But Laforgue does not drop easily into the romantic rôle of love-struck, moon-struck youth roaming the streets at night. With an evasive, self-protective flick of the spirit, he is instantly thanking his lucky stars for the fortunate let-off when, if his words had been read as gospel truth, his fate might have been to be *embourgeoisé* for the rest of his days and condemned to serve in a provincial piano-playing household! Note the dramatic positioning of the word 'convoi' and the over-rich rhyming (felt especially in such a small-scale verse-form) of 'heureuse...heure' and 'tu vois...convoi...son voyage': is this an example of mocking over-emphasis? The colloquial word 'panneau' (a trap or snare into which one falls), especially in its exclamatory form, has a definite puncturing effect, coming immediately after the romantic sugges-tion of a honeymoon in Scotland (a country enjoying a poetic aura from earlier in the century, thanks largely to the novels of Walter Scott); and the suspended syntax ('si, cet hiver,...') effectively delays the final line, enhancing the humour of this 'escape-clause' uttered like a sigh of relief. The reference to verses which were something of a pose and not a sincere expression of the heart provides a nice mirror-image, for it is also a comment on *Complainte de la lune en province*: we, too, are stepping into a snare if we expect to take the author at his word.

Lines 25–30. The final section, launched again by the grand rhetorical address 'Lune...', calls for a partnership between himself and the celestial body. Reading back reflections from the moon to the man, one imagines that he, too, is dilettante and nomad, without roots or human attachments; that he, too, floats in a pallid no man's land, having more in common with a bloodless planet than with the petty agitations of humanity. But a melodramatic penultimate fade-out is close at hand to erase such ethereal fancies: the high drama of 'je me meurs' dissolves into the ludicrous image of the province stuck in his heart like a mortal arrow, an incongruity made all the more bathetic by the final couplet, which not only ridicules all his own insistent rhetoric but deflates a whole tradi-tion of moon poetry (cf. a similar disrespectful attitude to the cosmos in Rim-baud's line, 'Mes étoiles au ciel avaient un doux frou-frou'). One should compare this with the end of *Locutions de Pierrots*, XII where an offhand colloquial tone dogs the 'serious' theme of death and self-obliteration, removing its tragic or romantic resonances. Laforgue's style here is at the furthest remove from, say, the suave melancholy of Verlaine's relapse into oblivion (cf. 'Et je m'en vais...', etc. in *Chanson d'automne*), and resembles Rimbaud's self-mocking anti-climax in *Ma Bohème*, where the plebeian or grossly physical image turns the sublime into the ridiculous (cf. '...un pied près de mon cœur' in *Ma Bohème*, and the parallelism here of '...dans le cœur' and '...dans les oreilles' which similarly devalues effusions from the heart). The final image of the poem is particularly clever: the antithesis of 'cœur' and 'oreilles', pin-pointing the basic separation of worlds, confirms the theme of 'exil'; it contains the undermining implication that the moon's contented non-commitment goes hand in hand with its senility and deafness, its blithe unconsciousness of any communication as it sails round in interstellar space; it makes the moon herself a bourgeois figure, well-off and complacently plugged for a good night's sleep; and it provides a last comic visual picture of the moon's face, with tufts of fleecy cloud protruding from its ears. Study the structural expertise of the poem: the function of the recurrent address; the neat associative logic in the transitions from one stage of development to another; the movement towards a more personal involvement in the later stages; and the significance of the fact that only the first and last couplets, which also contain the most caricatural images, refer to '*la* Lune' in the third person.

L'Hiver qui vient

Blocus sentimental! Messageries du Levant!...
Oh, tombée de la pluie! Oh! tombée de la nuit,
Oh! le vent!...
La Toussaint, la Noël et la Nouvelle Année,   4
Oh, dans les bruines, toutes mes cheminées!...
D'usines...

On ne peut plus s'asseoir, tous les bancs sont mouillés;
Crois-moi, c'est bien fini jusqu'à l'année prochaine,   8
Tous les bancs sont mouillés, tant les bois sont rouillés,
Et tant les cors ont fait ton ton, ont fait ton taine!...
Ah! nuées accourues des côtes de la Manche,
Vous nous avez gâté notre dernier dimanche.   12

Il bruine;
Dans la forêt mouillée, les toiles d'araignées
Ploient sous les gouttes d'eau, et c'est leur ruine.
Soleils plénipotentiaires des travaux en blonds Pactoles   16
Des spectacles agricoles,
Où êtes-vous ensevelis?
Ce soir un soleil fichu gît au haut du coteau,
Gît sur le flanc, dans les genêts, sur son manteau.   20
Un soleil blanc comme un crachat d'estaminet
Sur une litière de jaunes genêts,
De jaunes genêts d'automne.
Et les cors lui sonnent!   24

Qu'il revienne...
Qu'il revienne à lui!
Taïaut! Taïaut et hallali!
O triste antienne, as-tu fini!...   28
Et font les fous!
Et il gît là, comme une glande arrachée dans un cou,
Et il frissonne, sans personne!...

Allons, allons, et hallali!   32
C'est l'Hiver bien connu qui s'amène;
Oh! les tournants des grandes routes,
Et sans petit Chaperon Rouge qui chemine!...
Oh! leurs ornières des chars de l'autre mois,   36
Montant en don quichottesques rails
Vers les patrouilles des nuées en déroute
Que le vent malmène vers les transatlantiques bercails!...
Accélérons, accélérons, c'est la saison bien connue, cette fois.   40
Et le vent, cette nuit, il en a fait de belles!
O dégâts, ô nids, ô modestes jardinets!
Mon cœur et mon sommeil: ô échos des cognées!...

Tous ces rameaux avaient encor leurs feuilles vertes,   44
Les sous-bois ne sont plus qu'un fumier de feuilles mortes;
Feuilles, folioles, qu'un bon vent vous emporte
Vers les étangs par ribambelles,
Ou pour le feu du garde-chasse,   48
Ou les sommiers des ambulances
Pour les soldats loin de la France.

C'est la saison, c'est la saison, la rouille envahit les masses,
La rouille ronge en leurs spleens kilométriques   52
Les fils télégraphiques des grandes routes où nul ne passe.

Les cors, les cors, les cors – mélancoliques!...
Mélancoliques!
S'en vont, changeant de ton,   56
Changeant de ton et de musique,
Ton ton, ton taine, ton ton!...
Les cors, les cors, les cors!...
S'en sont allés au vent du Nord.   60

Je ne puis quitter ce ton: que d'échos!...
C'est la saison, c'est la saison, adieu vendanges!...
Voici venir les pluies d'une patience d'ange,
Adieu vendanges, et adieu tous les paniers,   64

Tous les paniers Watteau des bourrées sous les marronniers.
C'est la toux dans les dortoirs du lycée qui rentre,
C'est la tisane sans le foyer,
La phtisie pulmonaire attristant le quartier,   68
Et toute la misère des grands centres.

Mais, lainages, caoutchoucs, pharmacie, rêve,
Rideaux écartés du haut des balcons des grèves
Devant l'océan de toitures des faubourgs,   72
Lampes, estampes, thé, petits-fours,
Serez-vous pas mes seules amours!...
(Oh! et puis, est-ce que tu connais, outre les pianos,
Le sobre et vespéral mystère hebdomadaire   76
Des statistiques sanitaires
Dans les journaux?)

Non, non! c'est la saison et la planète falote!
Que l'autan, que l'autan   80
Effiloche les savates que le temps se tricote!
C'est la saison, oh déchirements! c'est la saison!
Tous les ans, tous les ans,
J'essaierai en chœur d'en donner la note.   84

L'Hiver qui vient

Section 1. This poem comes from Laforgue's *Derniers vers*, which represent a remarkable breakthrough into free verse and herald many experiments in this direction in twentieth-century poetry.

One is struck immediately by the abrupt, arresting style (and not least by the harsh modernism of the first word). Without warning or introduction, the reader is thrown into a terse, mobile 'stream of consciousness' style, with its fractures, switches and half-developed notations. It is a style which fulfils the implications of the first phrase, 'Blocus sentimental' (a play of words on 'blocus continental', the continental blockade), as if something were constricting sentimental or lyrical self-expression: here there is simply the direct translation of an intensity of emotion or state of crisis (evident in the interjections and exclamatory bursts), but no further self-analysis or sentimental elaboration (the persistent dots imply that so much has to be left unsaid). The impression is of hostile elements and urban ugliness which repress romanticism and choke poetic expression. One might contrast Laforgue's aggressive unsentimentalized treatment of the theme of autumn rain with Verlaine's 'O bruit doux de la pluie / Par terre et sur les toits'. Notice how the themes of time and space are woven implicitly into this opening, together with those of imprisonment and the prospect of escape. How do you explain the possessive adjective in 'toutes *mes* cheminées!': is it meant as a metaphor?

Section 2. The theme of the autumnal degeneration expands, the stylistic expression here being more fashioned than the mere juxtaposition of nouns and exclamations found in the opening section. With it comes the feeling of things which have gone beyond the limit, of irresistible destructive forces, of finality ('...tant les bois...Et tant les cors', 'c'est bien fini...notre dernier dimanche'), as well as a sense of homelessness and persecution ('On ne peut plus s'asseoir...', 'Vous nous avez gâté...'). A new element also appears at the end of this movement: the reference to an important human relationship spoiled in its parting stages (cf. other suggestions of abortive loves in Laforgue's work). But as if to confirm the efficacy of the 'Blocus sentimental', and the dispersing power of the hustling clouds, this is no more than a passing reference, a thread in the wind, never to be mentioned again. What effects are produced by the regularly cadenced 'Alexandrines' (in contrast to broken forms of the previous section), by the use of repetition and sound-echoes? Is there any associative link between the juxtaposed images of the hunting-horns and the fleeting clouds?

Section 3. Particularly noticeable is the way in which certain words and rhymes are picked up again from one section to another, giving continuity and stitching to this loosely articulated and pliable *vers libre*; rhyme pairings are frequently made between long and very short lines ('...du Levant...Oh! le vent!' or 'Il bruine...et c'est leur ruine'), creating a kind of stylistic concertina effect. Taking up the implications of the word 'gâté', the theme of damage and the ruin of frail constructions extends to another realm (how expressive is Laforgue's description of the spiders' webs?). This in turn prompts the very different, quasi mythical, view of the fruits of human industriousness ('Pactole', the river in Asia Minor always glinting with gold from which Cresus was supposed to gain his riches, is used symbolically to represent any source of great wealth or cornucopia), which finally collapses into the plaintive query as to the where-abouts of such golden suns, symbols of fertility and fullness, and introduces one of Laforgue's most obsessive themes: the death of the sun, described here as 'fichu' or 'done for' (note the reinforcement of the idea of death from 'ruine' to 'ensevelis' to 'gît', and compare this funereal emphasis with the wrapping of the sun in a shroud in *Complainte du Roi de Thulé*). Study the bitter play of contrasts (ironically inflated language set against colloquialism, the idealized against the naturalistic, health against illness, the land of milk and honey against the wasteland). Note the vigour of the style: the tireless repetitions and strings of assonance, the uncompromising nature of the imagery, the lively personi-fication, onomatopoeia and galloping syntax. What have the two similes in common? What does the call of the hunting-horns seem to represent: is there a certain incongruity or absurdity in their persistence (cf. '...font les fous')? ('Taïaut' is the cry which urges the hounds on when the prey is sighted; 'Hallali' the cry when the quarry is cornered and one is on the verge of a kill.) It is interes-ting that the poet's own place in this apparently self-generating stream of sound-language and association is only brief and parenthetical: a weary call for things to come to an end (cf. 'Crois-moi, c'est bien fini...') which is rapidly left behind.

Section 4. This section is introduced by rolling sound-waves which sustain the impression of constant movement; and in keeping with a style in which strands are lost, then picked up again and rewoven, the thought which was previously relegated to a hasty bracket ('...as-tu fini!') surges back in the form of the volitional 'Allons, allons...', 'Accélérons, accélérons...'. The infectious urgency of tone conveys determination to move with time rather than fight it, to face the inevitable, to cease to oppose one's resistance and expedite the kill. In what sense can this part be seen as an attack on naïve fancies? How do you explain the image of 'Don Quixotic rails' (cf. 'Et font les fous!' earlier)? (The 'chars de l'autre mois' are presumably the harvest waggons which have now disappeared, leaving only their ugly ruts in the ground as a proof of their passage and the implicit question in the air, 'Where do all the harvests go?') Perhaps it is paradoxical that, although stripping Nature of its illusions, Laforgue himself is clothing it richly in metaphor: as with the description of the ailing sun, depicted simultaneously as 'crachat' and 'glande' (and possibly also as a derelict tramp-figure), the movement of the clouds is now seen in both military and pastoral terms as soldiers in disarray and flocks driven roughly to the folds. Such multiplicity of imagery blends well into an atmosphere of collapse of unity and autumnal dispersion. How does Laforgue create a climate of violence here? What value is there in his use of colloquialism ('...qui s'amène', 'il en a fait de belles' and, previously, 'un soleil fichu')? Note that the theme of destruction returns (cf. the ravaged spiders' webs), stressing the disproportion between small protective constructions or human pretentions of ownership and order ('modestes jardinets') and these exorbitant universal forces. Such thoughts prepare for the laconic finale (the most cryptic style being reserved for the moment of personal confession) in which the idea of destruction is transferred from the outer world to that of the poet's own mind, emotions and dreams, which are haunted by the sound of tree-felling: how does Laforgue's treatment of this detail compare with Baudelaire's in *Chant d'automne* ('J'écoute en frémissant chaque bûche qui tombe')?

Section 5. The fatal rift between past and present is dramatized by the balanced opposition of '...avaient encor...ne sont plus', by the contrast between the gently poetic word 'rameaux' and the harshly alliterative '...fumier de feuilles', by the opposition of 'vertes' and 'mortes' in the rhyming position. In what way does Laforgue renovate the familiar poetic image of the wind-blown leaf (cf. Verlaine's *Chanson d'automne*) and give it a new vitality? Is the reference to leaves blown away to become, among other things, the stuffing for the mattresses of wounded soldiers an example of what has been called 'pseudo-pathetic, pseudo-patriotic exaggeration'; or is it intended to have a genuine shock-effect as a kind of 'odd man out' after the references to the destruction of leaves by the more natural means, water and fire? However one interprets it (and reading the tone is one of the difficulties with Laforgue, as it is with Apollinaire, another stylistic escapologist), it maintains the link with military imagery, it forces an awareness of death of a sombrely human kind, it harks back to the idea of 'litière', improvised and comfortless, and it evokes a human victim who perhaps, like the sun, 'Gît sur le flanc, dans les genêts, sur son manteau'. How appropriate is the phrase '...par ribambelles' as a description, not only of the leaves, but of the actual form of the poem?

Section 6. As previously with 'Allons, allons...', a new section is given dramatic impetus by initial repetition. Again we are swept into a bleak setting with no distracting embroidery or comforting human presence (cf. 'sans personne...sans petit Chaperon Rouge...où nul ne passe'). The description, moreover, acquires a surrealistic touch as the vast personified force of 'rouille' is seen to take over humanity (the militaristic verb 'envahir' renewing the suggestion of 'patrouilles'): one might compare Laforgue's vision here, especially since the word 'spleens' is so exposed, with that of the creeping, all-pervasive disease of damp in Baudelaire's poem *Pluviôse*... The originality and modernism of Laforgue's imagery and expression is striking: not simply the use of ingredients such as factory-chimneys and telegraph wires, which are to become increasingly common in subsequent poetry; but rather the imagination which conceives of ruts as rails and of rails as having the quixotic temperament, which sees (instead of Verlaine's vague 'interminable ennui de la plaine') splenetic wires trailing their tedium to infinity; or the linguistic boldness which coins an adjective like 'don quichottesques', and welds together spiritual mood and its spatial correlative in the startling phrase 'spleens kilométriques'. Is there the outline of a theme of human communication here (cf. 'Messageries du Levant' and the 'fils télégraphiques')? Notice the unchecked running-on of sentences.

Section 7. One could think of the form of the poem in several ways: as subterranean leitmotifs disappearing and then resurfacing, as windblown fragments dispersed and blown back in new combinations, or as a series of sounds and echoes fading and swelling (cf. 'que d'échos!' in the next section). Here the hunting-horn theme returns, associated more closely with the sense of distance, departure and disappearance: so there is a juxtaposition of different means of calling across space, one modern and unpoetic, the other more heroic and romantic; the former eroded by the wet, the latter shredded by the wind; both conveying a sense of dereliction, but the latter more insistent and plaintive. How would you describe the stylistic means in this section and what do they do for the atmosphere?

Section 8. The new development starts with a provocative *jeu de mots* (in saying 'Je ne puis quitter ce ton', is he referring to the actual word 'ton' which has occurred five times in a single line, or more generally to the changing tone in the wind which haunts him, or to the unconventional tone or style of writing which he finds forced upon himself?), and with a curt exclamation equally wide in meaning (does 'que d'échos!' refer to the 'échos des cognées' resounding in his sleep, or to the resonance of the horns which will not quite resign themselves to death, or to all the chains of echo and association which are dictating the movements of his pen?). A more fatalistic note penetrates the poem at this point ('C'est la saison, c'est la saison...Adieu...adieu'), after what has been a prolonged combat between two voices in himself, one dramatized in the form of the hunting-horns: the realist and the romantic, the voice of resignation and the voice of refusal. Notice how, as if in preparation for a finale, so many themes scattered through the poem are brought together again: 'vendanges' and 'paniers' revive the image of 'spectacles agricoles' and bounteous suns; the Watteau-type panier skirts and the rustic dancing ('bourrées') not only summon up the pastoral dream of a bygone age and so reinforce the idea of time irrevocable, but replay the theme of the unbelievable natural idyll or fairy-tale (cf. 'petit Chaperon Rouge'); 'les pluies d'une patience d'ange', on the other hand, links up with the earlier description of rain destroying the 'toiles d'araignées', spiders being usually thought of as absolute symbols of 'patience d'ange' but now fatally outplayed in the game of patience by the inexhaustible eroding power of the fine-fingered rain; the picture of human misery in cold and overcrowded slums gives more relevance to the original 'cheminées!...D'usines...'; while the final images of coughing, infusions and consumption explode the myth of 'plénipotentiaires' and grasp back brutally at the idea of illness and more particularly the similes of 'crachat' and 'glande arrachée dans un cou' which described the sun, showing that they were not put there for gratuitous shock-effect. In style, one notices the renewed use of savage contrast (between rustic summer dream and urban winter nightmare, between escapist fancy and brute realism); the tendency to indulge in linguistic play ('paniers...paniers Watteau') as a creative technique so that a deceptive playfulness is not far removed from the most shocking and undisguised views of winter misery; and the repetitive, alliterative or rhyming stress which gives key details a corrosive force ('C'est la toux…C'est la tisane', '*tisane*…ph*tisie*…mi*sère*', etc.). Remembering that Laforgue himself was to die at the age of twenty-seven from tuberculosis, one can understand his satire of the old world charm of Watteau's aristocratic shepherdesses surrounded by nature in blossom.

Section 9. The penultimate section is the satirical climax of the poem, a mock-answer to the question: is there no protection against the inhuman ravages of winter? It is a critique of bourgeois comfort which pretends to immunize itself against the destructive reality of the universe at large. How do you explain the image of the 'balcon des grèves' and 'l'océan de toitures'? Is there an element of the ludicrous in his inventory of human defences? Can you read an ironic tone in the style? What use is made again of antithetical visions? Note that, as in earlier instances (e.g. 'Soleils plénipotentiaires…', etc.), the most solemn and prolix language is hounded by the most down-to-earth, unpoetic or uncircumlocutory. (It is interesting in this vein to see which themes are stressed by the concluding lines of each section.) What seems to be the point of bracketing the final rhetorical question, with its accosting 'tu' form and colloquial opening? The 'tu' may refer to the now-absent person who was part of 'notre dernier dimanche', thus emphasizing separate worlds and the theme of *exil* (cf. 'mes seules amours'); or it may be a challenging address to the universal reader (the equivalent, in this new context, of Baudelaire's '*Tu* le connais, lecteur, ce monstre délicat, / – Hypocrite lecteur, – mon semblable, – mon frère!' in the poem *Au lecteur*), asking if he has truly penetrated the veil of distractions to see the bleak underside of life.

Section 10. 'Non, non!' is Laforgue's unambiguous final answer to cosseted illusions, and to his own falsely naïve question 'Serez-vous pas…'. Instead of the décor or *paradis artificiels* one finds an eerie planet sapped of its life-blood, and the frustrations of Time everlasting. Time just goes on and on, progressing but never getting anywhere (cf. the spatial equivalent of this in the form of the 'spleens kilométriques' of the telegraph wires which go on interminably; and the artistic equivalent in the 'Tous les ans, tous les ans…' by which the artist is doomed to repeat his puny efforts, year after year, to capture what defies grasp). The image of Time is a miniature parody of the legend of Penelope's web: Ulysses' wife, hard pressed by suitors in his absence, promised to make a choice when a web that she was weaving was finished, but each night she undid what she had put together during the day (cf. Laforgue's *Complainte du Roi de Thulé*, 'Broder…un certain Voile…De vive toile'). Here the image not only opens the poem on to a wider temporal perspective (which was where it began, cf. 'La Toussaint, la Noël et la Nouvelle Année'), but it draws together the references to 'toiles d'araignées' and 'patience d'ange', also aiming a last dig at the world of 'lainages', summed up in the unusually incongruous picture of Time preoccupied with the domesticated activity of knitting woolly house-slippers which will never materialize.

Note that the very last words remind one of the extent to which *L'Hiver qui vient* is a sound-poem, characterized by its multiplicity of voice. The work represents an original treatment of the theme of time (quite distinct from Lamartine's 'ô temps suspends ton vol'), opening the way for Apollinaire's unpredictable, supple and fragmented free verse some twenty-five years later.

Paul Valéry

(1871–1945)

La Ceinture

Quand le ciel couleur d'une joue
Laisse enfin les yeux le chérir
Et qu'au point doré de périr
Dans les roses le temps se joue, 4

Devant le muet de plaisir
Qu'enchaîne une telle peinture,
Danse une Ombre à libre ceinture
Que le soir est près de saisir. 8

Cette ceinture vagabonde
Fait dans le souffle aérien
Frémir le suprême lien
De mon silence avec ce monde... 12

Absent, présent ... Je suis bien seul,
Et sombre, ô suave linceul. 14

La Ceinture

Lines 1–4. 'Je n'ai pu comprendre cette pièce...Je ne sais point du tout ce qu'est cette ceinture', confesses Alain in his commentary on *La Ceinture*. And yet the progression of the poem from golden sunset ('au point doré...') to darkening night ('sombre, ô suave linceul') is not difficult to appreciate; nor is the theme of the contemplative poet confronted with the beauty of twilight. The real obscurity arises when one seeks to give meaning to the 'Ombre à libre ceinture' who dances across the scene, disturbing the serene communion of poet and world and foreshadowing nightfall and solitude.

The first movement of the poem (lines 1–8) is descriptive and the tone relatively impersonal. The opening stanza, with its two time-clauses, builds up an expectation of an event; the moment is one of special tenderness and fragility, balanced precariously between a time of blinding sunlight, now past ('le ciel... / Laisse enfin les yeux le chérir'), and an imminent blackness ('au point doré de périr'). Study the skill with which Valéry has introduced notions of colour: the associations of feminine beauty in the first line and the subsequent suggestion of a theme of love, the verbal inventiveness of inserting 'doré' into the expression *au point de* (cf. the phrase *au point du jour*), the ambiguity of the plural 'les roses' which could be a visual impression or an amorous symbol. The pink flush and changing tints of sunset seem to be time itself, indulging in a last act of easy movement and bravado before yielding to night. One might say that time was enjoying a moment of reprieve and liberty from its fatal cycles. The backcloth is now painted, ready for the entrance of the 'Ombre', a figure who, by dancing evasively in the face of ravishment and disappearance, is to show the same carefree attitude as 'le temps'.

Lines 5–8. The poet (discreetly hidden behind the impersonal 'muet de plaisir' – again note the inventiveness and concentration in Valéry's use of language) is captivated by the beauty of the moment. The verb 'enchaîne' brings in the first image of union or attachment; in this second stanza, the theme is played for the moment in a minor key, the link between 'le muet de plaisir' and the 'peinture' seeming to be based on no more than the charm of the picturesque. By what means (rhythmical, phonetic, syntactical, typographical) is the apparition of 'une Ombre' made so emphatic? Study the way in which Valéry underlines the unity of lines 1–8 as a cohesive section of development (look at the handling of the rhymes, the balanced syntax, the chiastic relationship between lines 3–4 and lines 7–8).

The 'Ombre' is an enigmatic figure partly because she comes as a disturbing personification into a scene which, visually, is quite familiar, partly because she could either be a simple shadow (seeming to dance in the fading light) or a more ethereal ghost-like presence (presaging the theme of death), partly because she is qualified by a specific yet puzzling phrase, 'à libre ceinture', with its paradoxical ideas of freedom and restraint. It has been suggested that she is a dusky cloud formation in the sky and the 'ceinture' a band of uncertain light the disappearance of which will break the poet's link with the world. Certainly there is the prospect, as yet only faintly suggested, of an intervention ('*Devant* le muet...') between the onlooker and the object of his contemplation.

Lines 9–12. But to penetrate further into this image of the belt it is perhaps worth distinguishing between the notions contained in 'enchaîne', 'ceinture' and 'lien', three words which forge a discernible pattern in the poem's structure. Both 'enchaîne' and 'lien' suggest the joining of two things and refer here to the poet's silent union across space with the natural world. The symbolic value of 'la ceinture', on the other hand, could well be one of interiority and isolation, since the belt only links with itself. The fact that the belt here is 'libre' and 'vagabonde' gives it an apparent freedom of movement (even if only a fleeting one before death); but it does not erase the idea of self-enclosure and containment which is the essential accompaniment and even a defining factor of this 'Ombre'. Perhaps she is the symbolic reminder that 'la ceinture' is the true image of the human condition, and that the poet's 'suprême lien' (the symbol of outward-reaching communion) can be no more than a wishful and ephemeral bond with the beauty of the world. The implications of solitude and detachment (the belt, because 'libre' and 'vagabonde' denies the immobile relationship, and being circular in its motions, disrupts the direct line of contemplation) forewarn the poet of his inevitable divorce from a higher beauty and shake the momentary ecstasy of his communion. His pleasure and adoration are on the point of dying, ready to be engulfed by passing time (in this respect, compare the poet's static silence with the attitudes of 'le temps' and 'une Ombre', two other victims of nightfall, as implied in the verbs 'se joue' and 'Danse'). Study the way in which Valéry has preserved a formal continuity between the first movement and this stanza; the expressive use of sound in these lines; the full associations of 'frémir' (fear, danger, excitement); the significance of the *points de suspension*. Note all the accumulated impressions of movement in this stanza; the suggestion of an evening breeze and possibly a nocturnal chill; the way in which what was originally expressed as a comparatively superficial, visual relationship ('couleur d'une joue...les yeux le chérir...peinture') is now made to seem all-important ('suprême'), more universal in significance, and given inner depth ('De mon silence').

Lines 13–14. The poem is a sonnet or, more strictly, a *quatorzain* since the division of a sonnet into three quatrains and a couplet is not traditionally admissible in French versification (although it is common in English Elizabethan poetry). Mallarmé uses the same configuration in *Au seul souci de voyager...* What are the advantages of establishing a series of quatrains and then isolating the final couplet? How does Valéry exploit them in this poem? Disturbed by the ripple of the 'ceinture vagabonde', the poet wavers between two apparently opposite states of mind, absence being the loss of the self in the meditation of beauty, and presence, the awareness of self, time and death (cf. *Les Pas*: 'Douceur d'être et de n'être pas'). Consciousness of self (the three dots after 'présent' show that it is becoming more and more acutely felt as night falls) finally snaps the 'suprême lien' and the poet is left to realize his own solitude. Note how the conclusion fulfils all that was foreboding in the second stanza: 'sombre' echoes 'Ombre' in sound and meaning, and the idea of enclosure and isolation in 'ceinture' is given sinister emphasis in the image of the 'linceul' (the pall of night, one presumes; cf. the last tercet of Baudelaire's *Recueillement*). The final sentence with its alliterative stress, rich rhyme, invocation and paradox marks the end of a movement towards a more personal and more direct expression, as if the *moi* of the poem has moved from absence to presence, from intercourse to introspection, from the notions behind 'enchaîne' and 'lien' to the symbolic import of 'la ceinture'. These transitions accompany the gradual fading of light, the gentle smoothing of dusk into night. It is a time of day which has often been thought of as subtly poetic; one should make a detailed comparison between this poem and others which draw their inspiration from the twilight hour (e.g. Hugo's *J'ai cueilli cette fleur...*, Baudelaire's *Harmonie du soir* and *Recueillement*). One could think here of the Orpheus legend, Orpheus being the traditional symbol of the poet: at the moment that he turned to cast his eyes on his loved one ('Laisse enfin les yeux le chérir'), that momentary glimpse, so long coveted, was turned into loss ('...au point doré de périr'), and Eurydice, swirled in gloom ('une Ombre à libre ceinture'), was snatched from the poet's eyes and taken back into the ultimate realm of darkness, leaving him emphatically alone ('Je suis *bien* seul') with an awareness of the incontrovertible force of death ('...linceul'). But there is perhaps an element of optimism here in that the poet alone, though frustratingly severed from the beauty with which he would wish to remain forever linked, does not himself sink into the grip of darkness but remains excluded in his own self-awareness.

Le Cimetière marin

Ce toit tranquille, où marchent des colombes,
Entre les pins palpite, entre les tombes;
Midi le juste y compose de feux
La mer, la mer, toujours recommencée!

O récompense après une pensée
Qu'un long regard sur le calme des dieux! 6

Quel pur travail de fins éclairs consume
Maint diamant d'imperceptible écume,
Et quelle paix semble se concevoir!
Quand sur l'abîme un soleil se repose,
Ouvrages purs d'une éternelle cause,
Le Temps scintille et le Songe est savoir. 12

Stable trésor, temple simple à Minerve,
Masse de calme, et visible réserve,
Eau sourcilleuse, Œil qui gardes en toi
Tant de sommeil sous un voile de flamme,
O mon silence!... Edifice dans l'âme,
Mais comble d'or aux mille tuiles, Toit! 18

Temple du Temps, qu'un seul soupir résume,
A ce point pur je monte et m'accoutume,
Tout entouré de mon regard marin;
Et comme aux dieux mon offrande suprême,
La scintillation sereine sème
Sur l'altitude un dédain souverain. 24

Comme le fruit se fond en jouissance,
Comme en délice il change son absence
Dans une bouche où sa forme se meurt,
Je hume ici ma future fumée,
Et le ciel chante à l'âme consumée
Le changement des rives en rumeur. 30

Beau ciel, vrai ciel, regarde-moi qui change!
Après tant d'orgueil, après tant d'étrange
Oisiveté, mais pleine de pouvoir,
Je m'abandonne à ce brillant espace,
Sur les maisons des morts mon ombre passe
Qui m'apprivoise à son frêle mouvoir. 36

L'âme exposée aux torches du solstice,
Je te soutiens, admirable justice
De la lumière aux armes sans pitié!
Je te rends pure à ta place première:
Regarde-toi!... Mais rendre la lumière
Suppose d'ombre une morne moitié. 42

O pour moi seul, à moi seul, en moi-même,
Auprès d'un cœur, aux sources du poème,

Entre le vide et l'événement pur,
J'attends l'écho de ma grandeur interne,
Amère, sombre et sonore citerne,
Sonnant dans l'âme un creux toujours futur!   48

Sais-tu, fausse captive des feuillages,
Golfe mangeur de ces maigres grillages,
Sur mes yeux clos, secrets éblouissants,
Quel corps me traîne à sa fin paresseuse,
Quel front l'attire à cette terre osseuse?
Une étincelle y pense à mes absents.   54

Fermé, sacré, plein d'un feu sans matière,
Fragment terrestre offert à la lumière,
Ce lieu me plaît, dominé de flambeaux,
Composé d'or, de pierre et d'arbres sombres,
Où tant de marbre est tremblant sur tant d'ombres;
La mer fidèle y dort sur mes tombeaux!   60

Chienne splendide, écarte l'idolâtre!
Quand solitaire au sourire de pâtre,
Je pais longtemps, moutons mystérieux,
Le blanc troupeau de mes tranquilles tombes,
Eloignes-en les prudentes colombes,
Les songes vains, les anges curieux!   66

Ici venu, l'avenir est paresse.
L'insecte net gratte la sécheresse;
Tout est brûlé, défait, reçu dans l'air
A je ne sais quelle sévère essence...
La vie est vaste, étant ivre d'absence,
Et l'amertume est douce, et l'esprit clair.   72

Les morts cachés sont bien dans cette terre
Qui les réchauffe et sèche leur mystère.
Midi là-haut, Midi sans mouvement
En soi se pense et convient à soi-même...
Tête complète et parfait diadème,
Je suis en toi le secret changement.   78

Tu n'as que moi pour contenir tes craintes!
Mes repentirs, mes doutes, mes contraintes
Sont le défaut de ton grand diamant...
Mais dans leur nuit toute lourde de marbres,
Un peuple vague aux racines des arbres
A pris déjà ton parti lentement.   84

Ils ont fondu dans une absence épaisse,
L'argile rouge a bu la blanche espèce,
Le don de vivre a passé dans les fleurs!
Où sont des morts les phrases familières,
L'art personnel, les âmes singulières?
La larve file où se formaient des pleurs.　　　　90

Les cris aigus des filles chatouillées,
Les yeux, les dents, les paupières mouillées,
Le sein charmant qui joue avec le feu,
Le sang qui brille aux lèvres qui se rendent,
Les derniers dons, les doigts qui les défendent,
Tout va sous terre et rentre dans le jeu!　　　　96

Et vous, grande âme, espérez-vous un songe
Qui n'aura plus ces couleurs de mensonge
Qu'aux yeux de chair l'onde et l'or font ici?
Chanterez-vous quand serez vaporeuse?
Allez! Tout fuit! Ma présence est poreuse,
La sainte impatience meurt aussi!　　　　102

Maigre immortalité noire et dorée,
Consolatrice affreusement laurée,
Qui de la mort fais un sein maternel,
Le beau mensonge et la pieuse ruse!
Qui ne connaît, et qui ne les refuse,
Ce crâne vide et ce rire éternel!　　　　108

Pères profonds, têtes inhabitées,
Qui sous le poids de tant de pelletées,
Etes la terre et confondez nos pas,
Le vrai rongeur, le ver irréfutable
N'est point pour vous qui dormez sous la table,
Il vit de vie, il ne me quitte pas!　　　　114

Amour, peut-être, ou de moi-même haine?
Sa dent secrète est de moi si prochaine
Que tous les noms lui peuvent convenir!
Qu'importe! Il voit, il veut, il songe, il touche!
Ma chair lui plaît, et jusque sur ma couche,
A ce vivant je vis d'appartenir!　　　　120

Zénon! Cruel Zénon! Zénon d'Elée!
M'as-tu percé de cette flèche ailée
Qui vibre, vole, et qui ne vole pas!
Le son m'enfante et la flèche me tue!

Ah! le soleil... Quelle ombre de tortue
Pour l'âme, Achille immobile à grands pas! 126

Non, non!... Debout! Dans l'ère successive!
Brisez, mon corps, cette forme pensive!
Buvez, mon sein, la naissance du vent!
Une fraîcheur, de la mer exhalée,
Me rend mon âme... O puissance salée!
Courons à l'onde en rejaillir vivant! 132

Oui! Grande mer de délires douée,
Peau de panthère et chlamyde trouée
De mille et mille idoles du soleil,
Hydre absolue, ivre de ta chair bleue,
Qui te remords l'étincelante queue
Dans un tumulte au silence pareil, 138

Le vent se lève!... Il faut tenter de vivre!
L'air immense ouvre et referme mon livre,
La vague en poudre ose jaillir des rocs!
Envolez-vous, pages tout éblouies!
Rompez, vagues! Rompez d'eaux réjouies
Ce toit tranquille où picoraient des focs! 144

Le Cimetière marin

Stanza 1. A poem which has been translated into all the major languages and which has become one of the most celebrated in French literature, *Le Cimetière marin* is a work fascinating not only in its final form but also in its genesis. Valéry traces its beginning to an obsessive rhythm which haunted his mind, an empty mould of meaningless syllables which he recognized as a decasyllabic line. Spurred on by the creative demon of form, he then accepted that his poem should be written in six-line stanzas, that it should be long, and that 'entre les strophes, des contrastes ou des correspondances devaient être institués'. For Valéry, these formal pre-conditions seemed to demand that the content should be:

> un monologue de 'moi', dans lequel les thèmes les plus simples et les plus constants de ma vie affective et intellectuelle, tels qu'ils s'étaient imposés à mon adolescence et associés à la mer et à la lumière d'un certain lieu des bords de la Méditerranée, fussent appelés, tramés, opposés...

These remarks are interesting in that they give an insight into the self-analytical workings of this particular poetic mind (poets are usually reticent about such things) and its faith in the creative power of form; but they also serve as a useful starting-point in a reading of the poem. We know that the poem will be an examination of the self, that this monologue will be staged in a very specific theatre (the Mediterranean, the sunlight, the cemetery at Sète), that it will involve forces of both the emotions and the intellect, and that the structure, avoiding the purely linear, will depend on echo and contrast, on shimmering variations of tone and rapid changes of thought.

The opening couplet, so balanced, so elevated in its literary inversions, so rich in phonetic patterns (e.g. 'tran*quille*...*co*l*o*mbes', '*tran*quille...*entre*'), introduces through description many of the major themes: peace ('tranquille'), purity ('colombes'), stability ('toit') and death ('tombes'). Even more importantly, it introduces the poet's imaginative power for we are to discover that the roof is the sea (with waves like overlapping tiles) and the doves are white-sailed boats (look at the last two lines of the whole poem). There is a feeling of satisfaction and visual enjoyment in the poet's words: the scene is one of eternal perfection, the overhead sun casts few shadows, poised at the solstice like an incorruptible arbiter and beating down evenly on all things, and the sea is ablaze with reflective images of divine power. Analyse the metrical structure of this first verse and consider whether Valéry has succeeded in infusing his decasyllables with the grandeur of the Alexandrine ('Le démon de la généralisation suggérait de tenter de porter ce *Dix* à la puissance du *Douze*'). Note how already in this and the following stanza a balance is established, to be intricately developed as the poem progresses, between the immobile and the restless, the permanent and the everchanging (human thought, presumably, being part of the restlessness, though for the moment magnificently saved from itself in this consummate vision).

Stanza 2. The poet's excited gaze is fascinated by the divine artistry present in the spectacle of the sunlit sea and by the infinite play of formation ('compose... travail...se concevoir...ouvrages') and disintegration ('consume'), of calm and everlasting motion. Time does not stand still but neither does it change; the poet is witnessing the Immutable in its incessant manifestations. So we have the abstract captured in the physical, the absolute in a pin-point of light, and the great unverifiable dream imposing itself as certainty. (For further comments on the language of this stanza, see the section on words and their tones in the Introduction.)

Stanza 3. Note the fluent transition, phonetically ('Temps scintille... temple simple') and by associative imagery ('Maint diamant...Stable trésor'). How appropriate is the introduction of Minerva at this point? The still, pensive waters of the sea return the poet's gaze and this sense of being contemplated brings about the first turning-point of the poem. The protagonist recognizes that the sea is his own correlative (cf. 'Masse de calme' and 'O mon silence', 'Toit' and 'Edifice dans l'âme'), and that, just as the sea has hidden depth and darkness beneath a burning surface, his soul too has a deep, interior architecture (cf. the ending of *Les Grenades*), crowned by this possibility for luminous meditative ecstasy. Study in this verse the accumulated suggestions of permanency; the enthusiastic sound-patterns, culminating in the overlapping 'mille tuiles, Toit'; the significance of the capital letter now given to 'Toit'. The original image of 'toit tranquille' has expanded to become 'temple' and finally 'Toit' (a kind of roof of the world and of consciousness, reflecting the divine).

Stanza 4. Having identified himself with the sea and become the centre of its gaze (cf. 'Eau sourcilleuse, Œil...' and 'Tout entouré de mon regard marin'), having joined the sacred ('Temple du Temps') and the ineffable (compare 'qu'un seul soupir résume' with 'mon silence'), the poet reaches the zenith of his contemplation (note the stress on height in these lines). He feels almost haughtily proud (cf. 'dédain souverain' with the earlier 'sourcilleuse'); and at this point of contact with the Absolute, the sea offers to the gods a shimmering reflection of their divine indifference. The protagonist and his correlative, the sea (cf. Baudelaire's lines 'Homme libre... La mer est ton miroir; tu contemples ton âme/ Dans le déroulement infini de sa lame'), seem to combine with the sky in a timeless unity; but this intense sensation of eternity cannot last, and is already threatened by the negative implications of the movement from 'paix' and 'calme des dieux' to 'dédain'. Note again the balance of opposite characteristics: massive presence and stability ('Temple du Temps'), and the proximity to airy nothingness ('qu'un seul soupir résume').

Stanza 5. The tone alters; the vocabulary becomes more sensuously physical and images of permanency give way to images of change and dissolution. The exquisite pleasure of the poet is an ambiguous one. He foresees his death, conceived of as a joyous self-sacrifice, as a transformation similar to that undergone by a fruit that one is eating or by some material object consumed by fire. The moment's access to eternity is felt as a passage from material form and substance into a quintessential sweetness, but it is simultaneously a foretaste of his own physical annihilation (the image of 'fumée' keeps the link with the idea of 'Temple' and sacrifice to the gods). Note how the heavens seem to reign serenely over this 'offrande suprême', so that the poet and the sea share the same fate, and the sky stands apart as a symbol of the Absolute. What senses are appealed to in this very rich stanza?

Stanza 6. The theme of change takes deeper root: change from pride (cf. 'sourcilleuse...dédain') to self-abandon, from contemplative 'oisiveté' (cf. 'O récompense...') to more firmly willed action; from the warm pulpiness of fruit to the intimations of coldness in 'maisons des morts' and 'mon ombre'. As the poet realizes his own mutability he turns towards the heavens (the Immutable) and confesses his pride in a gesture of self-immolation. He addresses the sky (the 'vrai ciel', not its reflection in the sea) and hopes to become the perfect focus of its gaze, fused in a vertical relationship with it, just as, previously, he was 'Tout entouré de mon regard marin'. But this divinity which is both luminosity and absence, vitality and void, leaves an unsettling sense of ghostliness and death; and the 'brillant espace', instead of absorbing him, projects his shadow. Examine the various ways in which Valéry evokes the unsubstantiality of the human spirit in stanzas 5 and 6.

Stanza 7. The willing sacrifice of the soul consumed by fire and light continues (cf. the close link between supreme fulfilment and self-abolition developed here with a similar idea in Rimbaud's *L'Eternité*). The poet now takes on the rôle of the sea which is to reflect light back to its source in recognition of the heavens' supremacy. Note that 'feux', 'Midi le juste' and 'pur travail', at first associated with the sea, become the poet's prerogative: 'torches...justice... pure'. He will act as a mirror for the Absolute (cf. the movement from 'regardemoi' in the previous stanza to 'Regarde-toi') so that it can know its own majesty. Trace the variations on the theme of the gaze which have appeared in the poem so far. Could one say that the *points de suspension* after the imperative fulfil a similar function to those in stanza 3? Like the sea, like the silvering of a mirror, like any object in sunlight, the poet has 'une morne moitié' (cf. 'Tant de sommeil sous un voile de flamme' in stanza 3) and it is this reminder of his own mysterious depths (which distinguish him so obviously from 'la lumière') that halts the process of fulfilment and forces the poet to look inward. In what way is the imperative made to seem ironic?

Stanza 8. The broad development of the poem up to this point has been from a vision of the sea and sky in reflective splendour; to the poet taking over the rôle of the sea and offering himself to the blazing look of the divine; to the awareness of his own evanescence and mortality in contrast to the Absolute, and his own duality of light and inner dark in contrast to the pure luminosity of the divine. At this moment, Valéry's meditation turns inwards to sound the realm of his own 'ombre'. The self is isolated in that area of poetic sensibility which lies between a feeling of total nothingness and an act of purity (e.g. the writing of a poem or any creative act which would translate being into perfection). The image of reflection returns in an auditory form ('l'écho de ma grandeur interne'); the self, if it cannot unite outwards and upwards with the Absolute, at least seeks confirmation of an inner grandeur and wants to achieve a personal unity between the surface *moi* and a deeper, more harmonious *moi* (apprehended by Rimbaud and expressed in his striking phrase 'JE est un autre'). But the 'creux' will never be filled ('toujours futur'); knowledge of the self will always be incomplete; and the poet, far from being accepted into the 'Temple du Temps', is aware of himself as the running victim of time. Explore the image of the 'citerne'.

Stanza 9. Now that one quest for pure communion has failed, exposing his own 'creux', the poet's thoughts turn back to the sea, the cemetery and the theme of death (prepared by 'tombes...maisons des morts...morne...amère... sombre'). The question is the first in the poem and, contrasting sharply with the confident 'le Songe est savoir', it stresses the changed mood of the protagonist. What image of the sea is evoked in the address 'fausse captive des feuillages, / Golfe mangeur de ces maigres grillages'? Does it complement any previous descriptions? What signs are there of a disenchantment with the sea as an authentic image of himself? The poet is the real prisoner (despite the parallel of a dazzling point of contact and a sombre underside, the poet–sea relationship is now one of contrast) in that he suffers the erosion and is inexorably pulled towards death. This despondent stanza finishes on a note of independence; the sea and her 'fins éclairs' may be indifferent but the spark which is the poet's intellect can think sympathetically of those buried in the cemetery, 'mes absents'. And although this single 'étincelle' seems meagre as a source of light compared with the multiple 'feux' of the sea in the first stanza, this sign of illumination gives man a special status: he can feel death within him and yet has the power to transcend it through thought.

Stanza 10. This leads to a closer identification, not with the sea or the sky, but with the earth and with the sacredness of the cemetery as a more human meeting-point (cf. '*mes* absents' and '*mes* tombeaux') of eternity and mortality, light and dark. Make a detailed comparison between this description of the cemetery and the earlier one of the sea (stanzas 1–3). Rather than risk dispersion in some vast spiritual adventure, the poet now prefers to link himself with the enclosed ('fermé'), the delimited and familiar ('Fragment terrestre'). How does the image of the sea initiated in the last line of this verse fit in with this change of attitude? (Note the similarity between this line and the last line of the previous stanza.)

Stanza 11. The sea and the cemetery are fused by Valéry's brilliant use of words: 'tranquilles' and 'colombes' recall the opening line of the poem; 'moutons mystérieux' suggest flecks of foam on the sea while actually referring to the white marble tombstones in the cemetery. The ornaments on the graves (doves and angels) are vain, unnecessary outward signs of death, the purity of which will be guarded by the sea ('chienne splendide') and the poet ('solitaire au sourire de pâtre'). So the poet here, in collaboration with the sea, envisages himself as a kind of shepherd of the dead, who need no more than this immaterial fire, this blaze of gold and these natural 'flambeaux' (whether cypress trees or tongues of flame from the sea and sky), and for whom the artificial forms of religion can only be trivia.

Stanza 12. The 'future fumée' and 'creux toujours futur' find their echo in the ideas of evaporation and absence which are associated with the cemetery; it is a place of ascetic purity (this explains the two imperatives 'écarte. . .éloignes-en') which offers the poet yet another path to follow in his examination of the self and the Absolute. Study the contrasts between this picture of harsh dryness and monastic austerity and the earlier image of ripened fruit and hedonistic enjoyment; the expressive and surprisingly specific second line of the stanza; the seeming paradox between asceticism and intoxication (is there perhaps an image of distillation of alcohol hidden in these lines?); the oxymoron of 'l'amertume est douce'; and the renewed calm and confidence of the poet witnessed in the reflective generalizations.

Stanza 13. The poet's meditation has brought him to a state of lucidity ('esprit clair') in which life seems to be clarified, chastened to its essentials, and in which the dead hold no mystery. The idea of heat and dryness directs the mind to 'Midi là-haut'. The central lines of this verse form a clear contrast to lines 46–8: the Absolute is self-knowing and self-sufficient while the poet is always waiting for the echo in the soundings of his inner being. Once again the *points de suspension* herald the poet's turning inward to contemplate his own self. He now recognizes that his image is not to be found in the dead, whose contradictions and obscurities have been eliminated in a kind of transparent wisdom while he is still 'secret changement'; and that his uniqueness is not as a pure mirror made to reflect the glory of the sun, but as a being of change and dissatisfaction marring the perfect glittering immobility of the Absolute.

Stanza 14. He alone, as a complex of emotions, conscience and effort (which imply movement, restlessness and conflict), stands apart as a foreign body from that 'sévère essence'. By his awareness of separation from the Absolute, he is the flaw in the harmony of the universe. Might the three nouns of the second line be connected with the idea of artistic creation and the poet's rôle? The exultant but somewhat negative pride of the poet, asserting the importance of man as an undermining imperfection created by the Absolute within itself (cf. this pride with the very different 'dédain' and 'orgueil' in stanzas 4 and 6), is short-lived, for death can eradicate the blemish of human isolation and convert men into accomplices of 'Midi'. The feeling of sympathy in the possessive adjectives of 'mes absents . . . mes tombeaux . . . mes tranquilles tombes' and in the shepherd-image fades as the 'peuple vague' of the cemetery is seen to be absorbed into the non-human. To what extent does Valéry achieve a balance of contrasts in this stanza?

Stanza 15. Ironically, the absorption of the dead into the soil is described in terms which recall the poet's ecstatic savouring of his own death and dispersion into the air in stanza 5. What is the effect of the paradox 'absence épaisse'; of the periphrasis 'la blanche espèce'; of the colour contrast? While the mineral and the vegetal draw sustenance from man's physical decomposition, his affective life and creative expressions disintegrate, leaving no trace. The disconsolate question heightens the tone of pathos in these lines which end on a gruesome concrete image expressing death's triumph over the individuality of emotions. Contrast the impersonality of the description in this stanza with the self-imagined distinction of 'Tu n'as que moi. . .' previously.

Stanza 16. The doleful tableau of death is rapidly followed by an extraordinary, contrasting picture of excited sexual seduction; but the excitement is created only to be doused by the brutal realism of the last line. What rhythm is established by the long enumeration? Does this little erotic scene appear incongruous in this poem? What justification would you give it? Note the expressive alliteration of the first line; the retention of the words 'feu' and 'brille' here as reminders of other scenes; the play on words in 'joue avec le feu'; the difference between the fate of 'Le don de vivre' in the preceding stanza and these 'derniers dons'. The unambiguous conclusion marks an important step in the poet's thoughts: after first taking the side of the dead, and then being inevitably deserted by them, he is finally forced to recognize that human life is no more than a brief spasm of movement which temporarily breaks the rules of eternal immobility.

Stanza 17. After this conclusive negation of the survival of the body or of anything which has constituted the physical joys of existence, it is natural that the poet should turn to question what fond hopes the soul, for its part, entertains. The spiritual quest and the optimistic self-sacrifice ('l'âme exposée aux torches du solstice') which appeared in the earlier part of the poem are both cast into doubt and finally scorned by the clear-minded poet (the address to his own 'grande âme' is meant as a challenging ironic echo of 'grandeur interne'); his meditations were as vain as ornaments on tombstones, and the sea and the sky offered false hopes of communion. What indeed can the soul hope for which could be more substantial than this play of appearances, glittering illusion? Contrast the unambitious use of the word 'songe' here with the earlier 'le Songe', and these 'yeux de chair' with the prestigious 'Œil'. Notice how images of substance ('toit... temple... masse') are replaced by images of superficiality ('couleurs de mensonge'). How is this tone of self-taunting sustained (cf. the contrasting tones of lines 100 and 101 which ridicule poetic pretentions while at the same time ridiculing metaphysical ones)? What aspects of poetic ambition are particularly mocked? Compare this movement of self-awareness with that in stanzas 5 and 8.

Stanza 18. In the growing cynicism of the poet, the pretentious monuments sculptured for immortality are rejected as deceitful, empty consolations, gilding the unpalatable. Human art, like the immortality it embellishes, is a 'beau mensonge'. This stanza takes up the ideas of stanza 11 but contrasts significantly with the calm, pastoral idyll of the shepherd and his dog guarding the 'blanc troupeau'. What is 'ce rire éternel'? Note how Valéry has juxtaposed contrasting words in this stanza to counterbalance, even cancel, each other (thus dramatizing contradiction and negation).

Stanza 19. The tone of disgust at false illusions drops briefly into one of black humour: 'profonds' suggests underground depth as well as depth of wisdom (and in this second sense is wryly contradicted by 'inhabitées'); the image of the dead lying drunk under the table (which is also the stone slab of the tomb) picturesquely recalls the idea of intoxication in stanza 12. The consideration of something outside the self once more initiates a process of reflection which leads the thinker back to his own state; the gnawing worms in the cemetery can be dismissed, for the real erosive force is within the poet himself as a part of his consciousness or, indeed, as consciousness itself. Its identity is left vague for the moment; only its presence is felt. Note the distance that has been covered, in this poem of debate about truth and falsity, between the early 'vrai ciel', seen as a brilliant source of certainty and salvation, and the present 'vrai rongeur', working in the inner dark and far more certain.

Stanza 20. The most intimate emotions ('amour... haine'), which were once proudly perceived as the source of 'le secret changement', the flaw in the diamond, are now the secret 'rongeur' which lives within the conscious mind, which thrives on the senses ('voit...touche'), the intellect ('veut...songe') and the body ('Ma chair lui plaît'), and even invades the refuge of sleep ('jusque sur ma couche'). The restlessness of consciousness is both creative and destructive, a form of self-love and self-torment, a proof of life (cf. 'cogito ergo sum') and the force which eventually wears man to nothing. The protagonist's dilemma has worsened in that he cannot reconcile himself to either the immobility of the Absolute or the mobility of human consciousness. Compare the concluding lines of stanzas 18, 19 and 20 (among other things, the as if involuntary presence of the sound 'vide' as a nagging accompaniment to the idea of life).

Stanza 21. The paradox of his situation makes the poet think of Zeno of Elea, a Greek philosopher, who maintained that neither movement nor life existed, an argument supported by a series of famous paradoxes: an arrow in flight, at any given moment, occupies its own length and therefore cannot be moving; Achilles will never catch the tortoise since, by the time he has reached the place where the tortoise was, the tortoise will always have gone a little further ahead. If these are true, then all movement must be illusion. According to Valéry himself, these lines 'ont pour rôle de compenser, par une tonalité métaphysique, le sensuel et le "trop humain" des strophes antécédentes'. The abstractions are certainly a long way from the erotic descriptions in stanza 16 and represent a kind of 'crise de l'intellect' just as they represented a 'crise des sens': on the one hand, sensual certainties destined to nothingness, on the other, intellectual ingenuities doomed to be locked in paralysing self-contradiction. The arrow here, in Valéry's terms, is probably the arrow of intellectual self-awareness, simultaneously moving and motionless, creative and useless, full of vitality and death-dealing. The mind's quest for the Absolute is equally paradoxical; like the 'creux toujours futur', the sun, the tortoise's shadow, will always be beyond the human grasp, so slow in its movements that it seems immobile but eternally evasive. The intellectual meditation has reached an impasse. How significant, in view of line 128, is the *enjambement* of 'Quelle ombre de tortue / Pour l'âme'?

Stanza 22. The prison of abstract thought woven by Zeno's sophistry is firmly rejected (the 'Non, non!' answering the repetition of 'Zénon'; 'Debout! Dans l'ère successive!' stressing the idea of spatial and temporal movement, a reconciliation with living time as opposed to the atemporal grandeur of the 'Temple du Temps') and the poet casts aside arid speculation ('forme pensive') in favour of a physical reawakening, and contemplation in favour of action. The 'naissance du vent' here (cf. 'm'enfante' in the previous stanza) is a birth, spontaneous and unselfconscious, with no opposite to negate it. The soul will be reconstituted through a baptism in nature, through bodily, not philosophical, awareness. What features are now present in the scene which were not there before?

Stanza 23. Affirmative, dynamic, the poet plunges into an atmosphere of irrational joy. There are suddenly several echoes of Rimbaud's *Le Bateau ivre*: in common words such as 'mer...mille...soleil...ivre...bleue', in less common words such as 'délires...peau de panthère...trouée' and in the depiction of a sea-monster; make a careful comparison between Valéry's conclusion and Rimbaud's poem (and note also the demands for purification which dominate the last lines of *Après le déluge*). The sea has become turbulent ('de délires douée'), full of bestial grace and with a sensual sheen ('peau de panthère') and exploding with thousands of suns which shoot through the 'chlamyde' (a cloak worn by the

Greeks, and perhaps symbolizing the discarded Greek philosophy of stanza 21). Study the implications of the image of the hydra. If one returns to the first stanza, one notices that it is not the stability of 'Midi le juste' which has been retained but the image (or rather the endless multiple images) of 'La mer, la mer, toujours recommencée', not the peace of the gods but the activity of 'Maint diamant d'imperceptible écume'. Instead of the eternal fire, the emphasis is on the sea's carnal cloak, appealing to the senses like flesh and fur. Instead of the 'ivre d'absence' of stanza 12, we have 'ivre de ta chair bleue'. And instead of offering itself as a mirror to the lordly brilliance of the heavens, it bites its own glittering tail, looping round and round on itself in a gesture of self-sufficiency (a 'parfait diadème' of another order). (It is important that, in a Mediterranean setting, the stillness of baking noon is often followed by an onshore breeze: hence the world breaking from the static vertical light and immobility replicates the poet's move-ment from meditative self-absorption into resolve and thrusting aspiration.) Note that this penultimate stanza is the only one to end on a comma, thus anti-cipating a dramatic continuity with the finale.

Stanza 24.　The final verse is one of excited movement, dispersion and violent rejoicing. The stable apprehension of the scene which began the poem disinte-grates; the 'temple simple à Minerve' and the 'ouvrages purs' offered to this goddess of wisdom and the arts crumble as the poet throws his work open to the wind, sea and light and the sea breaks its mood of calm meditation. The line 'Envolez-vous, pages tout éblouies' implies the retransformation of arduous thought and artistry into liberty of movement and involvement in life, and the flight of his pages is the liberation of the poet to a new recreative experience. What is the effect of the return to 'Ce toit tranquille'? In what way is the context different? The conclusion is a triumphant reaffirmation of human mobility and life's transience, chosen in preference to the immobility of the Absolute and the eternity of death; and a call to action which will bring down the curtain on tortuous meditation and act as its complete answer.

How far would you accept Gustave Cohen's comment on *Le Cimetière marin* : '. . .ce drame métaphysique, dont le pathétique est celui de l'intellect, est en même temps un drame lyrique' ?

Guillaume Apollinaire

(1880–1918)

La Tzigane

La tzigane savait d'avance
Nos deux vies barrées par les nuits
Nous lui dîmes adieu et puis
De ce puits sortit l'Espérance   4

L'amour lourd comme un ours privé
Dansa debout quand nous voulûmes
Et l'oiseau bleu perdit ses plumes
Et les mendiants leurs *Ave*   8

On sait très bien que l'on se damne
Mais l'espoir d'aimer en chemin
Nous fait penser main dans la main
A ce qu'a prédit la tzigane   12

La Tzigane

Stanza 1. The theme of love in Apollinaire's poetry is surrounded by elements of superstition, folklore and legend. They provide artistic colour, often of a bizarre kind. They give the theme a suggestive extension in time and tradition. Above all, they help to create an intriguing combination of the simple and the occult, of accessible human emotion and obscure impersonal force, which leaves the reader insecurely situated.

Apollinaire has chosen the simplest mode of presentation for this poem (a rapid narrative form, a straightforward syntax which fits plainly into the eight-syllable line, and the most elementary conjunctions), but it is one of the most sibylline. The first line has a particularly mysterious impact. 'La tzigane' as a first word introduces a sound foreign to the French language and a touch of exoticism, as well as associations with cartomancy, astrological predictions and a nomadic life beyond the fringe of normal society. The alliterations create an almost spell-binding effect. The phrase 'd'avance', in rhyming position at the end of the line and phonetically strengthened by several words in its immediate context, leaves us poised on the brink of a revelation as well as emphasizing the sense of fatality.

But the actual revelation is deliberately ambiguous. The word 'barrées' can mean obstructed as if by an impenetrable barrier, crossed through or crossed out.

One can interpret 'les nuits' in a variety of ways. The gypsy's foreknowledge may concern some negative influence in the life of the lovers associated with night-time: this could be the separation of the nights they have to spend apart, or a lack of fulfilment due to befall the nights they will spend together. More nebulously, 'les nuits' might represent those obscure forces accessible to the intuitions of fortune-tellers: the forces of night, the powers of darkness or some combination of black events. It is also possible to see in this image, if one thinks of palmistry, life-lines cut across (cf. 'barrées') by the line of night (disaster or death). (What would be your most immediate interpretation and how is it supported by details elsewhere in the poem?)

But the forthright expression of the following line (the specific nature of the Past Historic, the finality of 'adieu') seems to dispel the enigmatic vocabulary and fatalistic atmosphere. The gypsy is left behind, there is a pause ('. . . et puis') and the idea of a passage of time, however brief. This is enough for hope to take flight out of the dark hollow which had momentarily surrounded the lovers ('ce puits' could refer to the murky enclosure of the gypsy's tent or room, to the world of the dark and unfathomable on which they are only too happy to turn their back, or to the well of truth from which the fortune-teller draws her knowledge). One may suspect also, in this poem which relies so much on ambiguity and multiple meaning, that Apollinaire has put more than meets the eye into the apparently simple words '. . . et puis'. The fact that 'puis' is a rhyme and receives such a blatant echo only three syllables later throws more attention to it than its function as a mere adverb of time would seem to warrant. Could it be meant to trace in a suggestion of the couple's attitude as they depart, perhaps shrugging their shoulders and saying 'Well, what of it?' (cf. the belittling or challenging tone of the French 'Et puis après?'). If so, this gives a picture of the natural disinclination of young lovers to believe in misfortune, and ties in with the idea of resurgent hope in the last line. The echo 'puis. . .puits' would then be seen as a subtle play on words, with hope emerging, not only from the well, but from the couple's optimistic disregard for what has been predicted.

What is the effect of the position of 'Espérance', and its capital letter? What contribution does the pairing of '. . .savait d'av*ance*' and '. . .Espér*ance*' make to the thematic presentation of the stanza as a whole? Notice how, from a purely phonetic point of view, this final word gives a feeling of release after the prolonged use of the tight 'i' sound.

Stanza 2. But Hope is not easily fulfilled. One turns over a page in the life of the young couple, only to find that love, instead of being free, airy and spontaneous, has proved to be heavy and grossly physical (cf. the image of the dancing bear, no doubt kept chained). Like 'barrées' previously, the word 'privé' has several meanings: private, deprived and tamed (cf. the more modern 'apprivoisé'). Develop the implications of each of these meanings, showing how Apollinaire has left each with its relevance. Like the bear, love tries to dance and put on its show, but what should be graceful turns out to be ungainly. The words '. . .quand nous voulûmes', while suggesting a certain exercise of will over their love and an ability to prove its efficacy when they so desire, evoke something only spasmodic and lacking in spontaneity. What effect is achieved by the introduction of a new dominant sound into these two lines? The traditional bluebird of happiness also loses its beauty and is made as earth-bound as the dancing bear; while the beggars (a probable symbol of the deprived lovers in that they, too, are seeking charity from a niggardly fate) cease to voice their prayers of thanks.

These three details of the bear, the bluebird and the beggars are not only symbolic of the couple and their love, but also picturesque reminders of the world of the gypsy. It was a common feature of Rhineland gypsy performances (the Rhineland being the setting for a particularly influential period of Apollinaire's early love-life) to have trained animals, including one or two exotic birds (one of which might well serve as the bohemian fortune-teller's 'bluebird'), and to beg for money on the way. This clever intermingling of two areas of reference is a subtle indication that, in spite of their optimistic 'adieu', the lovers cannot shake off the clinging presence of 'la tzigane': her world seems inextricably linked to the strange malediction which moves with them. Contrast the mood of the last line of this stanza with that of the last line of the first stanza.

Stanza 3. The poem has passed in brief stages from prediction ('...savait d'avance') to reaction ('...sortit l'Espérance') to result ('...perdit ses plumes'). It now falls into philosophical reflection, born of experience, on the inescapability of fate. The words '...très bien' stress that the poet knows full well that love is doomed or, rather, that '...l'on *se* damne' and that man, in pursuing the impossible, is the accomplice to his own fate. (Notice how the opposite implications of the two religious words '*Ave*' and 'damne' are juxtaposed; and how '...se damne' throws back an echo to '...savait d'avance'.) But the knowledge does little to stop his dogged persistence (cf. the fruitless tenacity of '...quand nous voulûmes'). Although 'l'Espérance' is reduced to the more modest 'l'espoir', and 'l'amour' to the mere prospect of plucking a little love on the way through life, the lovers have not lost their ill-starred optimism. But this is never far away from their memory of the gypsy's prediction.

Significantly, Apollinaire again employs possible double references to bind together the lovers and 'la tzigane': 'en chemin' evokes the vagabond life, while '...main dans la main', a touching romantic gesture, may also contain the suggestion of palmistry. From such references, which carry ghost-like secondary images almost in the way that in children's picture-puzzles a tree's foliage can, if looked at in the right design, reveal an unexpected face, it is then only one short step to the final re-emergence of the gypsy-figure.

Look closely at the structure of the poem, especially the carefully counter-balanced subject-matter of the first and final stanzas, and the part the words 'la tzigane' play in this. How relevant to an accurate interpretation of the poem is the use of the various tenses (passing from Imperfect to Past Historic to Present to *passé composé*)?

Rosemonde

Longtemps au pied du perron de
La maison où entra la dame
Que j'avais suivie pendant deux
Bonnes heures à Amsterdam
Mes doigts jetèrent des baisers   5

Mais le canal était désert
Le quai aussi et nul ne vit
Comment mes baisers retrouvèrent
Celle à qui j'ai donné ma vie
Un jour pendant plus de deux heures   10

Je la surnommai Rosemonde
Voulant pouvoir me rappeler
Sa bouche fleurie en Hollande
Puis lentement je m'en allai
Pour quêter la Rose du Monde   15

Rosemonde

Stanza 1. This is another love-poem by Apollinaire, showing him in a typical rôle: that of universal lover wandering in the galleries of time and space, and not quite finding his own legend.

The element of time, advertised so prominently elsewhere in the poem, is stressed by the first word 'Longtemps', which stamps the poet as a lingering lover. But he is, as we soon learn, a lover in a world of his own, poised on the doorstep of someone who possibly knows nothing of his existence. What is the effect, in this stanza, of the clumsily articulated *enjambements* and the ill-matching rhymes? What intonation would you use in a reading of the first five lines: do they have an easy, conversational flow or an artificially worked structure? How does this affect one's view of the poet's attitude to his subject?

The particularly disjointed *enjambement* of '...pendant deux/Bonnes heures' makes one aware of the transience (or might it be the marathon duration?) of his amorous trek. It also highlights the ambiguity (implicit in the double meaning of 'a good two hours'). In what spirit is this slight play on words made: with sentimental nostalgia, with a touch of pique that he spent so long so fruitlessly, or even in a somewhat rakish manner?

The first four lines set the incident very precisely in time and place ('...au perron de...deux heures...Amsterdam'), making it seem an authentic 'real-life' happening. And yet the last line, with its unremitting gestures of affection, is strangely theatrical. (Notice how this line, after the appropriately meandering course of the introduction, brings things to a halt as it finally reveals *what* he was doing for such a long time. It is also the only line in the stanza which is not made to rhyme, however approximately, and so has a more isolated dramatic impact.)

Stanza 2. But the romantic actor has no audience. His love-mime, plaintively traced in the air at the end of the first stanza, is all the more poignant against this empty, uncommunicative décor ('...le canal était désert / Le quai aussi...'). (Contrast the rhythmical curtness of the first two lines here with the rhythmical pattern of the previous stanza: how does it reinforce the feeling of deflation?) The poet is a lover without partner or witness, who played his drama to himself, and now replays it in his memory to win the reader's admiration. There may well be a touch of boastfulness in the words 'Comment mes baisers retrouvèrent...', representing the vagabond Romeo's victory, followed as they are by the amorous fanfare 'Celle à qui j'ai donné ma vie'. But one cannot quite trust the poet's hyperboles; and the last line, as conclusive in its way as that of the first stanza, undermines the absolute quality of his proclamation '...j'ai donné ma vie', causing it to shrink from 'vie' to 'jour' to 'deux heures' and from something apparently everlasting into something quite transient, and creating yet another half-sad, half-humorous anti-climax. (How do the quality of the language, the rhythm and the juxtapositions produce a feeling of anti-climax? What might be the effect of the sudden use of the *passé composé* instead of the Past Historic here?) One could read the last two lines seriously: infatuated lovers do give their whole being quite sincerely in next to no time and will do so many times over. But there is certainly a touch of humour here at his own expense. Perhaps Apollinaire can see through his own foibles, as well as his little bit of mock-histrionics. Perhaps, too, it is as well that no-one saw, as his blown kisses may have been recognized for what they were: over-hopeful gestures to someone on the other side of a closed door.

Stanza 3. The plain statement that the episode, however long-lasting in the poet's own mind, took place on one day alone and for little more than two hours, confirms its transience and finality. With his kisses having found their mark and brought the affair to its conclusion, if only in the imagination, all that remains is to give this latest object of his pursuits an indelible place in the halls of memory, and to this end 'la dame', 'Celle à qui. . .' must have a name. How suggestive is the verb 'surnommai' here (as opposed to just 'nommer' or 'appeler'), especially in the Past Historic tense (as opposed to the Imperfect, which would put a completely different construction on the events)? 'Rosemonde' is a very evocative affectionate name: the rose is the symbol of love, its colour is often attributed to the happiest moments of life (cf. 'voir tout en rose'), the traditional image of Holland is of a flower-growing land, but more especially here the departing lover wants to remember the shape and colour of her lips (*mond* is, in fact, the Dutch word for 'mouth'). This idealization of the woman, captured and preserved in the one detail of those lips which his kisses sought and wishfully found, matches the earlier schematic picture of himself, summed up almost symbolically in the classic pose of fingers blowing kisses. And having stored away the name, he reluctantly goes on his way. What is the poet's mood in the final line? Is it more dispirited than hopeful? Do you see any ambiguity in the verb 'quêter'? Notice that this line, as well as rhyming within its own stanza, also rhymes with the first line of the poem: is this of any value?

The words '. . .la Rose du Monde' widen the idea of an amorous quest. The image of a cosmopolitan lover expands into that of a universal one (passing from the precise picture of a familiar Holland with its canals of Amsterdam, quay-sides and flowers, to the vagueness of some vast ideal). What he now seeks is not to love women in Holland or any other country under the sun, these being only manifestations of a greater need: a transcendent ideal of love which knows no boundaries. But is there anything new in this? For even in following Rosemonde as far as her doorstep and before even giving her a name, the poet was already chasing that inaccessible 'Rose du Monde'.

Jules Supervielle

(1884–1960)

Montévidéo

Je naissais, et par la fenêtre
Passait une fraîche calèche. 2

Le cocher réveillait l'aurore
D'un petit coup de fouet sonore.

Flottait un archipel nocturne
Encor sur le liquide jour. 6

Les murs s'éveillaient et le sable
Qui dort écrasé dans les murs.

Un peu de mon âme glissait
Sur un rail bleu, à contre-ciel, 10

Et un autre peu, se mêlant
A un bout de papier volant

Puis, trébuchant sur une pierre,
Gardait sa ferveur prisonnière. 14

Le matin comptait ses oiseaux
Et toujours il recommençait.

Le parfum de l'eucalyptus
Se fiait à l'air étendu. 18

Dans l'Uruguay sur l'Atlantique,
L'air était si liant, facile,
Que les couleurs de l'horizon
S'approchaient pour voir les maisons. 22

C'était moi qui naissais jusqu'au fond sourd des bois
Où tardent à venir les pousses
Et jusque sous la mer où l'algue se retrousse
Pour faire croire au vent qu'il peut descendre là. 26

La Terre allait, toujours recommençant sa ronde,
Reconnaissant les siens avec son atmosphère,
Et palpant sur la vague ou l'eau douce profonde
La tête des nageurs et les pieds des plongeurs.   30

Montévidéo

Lines 1–8. The title refers to the capital city of Uruguay, Supervielle's birth-place. In keeping with the general theme in his work of the mystery of the origins of life (cf. titles such as *Le Matin du monde* and *Commencements*), this poem attempts to reconstruct the variety of sensations awakened in a person seeing the world for the first time.

The use of the Imperfect 'Je naissais...' ('I was being born...') is quite rare. Why do you think Supervielle chooses it here and continues to use this tense throughout (what effect does it create that a succession of Past Historics would not)? One is projected into a half-real, half-unreal world, in which the new-born mind apprehends things simultaneously as physical sensations and pictures in the imagination. A child's first knowledge of the world may well be the impact of fresh air, sharpness of sound, an awareness of light and the acute tingle of a short slap. But such feelings are inseparable from the spontaneous images they generate. A rush of wind through an open window is the entry or exit of an elegant coach, its driver waking the dawn with a crack of the whip. Here the generous rhyme of 'fraîche calèche' knits together tactile impression and fanciful image as if they were one and the same thing. One might alternatively imagine that an actual coach passed by the window at that moment, the crispness of its sounds speeding in to blend with the other first sensations. These first lines are a pictur-esque example of the legend-making ability of the child's mind, which makes no distinction between reality and fiction. They present an original and unpretentious version of the well-known Classical legend of Apollo in his chariot chasing the dawn across the sky (cf. Rimbaud's treatment of this theme in *Aube*).

Lines 5–6, while introducing a new image, continue the idea of day-break. 'Flottait', brought into prominence by the inversion, creates a liquid, mobile impression before one knows anything of the source. To the sharpness and clarity of the first sensations, it adds a certain dreaminess and vagueness of outline. In the outside world it is that moment when daylight is not yet fully established and remnants of the night still linger, and the poet's eyes, it seems, are still veiled with a liquid haze.

The following couplet adds another colourful touch to the picture of morning and the world's prickling vitality. Stolid inanimate objects come to life, yawn and stretch; flat, dead surfaces acquire tint and texture which will vary through-out the day; and not just surfaces, but the innermost heart of things (the hard-worked and heavy-sleeping sand mattressed in the walls of brick and cement) are re-charged with life and mobility. Despite the fact that lines 5–8 have no rhyme, how does Supervielle give them an elegance and stylishness and avoid the prosaic?

Lines 9–14. Since the separate functional statement 'Je naissais', there has been no direct reference to the poet's own feelings. These have been depicted only in terms of nascent movements or stimuli in the outside world. Now the poet describes his own 'animation' in an equally fanciful and whimsical way. Does this little tableau of the activities of the soul seem frivolous? Notice the casual manner of the description and its peculiarly pictorial and concrete qualities. How do you visualize the image '...glissait/Sur un rail bleu, à contre-ciel'? Although these images would not be out of place in an animated cartoon, they suggest subtle qualities of the human soul: its facility of movement, its tendency to chase the ethereal and identify with it ('...se mêlant / A un bout de papier volant'), its ubiquity ('Un peu de mon âme glissait...Et un autre peu se mêlant') and its frustrated aspirations to be free from the obstructions of matter. The final picture ('trébuchant sur une pierre') suggests the experimental enthusiasm of the young child, walking for the first time, stumbling into its first obstacle, and proceeding thereafter with more caution and restraint.

Lines 15–22. These lines, slipping easily back from the hint of human spirituality to objects and creatures in the outside world, continue the humorous personified vision. The birds, in their dawn-chorus, seem to be answering a roll-call, but the morning, depicted as the benign paternal or regimental figure, is left comically stranded as the birds will not stay still and he is forced to start counting over and over again. The scents of the exotic eucalyptus for their part, as trusting and leisure-loving as any human, are suspended lazily in the air as if it were a hammock (the phrase 'l'air étendu', foreshadowing the reference to 'l'horizon' in the next stanza, seems to give horizontal visual outline and tangible density to the atmosphere).

Study the richness of the sensual impressions in the poem up to this point and the way in which they are interlinked with different elements, light, water, air. Note, too, the very approximate and unpredictable nature of the rhyming throughout the couplets, which creates an impression of the tentative and the ingenuous: sometimes they are perfect ('l'aurore...sonore'), sometimes they are replaced by assonance ('fenêtre...calèche'), sometimes by nothing at all ('sable...murs'). Such a technique might be thought appropriate to a poem describing a world not fully-fledged and perceptions which are part-complete, part-incomplete. What effect does the use of brief couplets have in lines 1–18?

The unexpected four-line stanza rounds off the preceding picture of a genial, inviting atmosphere, bringing to fruition the idea of daybreak, with this final spread of colour sweeping in from the Atlantic horizon to settle on every house, and confirming, by its use of personification, the intimate bond between the spirit of nature and human life. But at the same time this change to a different structure heralds a transition to the final quatrains and a new development: it anticipates the finale by setting all the diminutive images in a wider perspective ('l'Atlantique', 'l'horizon'), and by showing the narrator at a further distance from his subject ('Dans l'Uruguay sur l'Atlantique'), possibly on the verge of a more nostalgic mood.

Lines 23–26. The words 'C'était moi qui naissais...', replaying the theme of birth, contrast nevertheless with the initial 'Je naissais...': they now show the poet, not so much as the childlike participant in an awakening world, but more as an external observer on his former self. Similarly, the greater use of present tenses makes him a more general commentator on the nature of the world. The curious expression '...naissais jusqu'au fond...Et jusque sous la mer' indicates the birth of a self not made to move just in a superficial plane but to penetrate into the depths, not confined to the domain of one element (the radiant air) but extending mysteriously into the vegetal and marine realms, not belonging to the narrow setting of one room ('...par la fenêtre') but travelling out into the universal.

Is there any noticeable difference here between the function of octosyllabic lines and Alexandrines, between the use of couplets and a four-line verse? Does the change of form modify the mood or introduce more serious aspects of theme? (The one octosyllable remaining here may be seen as a token of continuity, so that the transition is made only gently; or as an appropriately curtailed line supporting the theme of a tardy, impeded growth.) One is aware now of a change of emphasis from references such as 'Flottait...sur le liquide jour', '...glissait / Sur un rail bleu', or 'Se fiait à l'air étendu', to '...jusqu'au fond sourd', '...jusque sous la mer' and '...qu'il peut descendre là'; of the contrast between images of a swift and spontaneous human birth and a laborious vegetable growth, between the undeceptive candour of the air and the false allure of the seaweed. The wind's inability to make the crossing into another realm throws into relief man's unique destiny: to break frontiers and transcend the elements.

Lines 27–30. The concluding stanza is the most universal in scope: 'La Terre' is its subject, Earth which is charged with a special oversight of men themselves. Like the morning which earlier counted up its birds, but on a grander scale, the Earth as the supreme solicitous figure ascertains that none of its family has gone astray. The Earth's rotation, progressively bringing light to every nook and cranny of the globe, is a fatherly tour of inspection and the ever-accompanying atmosphere its vast, sensitive feeler. It is the atmosphere which, with the coming of light, registers life, sounds, colours, scents and sensations (all delicately illustrated in the earlier part of the poem) and, above all, ensures that adventurous humans, the ones more likely to get lost, are still there. The verb 'Palpant' again gives a substantial, physical quality to the air (cf. 'l'air étendu') as well as a living, exploratory sense of touch. The last two lines bring the poem to a nicely symmetrical conclusion: sea water and fresh water, swimmers and divers, heads and feet are neatly opposed. After the grandiose tone of lines 27–8, the final image reinstates the humorous and picturesque vision, and it provides a last reminder that man is Earth's privileged child, an explorer and a wanderer, who can do what the wind cannot. His birth is a birth into several elements at once.

It has been said that Supervielle has the eye of a primitive painter or an innocent. Does such a comment seem appropriate to the style of *Montévidéo*? Critics also speak of the tentative and precarious quality of his vision of the world. Is there evidence of this here?

Haute Mer

Parmi les oiseaux et les lunes
Qui hantent le dessous des mers
Et qu'on devine à la surface
Aux folles phases de l'écume,   4

Parmi l'aveugle témoignage
Et les sillages sous-marins
De mille poissons sans visage
Qui cachent en eux leur chemin,   8

Le noyé cherche la chanson
Où s'était formé son jeune âge,

Ecoute en vain les coquillages
Et les fait choir au sombre fond.   12

Haute Mer

Stanza 1. Part of the attraction of this first stanza is the fantastical vision,
which invites one to imagine life in another element, in this case a poetic underwater realm. Already in the first line, there is a note of unreality in the juxtaposition of birds and moons, as if they moved as companions in the same sphere,
and in the idea of plural moons, ghosting about as commonly as birds themselves.
But this unreality becomes even more baffling as one realizes that these birds
and moons are actually under the sea. Note the richness of the different possible
meanings of the verb 'hanter': to frequent, to visit as a phantom, or persistently
to obsess. These creatures are not birds and moons as we know them, high in the
air, but their marine equivalents, living in the uppermost levels of the sea. And
just as moons known to man govern the movements of the tides, so these submarine moons exert their own mysterious influence on the surface of the sea,
tempting the human onlooker to guess at the nature of these underwater 'heavens'. How effective in sound and rhythm as well as associative suggestion are the
words 'folles phases'?

But the suggestiveness of the opening vision and its interplay of things from
different spheres, air and sea, *l'envers* and *l'endroit*, is by no means exhausted.
If one relates it to Supervielle's *Sous le large* one might well take the meaning to
be that the life-forms of the ocean, intrigued by the real nature of things in other
strata of existence, are yearning to know the realm beyond their own element.
In this sense, one can imagine them haunted by the flitting shapes of birds or the
outline of the moon, which they can only see refracted and disseminated through
the agitated surface of the water, or vaguely sense in the motions of the tide.

Stanza 2. The repeated 'Parmi . . .' ensures a continuity between the stanzas
and intensifies our anticipation of an as yet unidentified subject (due to be revealed
as 'le noyé'). It is a word suggesting that the subject in question is surrounded
thickly and on all sides by these many forms of marine life.

This stanza is built on somewhat paradoxical or self-contradictory phrases
which provoke the imagination as much as did the setting in the first four lines.
'Témoignage' could mean that the fish are 'bearing witness' (i.e. acting as a
living proof or illustration of something), or that they are 'witnesses' or onlookers
to something. How would you reconcile the use of the adjective 'aveugle' with
this word? 'Sillage' usually refers to a wake left behind on the surface of the sea.
How do you visualize 'les sillages *sous*-marins'? The expression 'poissons sans
visage', though justifiable when one thinks of the sightless fish living in the ocean
depths, comes as a grim and unexpected development of the idea of 'aveugle'.
These fish emit and absorb no communication. The physical proximity normally
associated with the preposition 'parmi' is negated here by the lack of responsiveness of everything in this environment. The final line is difficult to interpret: the
fact that the fish 'hide their route within themselves' is a further indication of
their reclusive, uncommunicative life, in which any knowledge of where they
have come from and where they are going to remains locked within.

Notice how Supervielle, unlike his technique in the first stanza which had no
rhyming outline, uses rhymes to make meaningful pairings between lines 5 and
7 and lines 6 and 8, and to give a greater rigour to his vision.

Stanza 3. The way in which the subject is revealed as 'le noyé', after such a prolonged preparation, comes as a shock. Seen in normal human terms, there is a hopeless finality about his state. But, though he has crossed the frontier between life and death, between one domain and another, he is still endowed in Super-vielle's poetic imagination with the power to seek and to listen. From the vision of an eyeless world which divulges nothing, one's attention turns to the pursuit, by the drowned man, of an elusive sound. But the significance of this coveted sound is mysterious. As opposed to the mere 'chant de la mer', this 'chanson' represents a more ordered and subtle quest, a harmony closely linked with the secret of his youth. The phrase 'Où s'était formé son jeune âge' is an unusual one: a song is a fleeting, unsubstantial thing, and yet here it is seen almost as the physical mould in which his young life was shaped. Perhaps he is seeking his own lost innocence, a childlike joy and freshness, a return to his origins (and here the sea appears as a kind of primeval cradle), or even the secret of genesis (notice that the poet has chosen to use 'jeune âge' rather than 'jeunesse').

But the search is a vain one. The final two lines reintroduce and push to the extreme the note of hopelessness. There is a common belief that the sea-shell, held close to the human ear, releases the sound of the sea. Perhaps 'le noyé' has heard this call. But paradoxically and tragically, the sea-shell which, taken out of its element, whispers the story of its origin, falls silent when once reimmers-ed in its native realm. So, a central theme of this poem is non-communication, either by looks or sounds. The drowned man's last gesture is one of resignation.

What are the qualities of the choice of the verb 'choir' and the use of the double nasal vowel at the end of the poem? Notice the exceptional concentration of sibilant sounds [s,ʃ,ʒ,z] throughout the poem, in many cases made to coincide with the rhythmical stress, and creating an insistent onomatopoeic effect. What is the significance of the structural development of the poem (look particularly at the first and last lines, and the progression from stanza to stanza)? Is there a second level of meaning and a touch of irony in Supervielle's title *Haute Mer*? Might one, as justifiably as in the case of *Sous le large*, look upon this poem as a fable?

Paul Eluard

(1895–1952)

L'Amoureuse

Elle est debout sur mes paupières
Et ses cheveux sont dans les miens,
Elle a la forme de mes mains,
Elle a la couleur de mes yeux,
Elle s'engloutit dans mon ombre
Comme une pierre sur le ciel.   6

Elle a toujours les yeux ouverts
Et ne me laisse pas dormir.
Ses rêves en pleine lumière
Font s'évaporer les soleils,
Me font rire, pleurer et rire,
Parler sans avoir rien à dire.   12

L'Amoureuse

Line 1. The poem begins with a surprise-image which removes it from prosaic realism into a realm of 'surreality'. It is a starkly physical image ('...debout... paupières'), but one which defies literal-mindedness and releases figurative possibilities. It establishes a feminine person as a mysterious persuasive force imposing itself on the vision. Although having tangible physical presence, she seems an almost weightless Peter-Pan-like figure. Is she the spirit presiding over poetic sight or dream, an agent of awakening or sleep?

Lines 2–4. These three lines describe an almost complete interpenetration of persons. She becomes part of his being, contained within the very shape of his hands and colour of his eyes: as if everything he touches or sees takes on her appearance and every isolated feature of himself becomes embodied in her.

Lines 5–6. After this simple celebration of the perfect echoing relationship in which woman and poet are indistinguishable one from the other, the final image of the stanza makes one wonder who is the dominant partner and who exerts the greater influence. 'Elle s'engloutit dans mon ombre', a strikingly dynamic image, gives the impression that she is drawn into the depth and vastness of his person, into the dark of his inner world, into the mystery that lies on the other side of closed eyes, becoming as inseparable and intimate as his shadow. The word 'ombre' is vague enough to leave all these possibilities alive. But the accompanying simile, normally expected to give clarification to an idea, is

disconcerting. It forces one to visualize what has preceded in a completely opposite way: a descent into darkness becomes projection upwards towards light, a
vague absorption into a murky background becomes a clearly delineated
silhouette against a bright sky, and an ethereal, nebulous creature becomes a
dense, hard object. The suggestion is that opposites are unified in her: she is
simultaneously contained within him yet powerfully outside him, unsubstantial
yet solid, descending and ascending, submissive yet endowed with kinetic force.
The poet is also illustrating dramatically how she instantly transforms darkness
into radiance as if they were one and the same thing (cf. 'Auréole du temps,
berceau nocturne et sûr' in Eluard's *La courbe de tes yeux...*).

Looking at the stanza as a whole, study the positional repetition of 'Elle...',
the unvarying word-order, and the way in which the simple main clauses are
loosely linked by commas and not made separate sentences. To what do these
features contribute? What makes the appearance of the verb 's'engloutit...' so
emphatic and the image in the last line so conspicuous?

Lines 7–8. In this simple two-panelled description of the wonder of woman,
these lines make the transition from what she is to the effect she has ('ne me laisse
pas...', 'Font s'évaporer...', 'Me font rire...').

The first line forms a structural link with the opening line of stanza 1. In
both, she is there as an insistent presence affecting his vision. But whereas earlier
she seemed to be closing his eyes to all but her, here she more clearly represents
open eyes, permanent wakefulness, the refusal to let him fall into lethargy. In
keeping with the idea of a shared identity, her eyes appear to have substituted
themselves for his own.

Lines 9–12. The final part of the poem continues to develop the play of
opposites fused in the magical 'Elle'. Waking, she affects his sleep. Dreaming,
she affects the world of day. Far from belonging to that traditional dream-world
of half-light which subsequently fades into oblivion, her dreams take place in
broad daylight and their burning brilliance outshines and outlives that of suns
(the plural here increasing the sense of her luminous power and diminishing the
sun's relevance as a unique life-giving force). She replaces the light of the real
world by another, more essential one (cf. the notion of a radiant dream-world
vitalized by a feminine presence in Desnos's poem, *J'ai tant rêvé de toi*). Even
more important is the effect on the poet. She releases the extreme contrasts of his
emotions, fusing his laughter and tears in the same way that she fuses dream and
the waking world; and just as 'ombre' was immediately transformed into 'ciel',
leaving the first stanza with a predominant image of radiance, so 'rire', by its
repetition and terminal position, leaves a dominant impression of joy. She also
opens his powers of expression for their own sake and for no particular purpose
other than to give an outlet to the intensity of his feeling.

What modulations are introduced in the last few lines by the disappearance of
of 'Elle...' as a subject, the changed location within the verse of the pronoun
'Me', the sudden accumulation of infinitives, the new pattern of rhythm in the
penultimate line, the particularly prolonged alliteration, and the use of the rhyming couplet?

The title *L'Amoureuse* tells that this is a love-poem. But is there a definite
nuance in the choice of the word *L'Amoureuse* rather than, say, *La Bien-aimée* or
L'Amante? Does the third-personal form ('Elle est...', 'Elle a...') have any
advantage here, as opposed to a direct address to a second person, which is not
an uncommon form for a love-poem?

Eluard has here evoked that multiplicity of feeling, insistent but undefinable (because it is too many opposites in one), awakened by a woman in love or, more appropriately, a woman who *is* love.

Sans âge

Nous approchons
Dans les forêts
Prenez la rue du matin
Montez les marches de la brume   4

Nous approchons
La terre en a le cœur crispé

Encore un jour à mettre au monde.

*

Le ciel s'élargira   8
Nous en avions assez
D'habiter dans les ruines du sommeil
Dans l'ombre basse du repos
De la fatigue de l'abandon   12

La terre reprendra la forme de nos corps vivants
Le vent nous subira
Le soleil et la nuit passeront dans nos yeux
Sans jamais les changer   16

Notre espace certain notre air pur est de taille
A combler le retard creusé par l'habitude
Nous aborderons tous une mémoire nouvelle
Nous parlerons ensemble un langage sensible.   20

*

O mes frères contraires gardant dans vos prunelles
La nuit infuse et son horreur
Où vous ai-je laissés
Avec vos lourdes mains dans l'huile paresseuse   24
De vos actes anciens
Avec si peu d'espoir que la mort a raison
O mes frères perdus
Moi je vais vers la vie j'ai l'apparence d'homme 28
Pour prouver que le monde est fait à ma mesure

Et je ne suis pas seul
Mille images de moi multiplient ma lumière
Mille regards pareils égalisent la chair   32

C'est l'oiseau c'est l'enfant c'est le roc c'est la plaine
Qui se mêlent à nous
L'or éclate de rire de se voir hors du gouffre
L'eau le feu se dénudent pour une seule saison   36
Il n'y a plus d'éclipse au front de l'univers.

*

Mains par nos mains reconnues
Lèvres à nos lèvres confondues
Les premières chaleurs florales   40
Alliées à la fraîcheur du sang

Le prisme respire avec nous
Aube abondante
Au sommet de chaque herbe reine   44
Au sommet des mousses à la pointe des neiges
Des vagues des sables bouleversés
Des enfances persistantes
Hors de toutes les cavernes   48
Hors de nous-mêmes.

Sans âge

Section 1.   The poem represents a quest for a kind of utopia, for a dream of a
rejuvenated world and, if one thinks of the title *Sans âge*, for an ideal of time
conquered and the enjoyment of an eternal freshness. Constantly implicit in the
background is the basic metaphor of dawn and light breaking over the world.
    There is a sense of purposefulness and anticipation in the first few lines: what
is it that impresses this feeling so strongly? Does the plural '...les forêts' add a
special note? Notice how Eluard uses, not elaborately developed similes, but
brief, arresting metaphors. Here he captures the quality of the air and light in the
most accessible concrete terms, appropriating the face of the world in terms of
familiar human structures ('...la rue du matin', '...les marches de la brume').
While bringing about an easy interpenetration of the human and the natural, so
central to the theme of the poem as a whole, these images also have a strong
descriptive quality (one thinks of a beam or pathway of light breaking through
mist or trees, and of mist rising in layers or swathes at different heights), and contain a wealth of symbolic meaning (e.g. at the top of the mist, as a kind of prize,
is light). The line 'La terre en a le cœur crispé', maintaining the close link between
natural elements and the world of man, is a variation in that it is now a personification, an affective rather than a visual image. To what does the pronoun 'en'
refer and how does it enhance the value of the image? One can read this line in
several ways: it suggests a frosty morning and the hard puckered surface of the
ground; it implies an animate being reacting physically, flinching beneath the
human tread; and above all it endows the earth with an ability to respond emo-
tionally, either in trepidation, eagerness or silent encouragement, to this human
pursuit of the ideal.
    Notice the emphasis of the imperatives, which set the poet up as a leader,

convey a sense of urgency and seem to call on man's adventurous or acquisitive spirit. The last line is a forceful reminder that day does not just break, dawn does not just rise, but that it must be risen, brought into the world. Develop the implications of this image. What is the poet's intention in isolating the final line? Do you think it comes more as an anti-climax than a climax?

Section 2. The tenses in the first two lines underline the division between a future to be attained and a past to be shaken off. On the one hand, confident in tone, affirmative in position, is 'Le ciel s'élargira', with its descriptive and symbolic connotations. On the other hand are the dereliction, baseness and obscurity of human lethargy, indifference and defeatism. Note the contrast between the freshness and vigour of the opening statement and the leaden alliteration, the trailing enumerations of the following sentence. The phrase 'D'habiter dans les ruines...' speaks of an enclosed and unconstructive world, without goal or project (cf. 'Nous approchons'), without dynamic upsurge or solidity (cf. 'Montez les marches...'), without openness to the grandeur of the world at large (cf. 'Le ciel s'élargira').

The next four lines, with their accumulation of future tenses, take up again the confident tone of prophecy. They speak of a deep interrelation between the earth and man, perfectly modelled on each other, the verb 'reprendra' implying a Paradise regained, an end to the divorce between man and his natural environment. The conquest of the wind, normally thought of as a free agent which cannot be swayed or deflected in its fanatical course, is an example of the elements no longer exercising their whims at the expense of human life but yielding to man's domination. Similarly, man will be no longer the victim, but the victor of time, with the unwavering light in his eyes (conviction, purity, illumination) undiminished by the destructive cycles of day and night. (Look back to images in *L'Amoureuse* which echo the line 'La terre reprendra la forme de nos corps vivants', and which develop the theme of a conflict between sleep and the world of open eyes, and a radiance outshining that of the sun.) Note the balance of these four lines: the studied variations of length, the way in which man's effect on the universe and the universe's lack of effect on him are juxtaposed.

This section culminates in a new four-line movement. What gives it a more generous rhythmical flow, a greater equilibrium? How is the idea of collective purpose and achievement reinforced? The idea of a conquering movement into space, already emerging in such phrases as 'Montez les marches de la brume' and 'Le vent nous subira', is concentrated in the words 'Notre espace *certain*...'. Space is seen, not as void or absence, but as a guaranteed possession, a measurable volume of expansiveness and possibility with which the poet can fill that hollow in human life gouged out by habit and indifference (what is the full value of the verb 'combler'?). Eluard conveys this by a striking intermingling of the notions of time and space, abstract and concrete: 'espace' and 'air pur' will fill in 'le retard'. The implicit image, developing the earlier opposition between 'Le ciel s'élargira' and '...l'ombre basse du repos', is that the light of this surreal dawn will rise high enough to pour into the vast pocket of sluggish life which illumination has never touched. The idea of eliminating a particular kind of attachment to the past leads naturally to the promise of 'une mémoire nouvelle': men will not be chained to the empty succession of what has been, but reunited with some essential, primordial source (cf. 'La terre *re*prendra...'), so that future and past come together in a new harmony. (How effectively does the verb 'aborder' conjure up an image?) There will also be a new language, replacing the normally deficient and jaded means of perception and communication. It will be 'un langage *sensible*', not abstract, but drawing from the very substance of the world, and so breaking down barriers of linguistic division and incomprehension.

Section 3. This section is again built on the broad opposition of dark and light, indifference and awareness, immobility and action. But it is developed at greater length, and in a more direct rhetorical way ('O mes frères...'). This gives a new tone which is both critical and compassionate. The 'nous' is split into '...mes frères' and 'Moi'. The rhyming words '...frères contraires' indicate that, although sharing the same destiny, these human brothers are as yet the negative image of the poet. They represent the static (cf. '...gardant'), a fact emphasized by 'Où vous ai-je laissés'. But despite the implied criticism that they have not kept up with the poet and have stayed behind on the route, there may also be self-criticism that somewhere the poet himself has failed to maintain contact.

Study the way in which details in this address fall into a pattern of contrasts. Where, in the poem, does one find counterbalancing images to '...gardant dans vos prunelles', 'La nuit infuse...', '...vos lourdes mains', '...l'huile paresseuse / De vos actes anciens' and '...la mort'? How well do you think Eluard has suggested the idea of a person setting off into the early morning and another slow to rise? To what effect does he employ run-on lines in the first six lines of this section?

From the strongly physical image ('Avec vos lourdes mains dans l'huile paresseuse') and the disparaging tone which accompanies it, one passes to the more grandiloquent 'Avec si peu d'espoir que la mort a raison' and then back to the saddened predicatory address 'O mes frères perdus'. In this context 'perdus' does not mean 'damned', but simply lost somewhere on the way (cf. 'Où vous ai-je laissés') and, more especially, unable to find their way, since their vision is clouded and their sense of touch dulled. As inspiration, the poet can only offer his own example ('Moi je vais vers la vie...'): notice the initial accentuation, the closely consecutive verbs, the monosyllabic emphasis and the vigorous alliteration which give force to this line, advertising the resurgent stimulus of the poet's idealism and sense of direction. The strange phrase '...j'ai l'apparence d'homme' testifies to an intuitive affinity to what he imagines to be his true nature and status, transcending all that is less than human. The sense of direction ('vers') is reinforced by a sense of purpose ('Pour prouver...'), and the final clause ends as a firm and resonant statement of faith that the earth corresponds exactly to man's needs.

The following movement is a fuller definition of the poet's luminous vision. Having laid himself open, with the words 'O mes frères perdus / Moi je vais vers la vie...', to the charge of poetic isolation, he passionately affirms that poetry is not locked in a world apart. For the radiance of his conviction is dispersed and reflected in the innumerable forms of the outside world, so that he no longer sees himself as a single, self-contained person or a separate corporal entity, but as a ubiquitous light which knows no boundaries. The words 'Mille images', 'Mille regards' and the rapid and varied enumeration impress the poet's multiplicity of spirit: as if he were a divine figure, he and the world seem to form one flesh, and animal, human and inanimate life are all one in him. It is at this point, as a blaze of gold bursts free from the 'gouffre', that the image of light and dark is given its most triumphant expression (what does the word 'gouffre' represent in the context of the poem and what is the suggestive power of '...éclate de rire'?). Contrasting natural elements (water, fire), acting in unison, reveal themselves in their pure form, unveiled, unadulterated, in excitement or pride at their own liberated beauty (cf. 'l'or éclate de rire de *se voir*...'). In view of the fact that the words '...pour une seule saison' are followed immediately by 'Il n'y a plus d'éclipse...' with its idea of perennial light, they must mean, not that water and fire are showing themselves in their purity just for a transient moment, for one season alone, but that they are joining in a single timeless season, as opposed to their two separate, contrary expressions of winter and summer. It is noticeable that everything is now translated, not in a future tense, but in the poetic present, thus reminding those 'frères contraires' that his realm is not one of distant objectives but an ideal spontaneously at hand.

Section 4. The finale is an unimpeded celebration of the nature of the new age, one facet after the other. Study the stylistic features: the virtual disappearance of verbs, the lack of punctuation which has a more noticeable effect here than elsewhere in the poem, the importance of repetition in its development and balance. In what way do they support the poet's theme?

The gesture of communication in 'Mains par nos mains reconnues' is in direct contrast to the inexpressiveness of '...vos lourdes mains dans l'huile paresseuse'. It is the fulfilment of the prophecy 'Nous parlerons ensemble un langage *sensible*'. 'Lèvres à nos lèvres...', with its similar echoing structure, not only continues the idea of language, but introduces into this climax of union the element of love. The vocabulary forms a particularly strong pattern: '...*se mêlent* à nous', '...à nos lèvres *confondues*', '*Alliées* à la fraîcheur du sang'. But what might seem, in the first two lines, to be simply a hymn of human reconciliation and love expands into a greater union between man and the universe. In a neat image, in which the warmth of the blood is transferred to flowers and the freshness of flowers transferred to the blood, Eluard strengthens the idea of an exchange of properties in which man's attributes flow freely into the heart of nature and vice versa (note the phonetic delicacy of these two lines, whose sound-echoes serve the same purpose as the preceding repetitions, namely, to suggest everything reflecting everything else). The air, too, (if one reads 'Le prisme' as the body of the atmosphere through which light is refracted on its journey to earth) seems to perform a human function in unison with man. Here one calls back to mind the prediction that 'La terre reprendra la forme de nos corps vivants' and the brief recurrent references throughout the poem to nature's physical form: 'La terre en a le cœur crispé', 'l'or éclate de rire...', '...au front de l'univers', 'Le prisme respire...' The two symbols of life, blood and breath, prepare the way for the plenitude of 'Aube abondante' which marks the fulfilment of the initial project: 'Encore un jour à mettre au monde'. This vision, harmonious, vital, dynamic, bounteous, also gives a sense of elevation. The words 'Au sommet ...Au sommet...' link with the early exhortation, 'Montez les marches de la brume'. The inexhaustible light of dawn lavishes itself everywhere, crowning the crest of all things, from the most diminutive to the most expansive and universal, with a consummate radiance. The image of 'sables bouleversés' is a fine example of Eluard's taste for intermingling literal and figurative meanings: sand is tossed over and over by the sea, and here no doubt, it is overwhelmed, 'bowled over' by the miracle. One cannot over-stress the importance of the last three lines as the culmination of the essential themes. Draw out the implications of 'Des enfances persistantes' (cf. the title *Sans âge*, the image of dawn and phrases such as 'Le soleil et la nuit passeront...' or 'Il n'y a plus d'éclipse...'); of 'Hors de toutes les cavernes' (cf. 'habiter dans...l'ombre basse', '...du gouffre' and images of darkness and enclosure); and, finally, of 'Hors de nous-mêmes' which is the peak of the poem (cf. images of man becoming porous to bird, rock, plain, etc.). Man is no longer imprisoned in the cycles of time, the enclosure of space, or the limits of his own self, but thrown open to the universal.

Henri Michaux

(1899–   )

Icebergs

Icebergs, sans garde-fou, sans ceinture, où de vieux cormorans
abattus et les âmes des matelots morts récemment viennent
s'accouder aux nuits enchanteresses de l'hyperboréal.

Icebergs, Icebergs, cathédrales sans religion de l'hiver éternel,   4
enrobés dans la calotte glaciaire de la planète Terre.
Combien hauts, combien purs sont vos bords enfantés par le
froid.

Icebergs, Icebergs, dos du Nord-Atlantique, augustes   8
Bouddhas gelés sur des mers incontemplées, Phares scintillants
de la Mort sans issue, le cri éperdu du silence dure des siècles.

Icebergs, Icebergs, Solitaires sans besoin, des pays bouchés,
distants, et libres de vermine. Parents des îles, parents des sources,   12
comme je vous vois, comme vous m'êtes familiers...

Icebergs

Section 1.   The sea has been the inspiration of many poems: a symbol of infinity,
a reflection of the moods of man, an image of the tides of human destiny,
the path of the exotic journey and so on: one thinks of Hugo's *Paroles sur la
dune*, Baudelaire's *La Musique* or Rimbaud's *Le Bateau ivre*. The iceberg is a
much rarer object of contemplation. Michaux here brings out the rich power of
suggestion of icebergs, the multiple spirit behind the monotony of colour, the
expressiveness behind the impassive front.

The first trace of a theme is that of the lack of limits, the freedom to move and
expand (cf. 'Je ne me sentis plus guidé par les haleurs' in Rimbaud's *Le Bateau
ivre*): is there a shade of difference between 'sans garde-fou' and 'sans ceinture'?
Is Michaux suggesting that, unlike a boat which is a foreign body on the ocean,
sealed against the water, icebergs know no such divisions and are both water
and not water, in a state of constant transfusion with the sea; or that, as pallid
frontier-posts marking the limits of the livable, they are always on the move,
subject to no fixed boundaries? The question of boundaries is relevant in the
following description, which turns them into a mysterious spiritual abode half-
way between this world and another, between life and life-in-death. They are
seen as a place of passage and repose for the souls of departed sea-

lovers, a vantage-point from which different creatures of nature, joined as one spirit, pause to contemplate a magical polar vision (cf. *Le Bateau ivre*: 'J'ai rêvé la nuit verte aux neiges éblouies'). What contribution is made to the surreal description by the choice of the dark-plumaged cormorant; the precise distinction of '...morts récemment'; the use of the verb 's'accouder' (cf. Supervielle's insertion of human physical gestures into an ethereal realm in which, strictly, they should be impossible); and the placing of the longest multisyllabic words, especially the rare 'l'hyperboréal', at the end?

Section 2.   There is an intensification of style and theme in the second section: on the one hand the repetition and doubling up of the word 'Icebergs', with its penetrating exotic sound; on the other the expansion of the spiritual note implicit in the word 'âmes' into a stronger religious theme. One might compare the image of icebergs as wintry cathedrals with Baudelaire's 'La Nature est un temple...' in *Correspondances* (though the sombre symbolism and richly provoked sensuality are both eliminated), and more particularly with the 'Féerique Eglise' and the 'navrants palais polaires' in Laforgue's *Complainte du Roi de Thulé*. But one notices the paradox that these are 'cathédrales sans religion': how would you explain this? In what way is the religious atmosphere enriched by the participle 'enrobés'; by the style of 'Combien hauts, combien purs...'; and by the idea of '...enfantés par le froid' (this detail also takes on a significance with reference to Laforgue and his King of Thule, both repelled by carnality and the grotesque blood-letting of the human birth–death cycle)? The picturesque use of the phrase 'calotte glaciaire' (the polar ice-cap) here suggests a zone of pure meditation, set apart from the agitations and impurities of the body of the world, while the outside view of 'la planète Terre' in a kind of cosmic perspective impresses the feeling of otherworldliness.

Section 3.   Again the slow, cyclic repetition draws the attention hypnotically back to the word 'Icebergs', the centre of these devotions. This section (though beginning with two pictorial images, the first depicting icebergs as the jutting vertebrae of the North Atlantic's backbone like the half-submerged spine of some timeless sea-mammoth and the second as frozen Buddha-figures, lost in impassive meditation and not of this world) then plunges into deeper and more abstract spiritual confines: Death, Anguish, Silence, Eternity. One passes from the more decorative properties of the ice-cathedrals to their latent mystery. What effects does Michaux derive here from the profusion of capital letters; from the tendency towards paradoxical expression (e.g. symbols of contemplative life set in oceans which are 'incontemplées'; death not as darkness but as signals of light roving the seas; the acute cry of silence which is mute but everlasting)? Note how the final phrases have the most intensely sibilant, one might say sibylline, sound.

Section 4.   After the climax of seriousness, on the fringe of the inhuman and the void, this final movement represents a kind of reconciliation. It still stresses the self-contained, self-sufficient serenity of icebergs, in a state beyond physical need or perturbation, their purity and their intactness. But it brings to fruition a mysterious balance of contradictions: freedom of movement and frozen immobility, splendour and bleakness, expressiveness and impassivity, inhumanity and homely hospitality, total solitude and kinship. For, although inaccessible ('Combien hauts...'), impenetrable ('...de la Mort sans issue', '...des pays bouchés'), irreconcilable with impurities ('...combien purs', 'libres de vermine') and indifferent to human time ('...de l'hiver éternel', '...dure des siècles'), the icebergs are sealed by a close bond with the poet himself. That they can bridge different orders is apparent in their drawing together of sailors and sea-birds, and more especially in that, being neither, they are intimately related both to land-mass and water (cf. the image of 'Péninsules démarrées' in *Le Bateau ivre*); but above all, while they move '...sur des mers incontemplées', the poet can say '...comme je vous vois', and while they are 'Solitaires' and 'distants', he can claim '...comme vous m'êtes familiers'. How effective are these last words as a conclusion? (Note the parallelism between the 'comme...comme' structure and the earlier 'Combien...combien'; is there a new tone here? what, if anything, is suggested by the incomplete punctuation at the end?)

Examine the sonorities of the poem ('fou...s'accouder...Bouddhas... bouchés', 'cormorans...morts...hyperboréal...bords...Nord...Mort', 'Icebergs... hyperboréal ... éternel ... glaciaire ... Terre ... mers ... éperdu ... vermine', 'ceinture...purs...dure...éperdu...issue'): Michaux's approach is not quite that of Mallarmé who, in *Le vierge, le vivace et le bel aujourd'hui...*, concentrates almost exclusively on the taut 'i' sound to suggest the rigours of the ice-realm; but the various similarities of sound do help the poem to 'congeal'. Study the structure: the slightly changing emphasis in each of the four parts; the organization of the verse-form so as to suggest the nature of icebergs (the use of repetition; the technique of apposition and verbless forms; the spaced para-graphing, each beginning at the same recognizable point). This is an unusual poem by Michaux in that, in contrast to the turbulence and energetic transformations which characterize so much of his writing, it is concerned with the serenity of the static.

Clown

Un jour.

Un jour, bientôt peut-être.

Un jour j'arracherai l'ancre qui tient mon navire loin des mers.

Avec la sorte de courage qu'il faut pour être rien et rien que 4
rien, je lâcherai ce qui paraissait m'être indissolublement proche.

Je le trancherai, je le renverserai, je le romprai, je le ferai
dégringoler.

D'un coup dégorgeant ma misérable pudeur, mes misérables 8
combinaisons et enchaînements 'de fil en aiguille'.

Vidé de l'abcès d'être quelqu'un, je boirai à nouveau l'espace
nourricier.

A coups de ridicules, de déchéances (qu'est-ce que la déché- 12
ance?), par éclatement, par vide, par une totale dissipation-
dérision-purgation, j'expulserai de moi la forme qu'on croyait si
bien attachée, composée, coordonnée, assortie à mon entourage
et à mes semblables, si dignes, si dignes, mes semblables. 16

Réduit à une humilité de catastrophe, à un nivellement parfait
comme après une intense trouille.

Ramené au-dessous de toute mesure à mon rang réel, au rang
infime que je ne sais quelle idée-ambition m'avait fait déserter. 20

Anéanti quant à la hauteur, quant à l'estime.

Perdu en un endroit lointain (ou même pas), sans nom, sans
identité.

CLOWN, abattant dans la risée, dans le grotesque, dans   24
l'esclaffement, le sens que contre toute lumière je m'étais fait
de mon importance.
Je plongerai.
Sans bourse dans l'infini-esprit sous-jacent ouvert à tous,   28
ouvert moi-même à une nouvelle et incroyable rosée
à force d'être nul
et ras...
et risible...   32

Clown

Lines 1–16. No modern writer has taken poetry deeper into the realms of experimental psychology than Michaux. He admits the reader into his inner poetic workshop, revealing not only what he calls his 'larves et fantômes fidèles' (bizarre dreams and recurrent apparitions wriggling from the subconscious) but also the tools of the trade and his multiple techniques. It is a poetry used as a means of piercing frontiers, of bringing together everyday life and 'the other side' (whatever form this may take). In the same process, it is almost always an implicit enquiry into the nature of identity.

The first four lines introduce an apparently common theme: the craving of a nostalgic temperament to know a new liberty and to voyage elsewhere. Only the form is different: the strangely self-contained phrases, the rhythmic repetition (what one critic has called 'limbering up') which gains in intensity as the phrases expand. In a few lines, however, the initial image, which might belong to Baudelaire's *L'Invitation au voyage* or Rimbaud's *Le Bateau ivre* (cf. '...dispersant gouvernail et grappin'), gives way to far more startling ones which proliferate dramatically; and in this context the metaphor of anchorage, boat and sea calls for a new interpretation. It also emerges that it is a poem concerned, not with remote idealism, but with efficacy; not with vague and hopeful self-abandonment, but with a ruthlessly directed operation on the self. It is, in fact, a poem of self-derision and self-demolition: a poem of purgation leading to almost total self-expurgation. For the main theme is the need to have the courage to do violence to oneself, to cast off all those familiar attachments by which one too readily recognizes oneself, to hack through sterile self-respect and the petty calculations of the logic-bound mind ('de fil en aiguille' implies a fiddling, piecemeal activity), to eliminate that false 'persona' which responds to social situations and has its echo in one's fellow men, and to reduce oneself unceremoniously to nothing. It is only when the poet has confirmed himself as a nobody that he is available to a superior function. What part is played in this thematic pattern by the idea of 'déchéance' or downfall (followed by its quizzical aside); the image of 'l'abcès'; the idea of 'pudeur' (which leads to the emphasis on 'dignes')? One is reminded here of Rimbaud's resolve, expressed in his *Lettre du Voyant*, to burst the walls of subjectivity and make himself the instrument of a communication with 'l'âme universelle': Rimbaud, too, speaks of self-alienation, 'JE est un autre' (though this is not quite the same as 'Vidé de l'abcès d'être quelqu' un'), noting scornfully that 'tant d'*égoïstes* se proclament auteurs' and 'si les vieux imbéciles n'avaient pas trouvé du Moi que la signification fausse, nous n'aurions pas à balayer ces millions de squelettes...'. Michaux is well known for his theory of poetry as 'exorcism'. Here the ghost to be exorcized (cf. the reference to fear) is the ghost of the self, the superstitious attachment most people cannot or dare not shake off. Note the pummelled vehemence of Michaux's expression and the tension that it generates. There is a fever and intoxication by rhythm which is the forerunner of a loss of ownership: could one see the phrases as coming in wave-movements? What are the different functions of repetition? Is it paradoxical that a poem concerned with 'rien et rien que rien' and a personal 'vide' should be so self-assertive, so charged with volition? Is there any justification for looking on lines 12–16 as a kind of verbal abscess?

Lines 17–23. The poem, from this point on, is alleviated. One would say that its motivating force had suddenly burst. Study the change of form: the verbless fragments following each other downwards in a limp sequence ('Réduit... Ramené... Anéanti... Perdu'); the way in which the past participial phrases, having little or no independent source of energy, change the mood in a flash from active to passive; the disappearance of the determined future tenses and the emphatic 'je' which governed them (cf. 'Vidé de l'abcès d'être quelqu'un'). The aspiration to downfall and nothingness is fulfilled ('Réduit... nivellement parfait... Ramené au-dessous... rang infime... Anéanti quant à la hauteur...'). So, too, is the desire to be elsewhere, severed from 'entourage' and 'semblables', for this is a remote region of experience so problematical that it may not even exist ('ou même pas') and a state so anonymous that one cannot even conceive of oneself as a personality. It is the total antidote to ridiculous human notions of self-sufficiency and self-esteem.

Lines 24–32. This final section hinges on the image of the clown. How do you interpret this central metaphor: what is the significance of its position immediately after the words 'sans nom, sans identité' and why should it merit the capital letters? Contrast this clown image with that of Laforgue's *Pierrots*: in this case no external features are described and the figure, belonging essentially to the abstract and metaphysical, cannot be visualized; nor is there any question of static posturing, for here salvation is in movement and self-inflicted violence. The strong emphasis on laughter throughout the piece ('ridicules... dérision... dans la risée... l'esclaffement... et risible') is equally crucial: even though this is not a humorous poem but an earnest and frenetic one, it focuses attention on the function of humour here and more widely in Michaux's work. Derision at his own expense provides a detachment and immunity from himself. Like irony, it exploits the discrepancy between appearances and reality, acting as a corrective (cf. 'Ramené... à mon rang réel'). It is the means by which he can explode the myth of the sanctity of the self and keep himself down to proper proportions. Hence the importance of the last word 'risible', where one might have expected 'ras' or 'nul' to be the more complete conclusion: to continue to find his human self pathetic, grotesque and laughable is the continued guarantee of that essential nullity and distance from himself which can be synonymous with a kind of resurrection. Develop the implications of the spiritual theme of the poem: the initial metaphor of the seas; the liquid imagery ('je boirai à nouveau l'espace nourricier', 'incroyable rosée'); the question of a communion between 'l'espace du dedans' (the title of the chief anthology of Michaux's work) and 'l'espace du dehors'; the idea of a return ('à nouveau', 'Ramené').

Beyond the word 'CLOWN', apart from the one verb ('Je plongerai') which gives the process a last kick towards the ultimate depths of nullity and renovation, and is a last reminder that the poem was launched on a distant wish, the verse-form gradually subsides to almost nothing. The last four lines, devoid of capitals and unemphatic, have no spirit of initiative. The words left hanging in the air suggest absence as much as presence. They are, moreover, vague adjectives, qualities without substance. Nouns and verbs, together with the 'je', are left behind and it becomes a poem without matter or resistance, without body or energy: a poem with 'nobody'. Michaux has described the workings of poetic 'exorcism' (which he calls 'le véritable poème du prisonnier') in this way: 'Dans le lieu même de la souffrance et de l'idée fixe, on introduit une exaltation telle, une si magnifique violence, unies au martèlement des mots, que le mal progressive-ment dissous est remplacé par une boule aérienne . . .' How appropriate are these words to the style, structure and development of *Clown*?

Robert Desnos

(1900–1945)

Non, l'amour n'est pas mort

Non, l'amour n'est pas mort en ce cœur et ces yeux et cette
bouche qui proclamait ses funérailles commencées.
Ecoutez, j'en ai assez du pittoresque et des couleurs et du
charme.   4
J'aime l'amour, sa tendresse et sa cruauté.
Mon amour n'a qu'un seul nom, qu'une seule forme.
Tout passe. Des bouches se collent à cette bouche.
Mon amour n'a qu'un nom, qu'une forme.   8
Et si quelque jour tu t'en souviens
O toi, forme et nom de mon amour,
Un jour sur la mer entre l'Amérique et l'Europe,
A l'heure où le rayon final du soleil se réverbère sur la surface   12
ondulée des vagues, ou bien une nuit d'orage sous un arbre dans
la campagne ou dans une rapide automobile,
Un matin de printemps boulevard Malesherbes,
Un jour de pluie,   16
A l'aube avant de te coucher,
Dis-toi, je l'ordonne à ton fantôme familier, que je fus seul
à t'aimer davantage et qu'il est dommage que tu ne l'aies pas
connu.   20
Dis-toi qu'il ne faut pas regretter les choses: Ronsard avant
moi et Baudelaire ont chanté le regret des vieilles et des mortes
qui méprisèrent le plus pur amour.
Toi quand tu seras morte   24
Tu seras belle et toujours désirable.
Je serai mort déjà, enclos tout entier en ton corps immortel,
en ton image étonnante présente à jamais parmi les merveilles
perpétuelles de la vie et de l'éternité, mais si je vis   28
Ta voix et son accent, ton regard et ses rayons,
L'odeur de toi et celle de tes cheveux et beaucoup d'autres
choses encore vivront en moi,
En moi qui ne suis ni Ronsard ni Baudelaire,   32

Moi qui suis Robert Desnos et qui pour t'avoir connue et aimée,

Les vaux bien.

Moi qui suis Robert Desnos, pour t'aimer   36
Et qui ne veux pas attacher d'autre réputation à ma mémoire sur la terre méprisable.

Non, l'amour n'est pas mort

Lines 1–5. In 1926, Desnos published a collection of seven poems under the title *A la Mystérieuse*. The two commentary poems as well as *J'ai tant rêvé de toi* and *A la faveur de la nuit* are all taken from this work, the dominant theme of which is that of love, sometimes a generalized love (*O douleurs de l'amour!*), more often a passionate love for the enigmatic woman of the poet's dreams. This woman-figure is obsessively present in Desnos's mind but always elusive ('Toi qui restes insaisissable dans la réalité et dans le rêve', he says in one poem; 'mon joli mirage et mon rêve éternel' in another). The mystery with which Desnos surrounds her (is she real or imaginary? does she even love him? does she even know him? is love dead or alive?) creates the tension which vibrates through *A la Mystérieuse*.

This poem, an emphatic statement of belief in love, begins with a rhetorical vigour. The categorical 'Non', followed so soon by the tugging 'Ecoutez' which arrests the reader's attention, seems intended to dispel any false impression one may have of the poet's feelings. It is also intended to dispel any remnants of his own previous tendency towards pessimism and despair. The first sentence owes much of its force to the initial Alexandrine with its insistent rhythm (the stress falling on three key-words ending in 'r'), to its repetitive grammatical form ('...en ce cœur et ces yeux et cette bouche') which accentuates the demonstrative quality of the address, and to the balanced opposition between '...l'amour n'est pas mort' and 'ses funérailles commencées'. In that the poet has previously been tempted to betray the value of love by his own words, the present text is a counter-proclamation. It is also a counter-proclamation (sharpened by the energy of the colloquialism 'j'en ai assez') in its renouncement of the superficial and trivial aspects of life, and perhaps, too, of poetry (e.g. a profusion of pictorial images or the search for stylistic originality, the bold but facile use of colour, and poetic 'charm' in the two senses of pleasant but insipid effects and spellbinding Surrealist imagery). Line 5, plunging into the affirmative 'J'aime l'amour', shows that, whatever may have happened to an individual affair, in loving love the poet saves it from death; and by juxtaposing 'tendresse' and 'cruauté' as the two qualities of love, Desnos is pledging his fidelity not only to its joys, but also to its pains and disasters, such disasters being not the negation of love as it might appear at the time, but part of its essence. There is a contrast between the emotional depth of the words 'tendresse' and 'cruauté' and those referring to the mere coating of things ('pittoresque...couleurs...charme'). Does this sentence make an effective conclusion to the opening movement?

Lines 6–8. The change from 'l'amour' to 'Mon amour', ambiguous in that it can mean love in the abstract or love as a person but touching nevertheless a more intimate lyrical note, marks a new stage in the poem. Again, the language is unequivocal ('...n'a qu'un seul nom, qu'une seule forme').

And yet, as if to contradict, the words 'Tout passe' come as a surprise. Similarly, the 'bouches', if they represent promiscuity and infidelity, should have no place in this vision; and the sentence 'Des bouches se collent à cette bouche' would seem to negate the image of a Desnos faithful to a single ideal of love.

But one cannot be confident that this is so. For, whatever the disconcerting implications of line 7, they are swiftly superseded by a reaffirmation of the unique unchanging value of his ideal, expressed now in an even more condensed form; and somehow his absolute can stand side by side with thoughts of transience and ever-changing appearances, it can pass through the fire of innumerable physical manifestations of love, and remain intact and reinforced.

Lines 9–20. Once more Desnos makes his transition by a neat and simple device: having moved from 'l'amour' to 'Mon amour', he now slips closer to the personal from 'Mon amour' to '. . . *toi*, forme et nom de mon amour'. Yet even here, in keeping with the dubious atmosphere in Desnos's poetry in which one cannot tell if one is dealing with a real woman or an ideal, with actual memories or a mythical pursuit, it is possible that the 'toi' represents, not a person, but the sum or quintessence of all loves, the *mystérieuse* who does not exist as one identifiable being but is synonymous with Love (cf. 'nom de mon amour'): in this way there would be no incompatibility between plural 'bouches' and single-minded devotion. The various hypothetical situations in which he imagines that she might remember his love represent possible future moments ('Et si quelque jour. . .Un jour. . .ou bien une nuit. . .Un matin'). But presumably he bases the choice of settings on some knowledge of previous meetings, so that this sequence is both projection into the future and reminiscence. Do the images appear to form a pattern or are they somewhat random (perhaps to indicate the fitful workings of memory)? Do they begin to sketch the faint portrait of a woman, her tastes and way of life?

After the extended conditional clause, which allows one for the first time in the poem to escape from the poet's rhetorical insistence and indulge in the luxury of descriptive detail, the sudden address to the loved one, 'Dis-toi', pursued as it is by an even more pointed imperative, pulls one back sharply and re-establishes the authoritarian tone. But the order is issued, not directly to the woman, but more intimately to that spirit within her which is, perhaps against her own wishes, the most sensitive receiver and agent of communication. (Notice, in such poems as *J'ai tant rêvé de toi* and *A la faveur de la nuit*, the tendency for Desnos to seek a relationship with a loved one who has lost her reality and is now a ghost or shadow.) His message is curiously phrased: 'davantage' is an unexpected addition to the apparently self-contained superlative '. . .je fus seul à t'aimer'. But it is all the more effective in suggesting that he was alone in loving her more, either more than her other lovers or more than the common norm of human love: where others may be erased by time (cf. 'Tout passe'), his was outlasting and can be proclaimed in defiance of death. There is an added element of surprise in the final clause. After the lyricism of 'O toi, forme et nom de mon amour', the poetic description of the 'rayon final du soleil' and the absolute expression of emotion in 'je fus seul à t'aimer davantage', the flat and prosaic 'il est dommage que', followed by the brisk revelation 'tu ne l'aies pas connu', form a curt if nostalgic anti-climax. Her lack of awareness and the difference of degree in their love seem to seal the poet in his own hyperbolic feelings and in the intensity of his own rhetoric (cf. the spell of words exercised in a world apart in *La Voix de Robert Desnos*).

Lines 21–25. The repeated 'Dis-toi', like the other repetitions in the poem, maintains both the insistent tone and the fluency of this airy love-letter, but the thought takes a new turn. Since it was the poet who said 'il est dommage...', one might expect the regrets to be his. But having revealed what she has never known, he anticipates regret on her part, and realizing the sterility of such an emotion, even though it has been exalted as a theme by prestigious poets in the past, forewarns her against it. Earlier in the poem, Desnos has turned his back on certain facile aspects of the literary in exchange for a deeper attachment. Here he refuses to adopt the well-worn posture of the poet who visualizes his loved one at a later age lamenting the missed opportunity of a love that she spurned (cf. Ronsard's lines: 'Vous serez au foyer une vieille accroupie, / Regrettant mon amour et votre fier dédain'); or who dramatizes the discrepancy between an ideal love and the imperfection of woman's response, or between what he has immortalized in verse and the perishable nature of her beauty and feelings (cf. the last stanzas of Baudelaire's *Une Charogne*). Unlike Ronsard and Baudelaire who foresee the decay of age, Desnos accepts no negative image of death. Even beyond life and in spite of the fact that 'Tout passe' she will have preserved all her physical attractions (cf. in *J'ai tant rêvé de toi* the line 'J'ai tant rêvé de toi, tant marché, parlé, couché avec ton fantôme...').

Lines 26–38. This concluding movement turns the focus finally on the poet's own part in this relationship. The confident statement 'Je serai mort déjà' implies that he is so totally incorporated within her living essence that he cannot imagine outliving her. Significantly, he does not see his mistress preserved in his poetry, but rather himself preserved in his immortal mistress. The words 'si je vis', when they come, are thus only a secondary consideration, a less conceivable possibility. Do these lines 26–8 represent the summit of the development of theme? Note the quality of the vocabulary (cf. lines 11–18), the choice of complementary words, the use of antithesis, the well balanced pattern of sounds. How is 'enclos' a better choice than 'enfermé'? What is the effect of suspending 'vis'?

Lines 29–31 are a perfect counterweight to what has preceded. If the poet should, by some chance, live on, it is she, or at least her most precious aspects, who will be enclosed and preserved within him. It is the inextinguishable physical reality and sensual influence of these aspects (cf. 'toujours désirable') that Desnos stresses above all, passing in each case from the general to a more particular nuance (from 'voix' to 'accent', 'regard' to 'rayon', 'toi' to 'tes cheveux'). The fact that he curtails this enumeration of her features with the inexplicit 'et beaucoup d'autres choses encore' is another sign of his disinclination to indulge in superfluous decorative description. He is a lover, not an artist. Thus he returns to the contrast between himself and the more consecrated poets: whereas Ronsard's or Baudelaire's fame lies in the greatness of his poetry, that claimed by Desnos lies purely and simply in the all-consuming quality of his love. What is the effect of introducing his own proper name into the poem (does it have any bearing on the theme of death? compare its value with the earlier mention of the specific 'boulevard Malesherbes')? Does the insistent 'Moi' form, in conjunction with the isolation of 'Les vaux bien', make the ending seem unduly arrogant and egocentric?

The final declaration (like so many recurrent phrases in Desnos's poetry which are not exact repetitions, but make a subtle adjustment on their second appearance) relinquishes the form of the past infinitive ('...pour t'avoir connue et aimée') and restores the idea of ever-present love ('...pour t'aimer'). It speaks in the same uncompromising voice encountered previously, which has no need for literary recognition nor for any other value than the exclusive one of loving, and for this (in contrast to those figures in literature who have spurned love) he is willing to spurn everything else on earth.

This poem is re-playing the age-old themes of unreciprocated love (cf. its treatment in *La Voix de Robert Desnos*), the passage of time, the workings of memory and possible regret, and especially that most conventional one, *amor vincit omnia*. Does Desnos succeed in turning these subjects into something original and personal? In view of the poet's own statement, 'j'en ai assez du pittoresque et des couleurs et du charme', would you say that he has effectively avoided these elements here? Desnos takes a somewhat anti-literary stance in the second half of the poem: does this mean that the style itself is largely free from conscious literary effects?

Comme une main à l'instant de la mort

Comme une main à l'instant de la mort et du naufrage se dresse comme les rayons du soleil couchant, ainsi de toutes parts jaillissent tes regards.

Il n'est plus temps, il n'est plus temps peut-être de me voir,   4
Mais la feuille qui tombe et la roue qui tourne te diront que rien n'est perpétuel sur terre,
Sauf l'amour,
Et je veux m'en persuader.   8
Des bateaux de sauvetage peints de rougeâtres couleurs,
Des orages qui s'enfuient,
Une valse surannée qu'emportent le temps et le vent durant les longs espaces du ciel.   12
Paysages.
Moi je n'en veux pas d'autres que l'étreinte à laquelle j'aspire,
Et meure le chant du coq.
Comme une main à l'instant de la mort se crispe, mon cœur   16
se serre.
Je n'ai jamais pleuré depuis que je te connais.
J'aime trop mon amour pour pleurer.
Tu pleureras sur mon tombeau,   20
Ou moi sur le tien.
Il ne sera pas trop tard.
Je mentirai. Je dirai que tu fus ma maîtresse
Et puis vraiment c'est tellement inutile,   24
Toi et moi, nous mourrons bientôt.

Comme une main à l'instant de la mort

Lines 1–3. The dense, multiple image with which Desnos begins this piece from *A la Mystérieuse* is clearly intended to have a challenging impact. Its lengthily developed and intricate form ('Comme...comme...ainsi...') contrasts with the abbreviated and often grammatically incomplete segments which come into prominence later in the poem. It is a kind of creative imaginative block which radiates in many directions and gives the poem its initial energy. What correspondences do you see, of a visual and a deeper figurative nature, between the three main elements in the image (hand, sun's rays, looks)? Notice how the poet has maintained a suggestive ambiguity, with the image of the sun interlocked in the same complex simile with the theme of disappearance and desperation, but looking forward to the idea of radiance in '...jaillissent tes regards'. In reading the sentence, one slips from the more tragic or sinister implications (death and shipwreck) to the image of a more splendid departure and finally to a spirit of upsurge, energy and expansive light. One might imagine that there is a development from negative to more positive, and yet one cannot escape the suggestion that these looks are themselves on the verge of extinction (cf. the use of the two words 'rayons' and 'regards' here with their use in *Non, l'amour n'est pas mort*).

Lines 4–8. But, however far they may spread, it seems useless for these looks to try to reach the poet or perpetuate a relationship which must, like all things, run its time. What is the value of the repetition, but with the addition in the second instance of 'peut-être', of 'Il n'est plus temps...'? The following images, moulded into a sudden galloping rhythm, are those of change and movement: 'la feuille qui tombe' representing time and the seasons and evoking the shape of a hand (Apollinaire often makes this association, as in *L'Emigrant de Landor Road*), and 'la roue qui tourne' representing space and distance and evoking the rolling ball of the sun. These two simple illustrations carry an apparently incontrovertible truth about the nature of the world ('...que rien n'est perpétuel sur terre'); and yet at this point in the poem, which could seem fatalistic, a brief and surprising phrase intervenes to negate all the preceding images of transience and set up love as an everlasting value. Line 8 echoes the spirit of the previous poem in that it shows Desnos willing himself to believe in love in the face of adverse evidence.

Lines 9–15. The succession of graphic images now introduced seems to surge up starkly from nowhere, unsupported by any main verb. Their gratuitous appearance makes one wonder if they are shreds of memory thrown to the surface, features of a dreamscape, or scattered details of a scene in front of him. But their crucial importance must surely be as poetic symbols. 'Des bateaux de sauvetage' and 'Des orages' give new substance to the original idea of 'naufrage' (the common rhyme helping to seal their affinity). How would you interpret the image of 'Une valse surannée'? Note that it is closely bound to the theme of the passage of time, and reminds one, especially in view of the fact that Desnos in *Non, l'amour n'est pas mort* makes a self-conscious link between himself and Baudelaire, of the 'valse mélancolique' of *Harmonie du soir* and more particularly the imagery of *Recueillement*. These lines make an unusual blending of time and space: the passage of time and the movements of the wind govern the same verb as if they belonged to the same order, a fusion reinforced by the curious phrase '...*durant* les longs *espaces* du ciel'. In this way the lines keep contact with the previous images (also governing a single verb) of the falling leaf and the turning wheel. The poet's summary of these various pictures as 'Paysages' and his subsequent dismissal of them is similar to the '...j'en ai assez du pittoresque et des couleurs et du charme' of *Non, l'amour n'est pas mort*. Here again, he is abandoning superficial colour and outmoded poetic charm, the irrelevance of visual or pictorial representations. One could also read in here that he is abandoning literary symbols as a suggested answer to his frustrations (for instance, the wishful solution proposed by such symbols as 'bateaux de sauvetage' and 'orages qui s'enfuient' which offer the prospect of salvaging something from a disaster). In their place, he pledges his allegiance to a single ideal more intimate and substantial than the scattered thread of visual images. What might be the significance of the line 'Et meure le chant du coq' as a conclusion to this phase of the poem: what connotations go with the cock-crow and could it have any relevance to the earlier reference to 'soleil couchant'? Lines 4–8 and lines 9–15 have a vaguely similar structure, which gives a clue to the pattern of meaning: both begin with a section concerned with time, movement and departure which is then followed by a wilful affirmation of love's timelessness; both pass from seemingly objective images to a strongly personal conclusion which seeks to negate them.

Lines 16–17. What effect does the repetition of the first image of the poem have at this point? How does the new context alter one's attitude to it? Notice the difference between the earlier pairing 'se dresse...jaillissent' and the present 'se crispe...se serre'. Is the idea of death more imminent, and is the close juxtaposition of '...meure le chant du coq' and 'l'instant de la mort', 'l'étreinte' and 'se serre' cruelly ironical? The poem owes much of its tension to its uncertainty of mood: there is throughout a feeling of precariousness (in the possible self-delusion of 'Et je veux m'en persuader', in that 'l'étreinte' is more an aspiration than a possession, in the merely wishful 'Et meure le chant du coq') which the affirmations of will-power do little to dispel. It is hard to know whether, at any given moment, optimism or pessimism, idealism or inevitability, has the ascendancy.

Lines 18–25. At this turning-point, the poem adopts a new style. What are its most noticeable features, and does it risk falling into the prosaic?

The threat of death has now crept closer to the poet himself; and it is only a logical step from '...mon cœur se serre' to the idea of crying, brought into prominence by the harping repetition of the one verb. Presumably the poet senses the onset of tears and since these have had no part in his love and are foreign to it tries to resist them. This is consistent with the attempt in the poem not to let his emotions relapse into the regretful, negative and pathetic (cf. the limp self-abandonment of the 'Et je pleure' in Verlaine's *Chanson d'automne*). And yet there is a sense of inevitability in 'Tu pleureras sur mon tombeau/Ou moi sur le tien', stressed by the shift to future tenses. It is strange that at a point in the text where the syntax becomes so elementary, the language so emotional and the style so patently subjective, the thought should be so elusive and confusing. There seems to be a definite link, for instance, between 'Il ne sera pas trop tard' and the earlier 'Il n'est plus temps...': Desnos is perhaps suggesting that, as a love relationship is disappearing and dying, it is too late to halt it; but that, once it is dead, it can be idealized and preserved and time is then forever at the lover's disposal. But this is not sure, and the paradox that after death it is not too late is left largely unexplained and out on a limb. And then once more the mood wavers, the last three lines forming an unexpected anti-climax (cf. *A la faveur de la nuit*) and causing the poem to founder. After the image of tears shed one for the other, there comes the revelation of a deliberate self-deceit (cf. 'je veux m'en persuader'): were they, in reality, ever joined as lovers? The tone of 'Et puis vraiment c'est tellement inutile' is oddly colloquial and spiritless and leads logically into the last line, which states quite flatly the imminence and unanswerability of the death of both of them. This resignation to a double death is the drawing together of the ideas expressed separately in previous images: first the woman's looks seen, and then the poet's heart seen, as 'une main à l'instant de la mort'.

Study the interplay of the ideas of death and immortality, illusion and reality, sincerity and deceit; of moods of hope and hopelessness, will and abandonment, love and loss of love; of enigmatic Surrealist imagery and patent sentimentality, of obscurity and simple lyricism. Would you say that it is a defect that Desnos has indulged to such an extent in ambiguity and contradiction, so that his themes (though obviously the universal ones of true love, time and death) have no clear contour; or has he successfully cultivated that blurred half-way world somewhere between evasiveness and accessibility, dream and reality, image and feeling, which could only lose its charm and its poignancy by being made explicit? Considering that this poem and the previous one *Non, l'amour n'est pas mort* have many details in common and seem to have been conceived in the same wave of inspiration, which of the two strikes you as artistically superior?

INDEX OF POETIC FEATURES